PHILOSOPHY FOR LIFE
AND OTHER
DANGEROUS SITUATIONS

PHILOSOPHY FOR LIFE
AND OTHER
DANGEROUS SITUATIONS

Ancient Philosophy for Modern Problems

JULES EVANS

New World Library
Novato, California

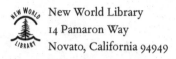 New World Library
14 Pamaron Way
Novato, California 94949

First published in Great Britain in 2012 by Rider Books, an imprint of Ebury Publishing, a Random House Group company. www.randomhouse.co.uk

Text design by Tona Pearce Myers

Library of Congress Cataloging-in-Publication Data
Evans, Jules.
 Philosophy for life and other dangerous situations : ancient philosophy for modern problems / Jules Evans.
    pages   cm
Originally published: London : Rider Books, 2012.
Includes bibliographical references and index.
ISBN 978-1-60868-229-4 (pbk. : alk. paper) — ISBN 978-1-60868-230-0 (ebook)
 1. Philosophy, Ancient. 2. Conduct of life. I. Title.
B111.E93 2013
180—dc23   2013019258

First New World Library edition, October 2013
ISBN 978-1-60868-229-4
Printed in Canada on 100% postconsumer-waste recycled paper

 New World Library is proud to be a Gold Certified Environmentally Responsible Publisher. Publisher certification awarded by Green Press Initiative. www.greenpressinitiative.org

10 9 8 7 6

To my mother and father, with love

"When evening comes, I return home and go into my study. On the threshold I strip off my muddy, sweaty, workday clothes, and put on the robes of court and palace, and in this graver dress I enter the antique courts of the ancients and am welcomed by them, and there I taste the food that alone is mine, and for which I was born. And there I make bold to speak to them and ask the motives of their actions, and they, in their humanity, reply to me. And for the space of four hours I forget the world, remember no vexation, fear poverty no more, tremble no more at death…"

NICCOLÒ MACHIAVELLI

Contents

LATE-AFTERNOON SESSION: POLITICS

EXTRACURRICULAR APPENDICES

Preface: Welcome to the School of Athens

POPE JULIUS II WAS A GREAT ENTHUSIAST for home improvement. Not content with commissioning Bramante to design the dome of St. Peter's Basilica, or Michelangelo to paint the Sistine Chapel ceiling, his Holiness hired a relatively unknown twenty-seven-year-old from Urbino, called Raphael, to paint a series of huge frescoes on the walls of his private library in the Vatican Palace. The frescos would represent the main subjects found in Julius's library: theology, law, poetry, and philosophy. It is the last fresco, which has come to be called *The School of Athens*, which is particularly admired today. In it, Raphael presents a group of philosophers from the ancient world, mainly from Greece but also from Rome, Persia, and the Middle East, gathered together in animated conversation. Academics are not certain exactly which philosophers are depicted in the painting. They're sure the two figures debating in the center of the painting are Plato and Aristotle, as they're holding their books. They're fairly sure the philosopher in the front left writing equations is Pythagoras, and the melancholy philosopher sitting alone is Heraclitus. The rather louche figure sprawled on the marble steps is probably Diogenes the Cynic. Socrates is in the back row, interrogating a pretty youth, and the smiling, garlanded philosopher on the far left may be Epicurus. What is clear is that this is a very heterogeneous group of philosophers, who put forward distinct and radical ideas, many of which were well beyond the limits of Catholic dogma. Epicurus was a materialist, Plato and Pythagoras believed in reincarnation, Heraclitus believed in a cosmic intelligence made of fire. And yet here they all are together, bursting out from the wall of the Vatican Palace.

The School of Athens is one of my favorite paintings. I love its balance between order and anarchy, the distinctness of the personalities but also the underlying unity in their ideas. I love how, at the center of the painting, in bright flowing robes, Plato and Aristotle are engaged in an argument, the one pointing up to the heavens, the other pointing down to the street. And I love the urban setting, how it's not clear if it's a temple, or a marketplace, or an arcade in some ideal city, where everyone can engage in the conversation, and the everyday is connected to the divine. As I look at the painting, I wonder: What would it be like to join in that conversation? What would it be like to study at the School of Athens, to listen to those great teachers, and "make bold to speak to them"? What do they have to say to *our* time?

This book is my dream school, my ideal curriculum, my attempt to render what it would be like to get a day-pass to the School of Athens. I've assembled twelve of the greatest teachers of the ancient world to teach us things that are often left out of modern education: how to govern our emotions, how to engage with our society, how to live. They teach us the art of self-help (Cicero writes that philosophy teaches us to "be doctors to ourselves"), but self-help of the very best kind, that doesn't focus narrowly on the individual, but instead broadens our minds and connects us to society, science, culture, and the cosmos. The course is not prescriptive — the faculty don't agree with each other (in fact, some of them actively dislike each other), and the book doesn't put forward one philosophy, but several. And yet, as in Raphael's painting, there is a unity underlying the diversity: all the teachers share an optimism in human rationality, and in the ability of philosophy to improve our lives.

In the morning roll call, Socrates, the headmaster of the school, will tell us why philosophy can help us and speak to our own age. Then the day's classes are divided into four sessions. In the morning session, the Stoics will teach us how to be Warriors of Virtue (so called because many of the modern Stoics we'll meet are soldiers). In the lunchtime session,

Epicurus will teach us the art of enjoying the moment. In the early-afternoon session, Mystics and Skeptics, we consider how our personal philosophies are connected to our ideas about the universe and the existence or absence of God. And in the final session, Politics, we consider our relationship to society, and the influence of ancient philosophy on modern politics, before Socrates conducts the graduation ceremony with a lesson on the art of departure. If that leaves you wanting to explore further, there's also a lot of extracurricular activities on my website, which has video and text interviews with some of the people you'll meet in the book, plus a "global philosophy map" showing philosophy groups near you (if you set up your own philosophy group, let me know and I'll add it to the map). And, of course, there are the wonderful books of the philosophers themselves, most of which are available on the site.

I want to re-create the openness and rowdiness you see in Raphael's painting, that sense of an animated street debate that anyone can join. Today, many people are rediscovering the ancients, and using their ideas to live better, richer, and more meaningful lives. We're rejoining that noisy, vibrant conversation that Raphael depicted so beautifully. We "make bold" to speak to the ancients. And they, in their humanity, reply to us.

1. Morning Roll Call:
Socrates and the Art of Street Philosophy

"And...ahem...how are you...feeling? Do you feel...okay?"

The awkwardness was unbearable.

This was in 1996, my first year at university. My undergraduate studies were going well, my tutors seemed pleased with my essays. But my emotions had abruptly gone haywire. Out of nowhere, I was suddenly beset with panic attacks, mood swings, depression, and anxiety. I was a mess, and I had no idea why.

"I'm doing fine, thanks, sir."

"Good."

The head of my department had been called in to check up on me. This was because, in my emotional incontinence, I had careered through my overdraft limit. My bank had contacted my college, who had alerted my head of department, a respected expert on Anglo-Saxon poetry, but not a big one for heart to hearts.

"You're not gambling, are you? Or doing drugs?"

I wasn't. But I had experimented rather recklessly with drugs in my last years at school. I wondered, was *that* what had messed me up? I came from a very loving family, and had been happy enough until recently. But I'd watched a few of my friends go off the rails, and some of them end up in mental institutions, and now my mental health was falling to pieces too. Had our drug-taking damaged our neural circuitry, condemning us to lifetimes of emotional dysfunction? Or was I just being a typical neurotic adolescent? How was I to know?

"Oh, I'm fine now, sir, really. Sorry for...the...er..."

"Well then."

There was a pause.

"I'm really enjoying *Sir Gawain and the Green Knight*," I offered.

"Yes it is a great book, isn't it?"

And, with relief, we both fled from the dark cave of the emotional, and headed back to the clearer air of the impersonal and academic.

I had a really good education, and I'm very grateful for it. My degree in English Literature gave me the chance to study wonderful books like *Sir Gawain and the Green Knight*, and to appreciate beautiful writing. I know I'm very lucky to have had that opportunity. What it didn't do, however, is teach me how to understand or govern my emotions, or how to reflect on the purpose of life. Perhaps that would be asking a lot of my overworked tutors (they weren't therapists, after all) but I believe that schools, universities, and adult education *should* offer some guidance to people, not just for their careers, but for life at its best and worst. That's what the teachers depicted in *The School of Athens* once provided: they taught their students how to transform their emotions, how to cope with adversity, how to live the best possible lives. I wish I had encountered their teachings in those difficult years. Instead, I found university to be more like a factory system: we clocked in, handed in our essay, clocked out, and then were left to our own devices. There seemed to be little institutional concern for undergraduates' well-being or the broader development of our characters.[1] Nor was there much hope among students that what we studied might actually be applicable to our life, let alone able to transform society. A degree was simply a preparation for the market, that big factory we were about to enter, the rules of which we were not capable of changing.

During the next three years at university, my academic studies went well, while my emotional life got worse and worse. The panic attacks came like earthquakes, wrecking my confidence in my ability to understand or control myself. I didn't feel I could talk about what was going on inside me, so I withdrew more and more into my shell, and this created a vicious circle, as my erratic behavior alienated my friends and attracted criticism, which only confirmed my belief that the world was a hostile and unfair place. I had no idea what was happening, and nothing I studied seemed much help in that department. What help could literature and philosophy possibly be to me? My brain was a neurochemical machine, I had broken it, and there was nothing I could do about it. Somehow, after university, I had to plug this broken apparatus into the great steel machinery of the market, and survive. I graduated in 1999 with a good degree and, to celebrate, had a nervous breakdown.

Eventually, in 2001, after five years of fear and confusion, I was diagnosed as suffering from social anxiety, depression, and post-traumatic stress disorder. Through my own research, I discovered that these emotional disorders could apparently be treated by something called Cognitive Behavioral Therapy. I found a CBT support group for social anxiety sufferers that met once a week in a church hall near me in London. There was no therapist present, but we followed a CBT course one of the group had bought from the internet.[2] We followed the handouts, practiced the exercises, and encouraged each other in our efforts to get better. And for some of us, it worked. In my case, I stopped having panic attacks after a month or so, and started to get more confident in my ability to reason with my violent emotions. It was a long journey back to health. It's not like you cross a border and are suddenly well again. I'm still getting better.

Ancient Philosophy, Modern Psychology

When I first came across CBT, its ideas and techniques seemed familiar. They reminded me of what little I knew of ancient Greek philosophy. By 2007, I had become a freelance journalist, so I started to investigate the origins of CBT. I travelled to New York to interview Albert Ellis, who'd invented cognitive therapy in the 1950s. I did the last interview with him before he died, and wrote his obituary for *The Times*. I also interviewed Aaron Beck, the other founder of CBT, as well as other leading cognitive psychologists over the next five years.[3] Through these interviews, I discovered the direct influence that ancient Greek philosophy had on cognitive therapy. Albert Ellis told me, for example, that he had been particularly impressed by a saying of the Stoic philosopher Epictetus: "Men are disturbed not by things, but by their opinions about them." This sentence inspired Ellis's "ABC" model of the emotions, which is at the heart of CBT: we experience an event (A), then interpret it (B), and then feel an emotional response in line with our interpretation (C). Ellis, following the Stoics, suggested that we can change our emotions by changing our thoughts or opinions about events. Aaron Beck likewise told me he was inspired by his reading of Plato's *Republic*, and "was also influenced by the Stoic philosophers, who stated that it was the meaning of events rather than the events themselves that affected people. When this was articulated by Ellis, everything clicked into place." These two pioneers — Ellis and Beck — took the ideas and techniques of ancient Greek philosophy, and put them right at the heart of Western psychotherapy.

According to CBT, and the Socratic philosophy that inspired it, what caused my social anxiety and depression was not repressed libidinal instincts, as psychoanalysis might argue. Nor was it neurological malfunctions that could only be corrected with pharmaceutical drugs, as psychiatry might argue. It was my beliefs. I held certain toxic beliefs and habits of thinking which were poisoning me, such as "I have permanently damaged myself" and "Everyone *must* approve of me, and if they don't, it's a disaster." These toxic beliefs were at the core of my emotional suffering. My emotions followed my beliefs, and I would feel extremely anxious in social situations, and depressed when those situations did not go well. The beliefs were unconscious and unexamined, but I could learn to examine them, hold them up to the light of reason, and see if they made sense. I could ask myself, "Why must everyone approve of me? Is that realistic? Perhaps I can accept myself and like myself even if someone else doesn't like me." It seems pretty obvious now, but through this sort of basic self-questioning, and through the support of my CBT group, I managed to shift slowly from my original toxic and irrational beliefs to more rational and sensible beliefs. And, in line with Ellis's ABC model of the emotions, my emotions followed my new beliefs. I gradually felt less anxious in social situations, less depressed, and more confident, cheerful, and in control of my life.

SOCRATES AND THE PHILOSOPHY OF EVERYDAY LIFE

Aaron Beck calls this technique of examining your unconscious beliefs "the Socratic method," because it was directly inspired by Socrates, the greatest figure in ancient Greek and Roman philosophy, and the headmaster of our school. There were people who called themselves philosophers for at least a century before Socrates, such as Thales, Pythagoras, and Heraclitus. But they either focused on the material nature of the universe, or they developed quite elitist and anti-democratic philosophies of life. Socrates, who lived from 469 to 399 BC, was the first philosopher to insist that philosophy should speak to the everyday concerns of ordinary people. He himself was of humble origins — he was the child of a stonemason and a midwife, unblessed with wealth, political connections, or good looks, yet he utterly bewitched his society, in an age which did not lack brilliant personalities. He never wrote any books. He didn't have a philosophy, in the sense of a coherent body of ideas which he passed on to his followers. Like Jesus, we only know of him through the accounts of others, particularly his disciples Plato and Xenophon. When the Delphic Oracle pronounced him the wisest person in Greece, he suggested that it was only because he realized how little he knew. But he was also aware of how little everyone else knew too. And what he tried to impart to his fellow Athenians — what he saw as his divine mission to teach — was a habit of questioning oneself. He said he considered it "a good of the highest order" to "examine myself and others," and "spend each day in discussion about the good."[4] Most people, he suggested, sleepwalk through life, never asking themselves what they're doing or why they're doing it. They absorb the values and beliefs of their parents, or their culture, and accept them unquestioningly. But if they happen to absorb wrong beliefs, it will make them sick.

Socrates insisted there's a strong connection between your philosophy (how you interpret the world, what you think is important in life) and your mental and physical health. Different beliefs lead to different emotional states — and different political ideologies also manifest in different forms of emotional sickness. For example, I placed too much value on the approval of other people (which Plato suggests is the classic sickness of liberal democracy) and this philosophy made me socially anxious. Through CBT, and through ancient philosophy, I brought my unconscious values into consciousness, examined them, and decided they didn't make sense. I changed my beliefs and this changed my emotional and physical health. My values were to some extent unconsciously picked up from my society. But I couldn't blame them on other people or on my culture, because I made a daily choice to accept them. Socrates declared that it's our responsibility to take "care of our souls," and this is what philosophy teaches us — the art of psychotherapy, which comes from the Greek for "taking care of the soul." It's up to us to examine our souls and choose which beliefs and values are reasonable and which are toxic. In this sense, philosophy is a form of medicine we can practice on ourselves.[5]

MEDICINE FOR THE SOUL

The first-century Roman statesman and philosopher Marcus Tullius Cicero wrote: "There is, I assure you, a medical art for the soul. It is philosophy, whose aid need not be sought, as in bodily diseases, from outside ourselves. We must endeavor with all our resources and strength to become capable of doctoring ourselves."[6] This is what Socrates tried to teach his fellow citizens, through his street philosophy. He'd strike up conversations with whoever he encountered on his walks around the city (Athens had a small population, so most citizens knew each other), to discover what that person believed, what they valued, what they sought in life. He told his fellow Athenians, when they put him on trial for impiety: "I go around doing nothing but persuading both young and old among you not to care for your body or your wealth" but rather to strive for "the best possible state of your soul."[7] Gently, humorously, self-deprecatingly, he would lead people to examine their life-philosophy and hold it up to the light of reason. Conversations with Socrates were the most ordinary, everyday experiences, and yet they changed you utterly. You were not the same person after you spoke to him. Briefly, you were awake. CBT tries to re-create this "Socratic method," and to teach us the art of questioning ourselves. During a session of CBT, you don't simply lie on a couch delivering a monologue about your childhood. Rather, you sit up and engage in a dialogue with your therapist, who tries to help you discover your unconscious beliefs, see how they shape your emotions, and then question those beliefs to see if they make sense. You learn to be Socrates to yourself, so that when a negative emotion knocks you off your feet, you ask, am I responding wisely to this? Is this reaction reasonable? Could I react more wisely? And you take this Socratic ability with you through the rest of your life.

The optimistic message at the heart of Socratic philosophy is that we have the power to heal ourselves. We can examine our beliefs, and choose to change them, and this will change our emotions. This power is within us. We don't need to kneel to priests or psychoanalysts or pharmacologists for redemption. Michel de Montaigne, the great Renaissance essayist, put it well. Socrates, he said, "has done human nature a great kindness, in show-ing it how much it can do of itself. We are all of us richer than we think we are; but we are taught to borrow and to beg...[And yet] we need little doctrine to live at our ease; and Socrates teaches us, that this is in us, and the way to find it, and how to use it."[8] Montaigne is right: *we are all of us richer than we think we are.* Yet we've forgotten what power is within us, so we go begging outside of ourselves for it.

WISHFUL THINKING?

Or is this an overoptimistic assessment of human reason? Does it demand too much of us? Some modern psychologists and neuroscientists would take issue with Socrates's optimism, would perhaps dismiss it as fatuous self-help. They would question, firstly, if we *can* know ourselves. They would point to how much of our decision-making appears to be uncon-scious and automatic, determined by our genes, or our neural chemistry, or our cognitive biases, or the situation in which we happen to find ourselves. They would point to the limits of human rationality and the weakness of our ability to question our emotional reactions. Some would challenge the idea that humans have the ability to change our habitual ways of thinking and acting, and would suggest we're condemned to make the same mistakes over and over.[9] In fact, some scientists would actually challenge the idea of free will and consciousness, which they would suggest are mystical superstitions. We are material beings, in a material universe, and just like everything else in the universe we are ruled and determined by physical laws. So if you happen to be born with a strong disposition to depression, social anxiety, or any other emotional disorder, then unfortunately for you, the chances are you will always have it. Your one hope for coping with that biochemical disorder is to try to balance it with other chemicals. A material solution to a material problem. Your consciousness and reason don't come into it at all.

Yet there is growing evidence that Socrates was right. First of all, there is evidence from neuroscience that shows that when we change our opinion about a situation, our emotions also change. Neuroscientists call this "cognitive re-appraisal," and they trace its discovery back to ancient Greek philosophy.[10] Their research suggests that we have some control over how we interpret the world, and this gives us the ability to modulate our emotional reactions.

Secondly, CBT has shown, in many randomized controlled trials, that people can challenge and overcome even deeply entrenched emotional disorders. Researchers have found that a sixteen-week course of CBT helps around 75 percent of patients to recover from social anxiety, 65 percent to recover from PTSD and as much as 80 percent from panic disorder (although the CBT recovery rate is under 50 percent for OCD).[11] For mild to moderate depression, CBT helps around 60 percent of patients recover, which is roughly the same as a course of antidepressants, although the relapse rate is much lower after CBT than after a course of antidepressants.[12] This evidence base suggests that we can learn to overcome ingrained habits of thinking and feeling. Daniel Kahneman, the Nobel Prize–winning psychologist, who is often pessimistic about our ability to overcome irrational cognitive biases, is optimistic on this point. He told me: "CBT has clearly shown that people's emotional responses can be re-learned. We're continuously learning and adapting."[13]

LEARNING NEW HABITS

Neuroscientists have a word for this remarkable ability of the human brain to change itself: "plasticity." The ancient Greek and Roman philosophers were early champions of plasticity. In the words of the Stoic philosopher Epictetus: "there is nothing more tractable than the human psyche."[14] They understood, as we are beginning to understand, how much of our moral character is made up of malleable habits: indeed, the word "ethics" comes from the Greek word *ethos*, meaning "habit." Contemporary psychologists like Daniel Kahneman suggest we have "dual processor" brains, with one thinking system that is mainly automatic and habit-based, and another thinking system capable of more conscious and rational reflection. The conscious-reflective system is slower and more energy-intensive than the automatic system, so we use it a lot less.

If philosophy is going to change us, it needs to work with both systems. And that was what ancient Greek philosophy did. It involved a two-fold process: first make the habitual conscious, then make the conscious habitual. First, we bring our automatic beliefs into consciousness through Socratic examination to decide if they are rational. Then we take our new philosophical insights and repeat them until they become new automatic habits. Philosophy is not merely a process of abstract reflection, but a practice. "We acquire the virtues by practice," Aristotle wrote. We cannot "take refuge in theory, like patients that listen attentively to their doctors but do none of the things they are told to do."[15] Philosophy is a training, a set of daily mental and physical exercises that become easier with practice. Greek philosophers often used the metaphor of gymnastics: just as we strengthen our muscles by repeated practice, so we strengthen our "moral muscles" through repeated practice of certain exercises. After enough training, we naturally feel the right emotion in the right situation, and do the right thing. Our philosophy becomes "second nature" and we achieve what the Stoics call "a good flow of life."[16]

This is not an easy process. It takes a lot of energy and courage to change our automatic habits of thinking and feeling, and it also requires humility: no one likes to admit their way of seeing the world might be wrong. We cling to our beliefs, even when they drown us. The fact that CBT only works for 60–70 percent of people suffering from emotional disorders suggests that the Socratic capacity to know yourself and to change yourself is just that: a capacity. The Greeks didn't claim that humans are born free, conscious, and perfectly rational beings. They suggested that humans are, in fact, deeply unconscious and automatic creatures who sleepwalk through life. But they insisted that most of us can use our reason to choose wiser paths in life, if we really work at our philosophical practice. Our ability to reason with our emotional habits may itself be genetically and environmentally determined, but I believe we almost always have *some* wiggle room, *some* capacity to challenge our automatic programming, and with practice almost all of us can become somewhat wiser and happier. That limited ability to know ourselves and change ourselves can mean the difference between a life of utter misery, and a life of moderate content.[17]

PHILOSOPHIES FOR LIFE

Socrates's idea that philosophy can really change people and bring them happiness has been mocked for centuries, even by philosophers like David Hume, the eighteenth-century Scottish thinker, who was gloriously dismissive of the therapeutic power of philosophy. Hume, who was perhaps being intentionally provocative, wrote that most humans "are effectually excluded from all pretensions of philosophy, and the medicine of the mind, so much boasted... The empire of philosophy extends over a few, and with regard to these, too, her authority is very weak and limited."[18] I would argue that Ellis and Beck proved Hume wrong. They've proved that philosophy, even in a very simplified and basic form, *can* help millions of ordinary people to live happier and more examined lives.

Nonetheless, it is inevitable that, in turning ancient philosophy into a sixteen-week course of CBT, cognitive therapists had to truncate it and narrow its scope, and the result is a rather atomized and instrumental form of self-help, which focuses narrowly on an individual's thinking style and ignores ethical, cultural, and political factors. The ancient philosophies we're going to meet certainly offer us quick and useful therapeutic tools. But they're more radical than that. They also offer critiques of society, and political ideas about how society should be run. And they offer various theories about God, the meaning of life, and our place in the universe. Self-help in the ancient world was far more ambitious and expansive than modern self-help. It linked the psychological to the ethical, the political, and the cosmic. And it didn't offer people short-term fixes to be practiced for a month or two until the next self-help fad arrived. It offered people an enduring way of life, something to be practiced each day for years, to radically transform the self — and perhaps to transform society. Today, many people are looking for a philosophy for life, and have gone back to the philosophers of antiquity to find something they can live by. All the people you'll meet in this book have had their life transformed by ancient philosophy — and many of them would say, like me, that their life was saved by it. They come from every walk of life: soldiers, astronauts, hermits, magicians, gangsters, housewives, politicians, anarchists. They've all discovered that philosophy really works, even in the most dangerous and extreme situations.

STREET PHILOSOPHY

The idea of "philosophy as a way of life" is quite far from the contemporary academic model of philosophy, where students are taught a theory and then tested in that theory. For the ancient Greeks, as I've said, philosophy was a much more practical, intimate, and communal process. A student had to bring all of themselves to the practice of it, not just their intellectual faculties. How and where could that sort of philosophy be practiced today? One response has been to try to take philosophy back to the streets, where Socrates himself used to practice it. In 1992, a young French scholar called Marc Sautet irritated his academic peers by declaring that philosophy had become overinstitutionalized and divorced from the concerns of ordinary people. As an alternative, he set up the *Café Philosophique*, which met in the

Café des Phares in Paris every Sunday morning. Anyone could turn up, vote on a topic to be discussed that day, and take part in a large group Socratic dialogue (there could be two hundred people at these events, crammed into the café). Thanks to the internet, the movement rapidly went global: there are now around fifty Socrates Cafés all over the world.[19]

Other grassroots philosophy movements followed Sautet's lead. In Liverpool in 2000, three working-class Liverpudlians set up a movement called Philosophy in Pubs, and there are now thirty PIPs across the UK, and fourteen in Merseyside alone, making Liverpool the undisputed world capital of grassroots philosophy. One of the founders, Rob Lewis, told me he'd taken a philosophy course when he was unemployed. It had been "a massive turning point" in his life. He says: "Practicing philosophy helped me overcome the sense of alienation that many of us feel at times, which comes from being in a society that wants to judge you to see what life chances you might be worthy of." The idea of PIPs, from the beginning, was to take philosophy beyond academia, beyond what Rob calls the "chattering classes," and to bring its power to the working classes. One of the founders, Paul Doran, tells me: "I'd like it if in ten years' time, it would be considered completely normal to go into any pub in Britain and say, 'What night does your philosophy club meet?'"

These grassroots philosophy organizations often have a slightly anti-academic spirit. The popular philosopher Alain de Botton, for example, set up an organization called the School of Life in 2008, in a bid to free philosophy from the rigid institutionalism of academia. Academic philosophy, he complained, no longer teaches us how to live: "Oprah Winfrey asks more of the right questions than the humanities professors at Oxford"[20] (there goes his invitation to high table). I have some sympathy with this view. I remember asking one academic expert in Stoicism whether he'd ever used Stoicism in his own life. He replied: "Good Lord, no. Thankfully my life has never got *that* bad." He seemed to see ancient philosophy as a dusty museum relic. But other academics are less dismissive of the contemporary usefulness of ancient philosophy, such as Pierre Hadot, A. A. Long, Michael Sandel, and Martha Nussbaum.[21] At the philosophy group I help to run, the London Philosophy Club, we've hosted many academic philosophers who have given up their time to share their expertise with us, for free. Street philosophy and academic philosophy are not rivals — they need each other. Without academic philosophy, street philosophy becomes incoherent. Without street philosophy, academic philosophy becomes irrelevant.

New Philosophical Communities

Neither the School of Life, nor Philosophy in Pubs, nor the London Philosophy Club demand that their members follow a particular philosophy or ethical way of life. They're liberal forums where strangers meet up to discuss various philosophies without having to commit to any one. In that sense, they're different from ancient philosophical schools set up by descendants of Socrates, like the Cynics, Platonists, Stoics, or Epicureans. As we'll see, those ancient schools were more like communes or sects, whose members would commit to a radical and countercultural way of life. But we're also seeing the rise of new philosophical communities today that are closer to that ancient model. We'll meet the New Stoics, for example, who are a group of contemporary Stoics from around the world. We'll meet Action for Happiness, a movement committed to the spread of rational hedonism. We'll visit an anarchist commune camped out on the pavements of London like the Cynics of antiquity. We'll meet the School of Economic Science, a Platonic community with around twenty thousand followers. We'll meet the Landmark Forum, which claims to have trained over one million people in its shock Socratic philosophy. We'll go to Las Vegas to attend a global gathering of the Skeptics, a grassroots movement with several million members. Some of these philosophical communities are substitutes or rivals to traditional religions. This of course poses a challenge of historical reconstruction: no ancient Greek or Roman philosophies have remained living traditions since their establishment two millennia ago, so modern followers need to try to piece the fragments back together and construct new traditions. And it also poses an organizational challenge. Can these communities really replace traditional religions, without turning into cults?

THE POLITICS OF WELL-BEING

Ancient philosophical therapy also had an important political component. As we've seen, our beliefs can make us sick or help us to flourish. We pick up many of our beliefs from our culture and our political and economic system, so any trainee-philosopher has to decide what relationship to adopt toward their society. The teachers in our faculty put forward different solutions. The Stoics and Skeptics, for example, declared their inner independence from the toxic values of their culture, but didn't try to evangelize or change other people. They were pessimistic about ordinary people's interest in philosophy or desire to change. The Epicureans and Pythagoreans took a similarly pessimistic view of the influence of philosophy, and withdrew from society into philosophical communes. But some members of our faculty had greater hopes for philosophy, and thought it could genuinely transform society. Our last session, on politics, will examine the political visions of Diogenes, Plato, Plutarch, and Aristotle, and explore how people are trying to bring their visions into reality today.

The idea that a whole society could be brought under a single philosophy or religion of the good life has been strenuously resisted in Western liberal societies ever since the nineteenth-century philosopher John Stuart Mill insisted that people should be left to pursue "our own good in our own way."[22] The two great lions of postwar liberal philosophy — Sir Karl Popper and Sir Isaiah Berlin — likewise warned that the search for a single formula for the good life was a "metaphysical chimera."[23] A whole nation will never agree to one model of happiness, so any attempt by a government to impose one philosophy on its citizens would necessarily be coercive and despotic. Governments, Berlin insisted, should protect their citizens' "negative liberty" — their freedom from interference — while leaving them alone to pursue their own "positive liberty," their own model of personal and spiritual fulfilment.

BEYOND LIBERALISM

Yet, in the closing years of the twentieth century, and in the first years of the twenty-first, a feeling grew among intellectuals and policy-makers that pluralism and moral relativism had gone too far, and that neo-liberal individualism had left us atomized, disconnected, and lacking a sense of the common good. Aristotle and Plato's idea that governments should encourage the spiritual flourishing of their citizens returned to the mainstream of Western thought. Indeed, today it has become an overwhelming consensus.[24] What gave policy-makers this sudden confidence that governments could make people happier? In large part, it was the success of cognitive therapy. Aaron Beck and Albert Ellis appeared to have proven, scientifically, that people could be taught to overcome emotional and behavioral disorders. Then, in the late 1990s, a student of Aaron Beck's at the University of Pennsylvania, Martin Seligman, suggested psychology should help people not just to overcome emotional disorders, but also to flourish, and live the best possible lives. He called his new field Positive Psychology. Just as Beck and Ellis were inspired by ancient Greek philosophy, so Seligman and his colleagues explored the ideas and techniques of ancient Western and Eastern philosophies, and then tested them out empirically to see which ones really worked. As Christopher Peterson, Positive Psychology's "director of virtues," quipped: "Aristotle never had the benefit of a seven-point scale."[25] Through this synthesis of ancient philosophy and modern psychology, Seligman and his colleagues hoped to build an objective "science of flourishing," and then to bring this science into the heart of Western politics. Imagine, Seligman declared, if governments and corporations around the world taught their citizens and employees the science of well-being — just as the Medici family imparted Platonic philosophy to Renaissance Florence.[26] Wouldn't that be amazing?

This new movement, which Seligman called the "politics of well-being," has been remarkably successful in attracting political and financial backing. In the UK, for example, the government agreed to spend over half a billion pounds training six thousand new cognitive therapists to provide CBT to the nation. Most children in English schools also now take a national curriculum subject called Social and Emotional Aspects of Learning, which teaches them how to be "emotionally intelligent," and which includes techniques from CBT. In the United States, every soldier in the army now takes a course in "resilient thinking," designed by Martin Seligman and his team and launched in late 2010, in a bid to reduce the incidence of post-traumatic stress disorder and suicide among the troops. As we'll see, at the heart of the program are cognitive techniques taken from CBT and ancient philosophy. In the UK, one think-tank has suggested Seligman's resilience course should be taught to all six million workers in the public sector. Even more ambitiously, in late 2011 the president of the European Council, Herman Van Rompuy, sent a book on Positive Psychology to two hundred world leaders, asking them to make well-being the goal of public policy in 2012, by teaching Positive Psychology to "the man and woman on the street." And governments around the world, including in France, Belgium, Bhutan, Finland, Austria, the UK, and Germany, have in the past few years started to measure "national well-being" and to suggest that the overriding aim of governments should be the flourishing of their citizens, just as Aristotle insisted.

The Danger of an Illiberal Politics of Well-Being

There are many aspects of this movement that I support, particularly the British government's boldness in expanding the provision of mental health services. I myself was greatly helped by CBT, and if some of the millions of people helped by CBT go on to explore the ancient philosophical roots of it, all the better. Having grown up during the arid years of neo-liberalism, I'm also excited that ancient Greek ideas about flourishing and the good life are back in the classroom, in the workplace, and at the heart of politics. But the sheer speed and scale at which this movement is moving into public policy makes me uneasy. The new politics of well-being could easily become illiberal and coercive, if scientists and policy-makers try to argue that they have "proved" a certain model of the good life, and therefore there is no need for democratic debate or consent. There is a danger of leaping too hastily from the *Is* of empirical evidence to the *Ought* of ethics and politics, and ending up with a rigid and illiberal dogma of how people *must* think, feel, and live.

This danger was most apparent to me in the neuroscientist Sam Harris's recent book, *The Moral Landscape*. Harris argues that the only reasonable foundation for ethics is a concern for the well-being of all sentient creatures. Science, he insists, can tell us facts about well-being, and therefore science — and only science — can tell us what the good life is. His book provoked a lot of indignation among priests and philosophers. But I don't have any problem with his insistence that science can and should inform moral debate. The ancient Greeks would entirely agree: their philosophies, as we'll see, combined biology, psychology, and physics with ethics and politics. Any reliable ethical code should try to fit with the available scientific evidence about our nature and the nature of the universe. If science tells us, for example, that humans are powerless to know or change our thoughts or emotions, that's bad news for Socratic ethics. If, on the other hand, the scientific evidence from CBT suggests that we *can* use our reason to change our thoughts and emotions, that's good news for Socratic ethics. Harris is right so far.

Then Harris takes a bold leap into political philosophy. If science can tell us precise facts about human well-being and morality, then it should be used to guide national and international politics. We should use it to design better social, legal, and political institutions, and to construct a universal moral framework in which the customs and morals of all individuals and societies can be weighed, measured, and judged. Harris looks forward to the day when an international committee of scientific experts watches over us and gives us clear and precise guidance as to the morality of our actions. This vision reminds me of the power and authority once assigned to the Vatican, where a committee of theological experts, guided by the "moral science" of Aristotle and Thomas Aquinas, watched over Christendom and dispatched moral judgments on the rulers within it. More recently, it is reminiscent of Positivism, the strange philosophical cult invented by Auguste Comte in the nineteenth century. Comte insisted he had finally turned the wisdom of ancient philosophy and Catholic theology into a cast-iron science, and that governments simply had to hand over power to a committee of scientific experts.[27] John Stuart Mill, an early enthusiast for Positivism, came to see the danger of this vision. If it became a reality, he warned, it would lead to "a despotism of society over the individual, surpassing anything contemplated in the political idea of the most rigid disciplinarian among the ancient philosophers."[28]

And yet Harris's Positivist vision is already becoming a reality. In late 2010, British prime minister David Cameron ordered the Office for National Statistics to define and measure national well-being (a poisoned chalice if ever there was one).[29] The ONS created an "expert committee" who quickly arrived at an official government definition of well-being. The committee was entirely made up of economists and social scientists, without a single philosopher, or artist, or priest. There was no real democratic debate over how well-being should be defined, other than a whistle-stop "national conversation" tour by ONS officials around the country. The ONS reported that, to their surprise, many people who attended these events said that religion was important to their idea of well-being.[30] But naturally God didn't make it into the ONS's scientific formula for well-being. How could science measure a person's closeness to God? Despite the absence of God, the ONS insisted it had found an objective definition of well-being, and could measure it in the population using questionnaires. Critics of the initiative say the ONS is only measuring happy feelings, a purely Utilitarian or Epicurean definition of well-being. But the ONS says it also measures "eudaimonic" well-being, from the ancient Greek word *eudaimonia*, by which Aristotle, Plato, and the Stoics meant "virtuous happiness." The ONS says its questionnaires measure a person's *eudaimonia* by asking them "How worthwhile is your life on a scale of one to ten?" The data from this question, the ONS says, will give us an accurate scientific measurement of the nation's spiritual flourishing. Really? The answers might, perhaps, give us some very crude idea of a person's own assessment of their flourishing, but it can't tell us how they *actually live*, how they treat others, or the wider impact and moral value of their life. Do we really think a brief questionnaire can measure the virtue, meaningfulness, impact, and cosmic value of a person's life, assign them a number, and then rank them in a global moral hierarchy? That would ascribe skills to statisticians normally reserved for omniscient deities.[31] In the words of Aristotle: "It is the mark of an educated man to look for precision in each class of things only so far as the subject admits."[32]

DEMOCRATIZING THE POLITICS OF WELL-BEING

Any philosophy of well-being involves values, beliefs, and judgments about big questions like: "Why are we here?," "Is there a God?," "What does it mean to flourish?," and "How should we order society?" Empirical research can tell us some interesting things about these questions, but we also need to exercise our practical moral judgment, or what the Greeks called *phronesis*. As Socrates insisted, the practice of reflecting on these questions, alone and with other people, and choosing your own response is itself an important part of the good life. Governments shouldn't deny people that process, and force them to fit into a prefabricated model of well-being designed by "experts." That denies them autonomy, reasoning, and choice — all of which, I suggest, are an important part of human flourishing.[33] And well-being scientists shouldn't hide their own moral assumptions behind spurious claims of scientific objectivity. Instead, the different ethical approaches to well-being should be unpacked and explored, so that people can make up their own minds. We have to find the right balance between the Greeks' idea of "the good life," and a liberal, pluralist politics which respects people's right to ask questions and choose how to live. Otherwise the politics of well-being will rapidly become intrusive, illiberal, bureaucratic, and deeply resented. We can lead people to the well of philosophy, but we can't force them to think.

THE FOUR STEPS OF THE SOCRATIC TRADITION

What I have tried to show in this book is that Socrates and his descendants did not come up with one definition of well-being, but several. All the approaches we'll meet in the school are branches of what I call the Socratic tradition. They all follow these three Socratic steps:

1. Humans can know ourselves. We can use our reason to examine our unconscious beliefs and values.
2. Humans can change ourselves. We can use our reason to change our beliefs. This will change our emotions, because our emotions follow our beliefs.

3. Humans can consciously create new habits of thinking, feeling, and acting.

These three steps are, in essence, what CBT teaches. There's a good evidence base for these steps, and what they teach are "thinking skills" rather than particular moral values, so I don't see a problem with governments teaching these skills to people in schools, universities, mental health clinics, armies, and elsewhere. However, all the philosophies we'll meet then take a fourth step:

4. If we follow philosophy as a way of life, we can live more flourishing lives.

This is where things get a bit more complicated, when you try to decide what exactly makes a life "flourishing." This is where values, ethics, and practical reasoning come in. The first three steps teach you how to drive your mind. The fourth step tells you where to drive it to. All the philosophers in our faculty take the fourth step, but in different directions. They have different conceptions of the good society. And they have different conceptions of the purpose of life — some believe the ultimate aim of life is unity with God, while others doubt that the gods exist or have any relevance to human life. They have a lot in common (they all agree on Steps 1, 2, and 3) but they also have fundamental differences when it comes to Step 4. Perhaps, then, ancient philosophy can offer us some common ideas and techniques for the good life. Perhaps it even offers a meeting place between believers and nonbelievers, and between the sciences and the humanities. But there will always be *some* disagreement. I don't think any of the philosophies we'll meet are perfect, and you will never get an entire population to sign up to one of them. The Himalayan kingdom of Bhutan is often held up as a model of how a whole country can sign up to one philosophy of well-being. But Bhutan is a tiny, monocultural, semi-literate, mainly rural country with a population smaller than Birmingham, ruled by a king. It is much easier for Bhutan's government to impose one common philosophy of the good (Buddhism) than a large, secular, multicultural, liberal state. Because of that, neither governments nor corporations should try to impose one model of well-being on their members, but instead should teach the various different approaches to the good life, then let people decide for themselves.

THREE QUESTIONS FOR EACH PHILOSOPHY

For each different philosophy we'll meet, I've asked three questions. Firstly, what self-help techniques can we take from this philosophy and use in our lives? Secondly, could we embrace this philosophy as a way of life? And, finally, could this philosophy form the basis of a community, or even a whole society? For each philosophy, I have drawn on interviews with people who have used its ideas in their own lives to overcome serious problems and improve their lives. Most of the time, they were conscious that the techniques come from ancient philosophy, and in many instances, the people interviewed consciously subscribe to one of the ancient schools and try to follow it as a way of life. All of them are living philosophy, and they're all far more serious in their practice than I am. It is worth saying at the outset that, although philosophy helped me a lot, I don't consider myself a philosopher, but rather a journalist who is curious about how people apply these ancient ideas in modern life. With that in mind, it's time we heeded the words of Seneca: "There is no time for playing around. You have been retained as counsel for the unhappy. You have promised to bring help to the shipwrecked, the imprisoned, the sick, the needy, to those whose heads are under the poised axe. Where are you deflecting your attention? What are you *doing?*"[34] Quite right, Seneca, it's time we began our classes. Our morning session begins in the Arabian Desert, where Rhonda Cornum is about to have a very rough landing.

The Warriors of Virtue

2. Epictetus and the Art of Maintaining Control

RHONDA CORNUM WAS WORKING as a flight surgeon in the 101st Airborne Division during the First Gulf War in February 1991, when she was sent on a mission to rescue a fighter pilot who had been shot down. Her own helicopter was shot down, and crashed into the Arabian Desert at 140 miles an hour, instantly killing five of the eight crew. Cornum survived, although both her arms were broken, a ligament was torn in her knee, and she had a bullet lodged in her shoulder. Iraqi soldiers surrounded the crashed helicopter, and dragged Cornum out by her broken arms. They put her and another member of the crew, Sergeant Troy Dunlap, into the back of a truck. As the truck bumped along the desert road, one of the Iraqi soldiers unzipped Cornum's flight suit and sexually assaulted her. She couldn't fight him off, and tried not to scream, but every time he knocked her broken arms she couldn't help crying out. Eventually he left her alone. Sergeant Dunlap was chained up next to her, unable to help. "Ma'am," he said quietly, "you're really tough." "What'd you think, I'd cry or something?" she said. "Yeah, I thought you would." "That's okay, Sergeant," Rhonda said after a while. "I thought you'd cry too." They were kept prisoner in an Iraqi military compound for eight days. Cornum has said of the experience: "Being a POW is the rape of your entire life. But what I learned in those Iraqi bunkers and prison cells is that the experience doesn't have to be devastating, that it depends on you."[1]

Rhonda tells me: "When you're a POW, your captors control pretty much everything about your life: when you get up, when you go to sleep, what you eat, if you eat. I realized the only thing I had left that I could control was how I thought. I had absolute control over that, and was not going to let them take that too. I decided, well, there was the old mission of rescuing the fighter pilot, and now circumstances had changed, and I had a new mission, to get through this." She did survive, and didn't give away any confidential information. Nor did she feel herself permanently traumatized by her experience. She told one interviewer: "You're supposed to look at being sexually molested as a fate worse than death. Having faced both, I can tell you it's not. Getting molested was not the biggest deal of my life." Cornum clearly possesses in abundance the character-trait that Americans call "grit," and that the British call a "stiff upper lip." This attitude, which is the essence of Stoicism, doesn't mean she hid or denied her emotions, as the popular understanding of the word "stoic" might suggest. Rather, her emotions followed her recognition that there was simply no point in panicking over aspects of her situation that were out of her control, and that it made a lot more sense to focus on what she *could* control. And she insists that people like me, who aren't as naturally tough as her, can learn this resilient attitude. She tells me: "There are people who are just naturally resilient, who look at problems as challenges to be overcome. Some people even see adversity as opportunities to excel. I recognized that I had those skills, and others didn't. What we have learnt since then, is that the thinking skills that lead to resilience can be taught."

In 2009 Cornum was put in charge of a new $125-million Pentagon program, called Comprehensive Soldier Fitness, which aims to teach resilience to each of the 1.1 million soldiers serving in the US Army. The program, which the journal *American Psychologist* described as "the largest deliberate psychological intervention in history,"[2] was developed by Martin Seligman, the founder of Positive Psychology.[3] Seligman's concept of resilience is based on the idea, originally from Greek philosophy and then picked up by CBT, that you can teach people how their beliefs and interpretive styles lead to their emotional responses, and then teach them how to dispute their irrational beliefs Socratically, and to replace them where necessary with a more philosophical perspective. The aim, in the words of the program's promotional video, is to teach American soldiers how to "take control of your emotions, before they take control of you." In other words, the US Army is trying to raise a generation of resilient philosopher-warriors, using the same philosophical ideas and techniques that Athenians, Spartans, Macedonians, and Romans used to cope with their own gruelling campaigns, at the dawn of Western civilization.

Is It Really All Down to Your Thoughts?

There's an obvious objection to this sort of therapy: Are emotional disorders really always the fault of your beliefs? Aren't they sometimes caused not by your beliefs, but by the terrible situation you're in? Focusing too narrowly on a person's thinking might ignore the environmental stresses that are harming them. The reason that only 3 percent of UK troops serving in Iraq were found to be suffering from post-traumatic stress disorder, as opposed to around 17 percent of US troops, is not necessarily because American troops have less resilient beliefs. It may be because they were in some of the worst fighting, and were serving tours that were twice as long as their British allies.[4] Nonetheless, even in truly dire situations like the Iraq War, we do still preserve some control over our situation: our response to it. No one can take that freedom away from us. And we can steer our way through the worst situations, by focusing on what is in our control, without driving ourselves crazy about what we can't immediately control. Cornum told a group of troops in 2010: "I approached every problem I encountered, whether it was failing an exam or a disease or getting shot down and shot up the same way: I would fix what I could fix and I wouldn't complain about what I couldn't."[5] Cornum doesn't think of herself as a Stoic, but the technique she practices and teaches was actually best described by a Roman Stoic philosopher in the second century called Epictetus.

THE SLAVE PHILOSOPHER

Epictetus was born into a situation of minimal control. He was born a slave, in the town of Hierapolis, in what is now Turkey, in AD 55. His name means "acquired." Some accounts suggest he was beaten up and tortured by his first owner, and his leg was broken so badly he stayed lame his whole life. However it happened, he was certainly lame, poor, without family or freedom for most of his life. But he was lucky enough to have an enlightened second owner, called Epaphroditus, who allowed Epictetus to study under the greatest Stoic philosopher of his day, Musonius Rufus. The word "Stoic" comes from the *Stoa Poikile*, or "painted colonnade" in the corner of the Athenian marketplace, where the original Stoics gathered to teach their street philosophy to anyone who wanted to listen — male or female, freeman or slave, Greek or barbarian. Stoicism arose in the third century BC, a century after the death of Socrates, when Greek city-states were being conquered by marauding empires. Its philosophy was a means of coping with that chaos: Stoics claimed that if you use your reason to overcome attachments or aversions to external conditions, you can stay unperturbed under any circumstances — even if your country has been conquered and a tyrant is torturing you on the rack (this idea is one of many similarities between Stoicism and Buddhism, which I explore further in the appendix). Their philosophy of inner freedom and external defiance spread to Rome in the first century BC, where it was taken up by leading Roman politicians and used as a philosophy of republican resistance to imperial tyranny, in a movement known as the "Stoic opposition." Like Jedi knights resisting the Galactic Empire, the Stoic opposition were constantly clashing with the imperial government and being imprisoned, exiled, or executed.

Epaphroditus eventually freed Epictetus, but he made the unusual career decision of becoming a Stoic philosopher himself, which immediately put him in the crosshairs of the imperial regime. Epictetus was exiled when the emperor Domitian banished all philosophers from Italy in AD 94. He travelled to Nicopolis, a bustling town in western Greece, and there carried on his teachings. He was never particularly well off, but the influence of his ideas carried through time and space. It is said the emperor Hadrian travelled to Nicopolis to talk to the old man. The emperor Marcus Aurelius, Hadrian's heir and a great philosopher in his own right, was probably more influenced by Epictetus than by any other thinker. And thanks to a student of his, Arrian, who took notes in his lessons, his ideas have passed down into the modern age: Thomas Jefferson, Lawrence Sterne, Matthew Arnold, J. D. Salinger, and Tom Wolfe all used his ideas in their own work and lives. His *Discourses* helped me overcome my own emotional problems more than any other book of philosophy.

EPICTETUS'S PHILOSOPHY OF RESILIENCE

Epictetus drew on his traumatic life to inform his philosophy of resilience. At any moment, as a slave, you could be beaten up, tortured, or executed. As a Stoic philosopher, you also faced the constant prospect of imprisonment or execution. How, then, could a Stoic stay calm and mentally strong in the midst of so much uncertainty and oppression, when their ability to control their own destiny was so hampered? How could they hope to remain the "captain of their soul"? Epictetus's answer was to remind himself constantly what is in his control and what isn't. On the first page of his *Handbook*, we read: "Some things are up to us, and others are not." Epictetus makes a list of the things that are not in our control (I've added a few):

NOT IN OUR CONTROL
Our body
Our property
Our reputation
Our job
Our parents
Our friends
Our co-workers
Our boss
The weather
The economy
The past

The future
The fact we're going to die

Of course, some of the things on the list are not entirely out of our control either. Our body is, to some extent, under our control — we can eat healthily, we can exercise, we can even go to a cosmetic surgeon to try to make our body as perfect as possible. But it is still, ultimately, weak, fragile, out of our control, and eventually, despite our best efforts, it will die. So what is under our own control? Epictetus draws up another list:

IN OUR CONTROL
Our beliefs

And that's pretty much it. This may seem like a very limited field of control. And yet this small window is the basis for human freedom, autonomy, and sovereignty. We have to learn, Epictetus says, to exercise our power over Zone 1 — over our thoughts and beliefs. That is our sovereign domain. In Zone 1, we are king, if we choose to exercise our sovereignty. We always have a choice what to think and believe. The Stoics insisted that no one can ever force us to believe something against our will. No one can brainwash us if we know how to resist them. Epictetus said: "The robber of your free will does not exist."[6] However, we have to accept that we *don't* have complete sovereignty over Zone 2 — over external events. In fact, we only have limited control over what happens in the world. We have to accept this, otherwise we're going to be angry, afraid, and miserable for most of our life.

How Mistakes about Control Cause Us Suffering

A lot of suffering arises, Epictetus argues, because we make two mistakes. Firstly, we try to exert absolute sovereign control over something in Zone 2, which is not in our control. Then, when we fail to control it, we feel helpless, out of control, angry, guilty, anxious, or depressed. Secondly, we don't take responsibility for Zone 1, our thoughts and beliefs, which *are* under our control. Instead, we blame our thoughts on the outside world, on our parents, our friends, our lover, our boss, the economy, the environment, the class system, and then we end up, again, feeling bitter, helpless, victimized, out of control, and at the mercy of external circumstances. Many mental illnesses and emotional disorders come from these two fatal mistakes. This is true even of psychotic illnesses, which often manifest as failures to establish the proper boundaries of the self, and to understand what is in your control and what isn't. Schizophrenics, for example, often have paranoid fantasies that their minds are being controlled by external forces — the FBI, the Mafia, aliens, demons, and so on. They are terrified of their thoughts being invaded or possessed by these external forces, and they grant their thoughts and the voices they hear an absolute power over them. On the other hand, they may also have grandiose messianic fantasies of being able to save the world through their thoughts. Their swings from paranoid victimization to messianic grandiosity come from an inability to draw a realistic line between what is under their control and what isn't.[7]

Less serious emotional disorders also stem from a confusion about what we control and what we don't. A person with social anxiety, for example, becomes obsessed with what other people think of them. They become nervous, paranoid, angry, and hopeless, all because they are completely fixated on other people's opinions — which are out of their control. Their intense focus on Zone 2 is a recipe for paranoia, helplessness, and alienation. Likewise, a person with depression will often blame external factors for their bad mood. They will blame the past, or their parents, or their co-workers, or the economy, or global politics. They constantly abrogate responsibility for their own beliefs and feelings. And this only makes them feel more helpless, out of control, and depressed. A 2010 study by the Institute of Psychiatry of the mental health of British soldiers serving in Iraq and Afghanistan found that the main cause of emotional suffering among the troops was not battle-related. It was getting phone calls from their wives, in which their wives complained about problems back home — problems which the soldiers were powerless to do anything about. The feeling of being out of control and powerless to help one's loved ones is more demoralizing than any Taliban bomb.

THE SERENITY PRAYER

The next time you're in a really difficult or stressful situation, look at how the people around you react. Some people will start panicking, because they focus on aspects of the situation they can't control. But others will stay calm, and immediately focus on what they can do, right now, to change the situation and get a handle on it. Resilience and mental health come from focusing on what is in our control in a situation, without driving ourselves crazy over what is not. The US Army's Leadership Manual puts it in very Epictetan terms: "It is critical for leaders to remain calm under pressure and to expend energy on things they can positively influence and not worry about things they cannot affect."[8] This attitude is summed up by the Serenity Prayer, which is read at the end of each meeting of Alcoholics Anonymous. It says: "Lord, give me the serenity to accept the things I cannot change, courage to change the things I can change, and the wisdom to know the difference."

It is also an attitude advocated by Stephen R. Covey, the author of the self-help bestseller *The 7 Habits of Highly Effective People*. Covey advises us to be "proactive": "You need to develop the awareness 'I am a separate person to all that's happened to me — my moods, my impulses, even my genetic make-up. I have the capacity to take responsibility. I am responseable.' We have the power to choose our response even in situations we have little control over. Between the stimulus and the response lies a space, and in that space lies our freedom and power." Covey, like Epictetus, suggests that we should "imagine two circles" — an outer circle which Covey calls the "circle of concern," which includes things that we might worry about but can't really affect. And a smaller inner circle that Covey calls the "circle of influence," which includes things we can control, over which we should take responsibility. The more we focus our energy on the circle of influence, Covey suggests, the happier and more effective we will be.

Now this doesn't mean that we should stop caring about broader world affairs, on the basis that, say, someone living in the UK can't really control what happens in the Sudan or Bangladesh. We may have limited control over events in other parts of the world, but we still have some control, and *some* influence. The choice to buy an SUV, for example, has some impact on living conditions in Bangladesh. Epictetus was a Stoic, and the Stoics were anything but introspective, apolitical hermits. They very much believed in doing what one could to help one's fellow man. But that does not mean giving way to helpless despair or impotent rage because you can't save the world on your own. You do what you can to improve the world, while recognizing and accepting the limits of your control. Likewise, if you're in an adverse situation in your personal life, do what you can to improve your situation. If you're in a bad job, try to leave it. If you're being bullied, tell someone, or confront the bully. But sometimes we all come up against something adverse that we can't immediately change — particularly events that have already happened. Then we just have to tolerate it, for the time being. We have to bide our time, and wait for the situation to change. In the meantime, we can use the opportunity to develop our inner freedom and capacity to rise above events. Adverse situations can be seen as opportunities to sharpen our agency and inner freedom. Epictetus once said: "It is circumstances which show what men are."

Not Blaming Ourselves
for What Is Out of Our Control

Epictetus's technique of defining the limits of our control is particularly useful when we're children and adolescents, because then we're very much at the mercy of circumstances and of other people — particularly our parents. I want to look at two examples of children who suffered traumatic childhoods, to show how Epictetus's lesson can be used to get through adversity. The first example was told to me by William Knaus, a wonderful, kind, wise old man, who is the pioneer of teaching cognitive therapy in schools, which he has been doing since 1971 through an approach called Rational Emotive Education. In the early 1970s, Bill started treating a five-year-old girl, who we'll call Anna, who was living in a foster home. He says: "She was a very hyperactive child, she couldn't sit in one place, and her IQ was measured in the sub-normal range." Knaus started to piece together her history. He says: "She had utterly disturbed and destructive parents. Her mother, in her mid-twenties, used drugs, and needed a lot of money to support her habit. She would sometimes fight with her drug pushers. Anna had witnessed an incident once where a pusher attacked her mother in a grocer's store, and she'd ducked, and someone else had been stabbed and killed."

Her father, in his fifties, was an alcoholic, and sexually abusive. When she was three, her father had taken her into a pornography studio, and he and several other men had sex with her while it was videotaped. The memory of it was very sharp in her mind, as if it was in slow motion. "Did that explain why she was all over the place?" says Knaus. "Yes, it did. Her parents had put her through horrific experiences." Cognitive therapy can show dramatic results in a short period, but in Anna's extreme case, it took longer. Over the next two years, Bill tried to teach Anna a framework for establishing resilience, teaching her to understand where her feelings came from, and why people responded like they did to her erratic behavior. He helped build up her sense of self-efficacy, her sense of being in control of her feelings and her environment. But he says: "She still had that horrific image of abuse in her mind, and she still viewed herself as a horrible person because of all the things that took place."

One day, when she was seven and a half, just over two years after beginning therapy, Anna came in to see Bill, and was ready to talk about the experience and her attitudes to it. Bill says:

> The idea is to teach the child concepts which they can apply in real-life situations. So we looked at control as a concept. I said to her, when you look at the ocean, and you see the waves lapping in to the shore, can you tell them to stop? "No, nobody can stop the waves." What if you're on a picnic, and it's raining, could you stop the rain? "No. Why are you asking me silly questions?" Well, can you decide what to wear to school? "Yeah, sometimes." Can you choose what TV show you want to watch? "Yeah, sometimes." Can you decide what you draw or write about? "Yes, usually." And what you think about? "Yes, usually." So we discussed the idea of there being some things you can control and others you

can't. Then I asked her, the thing that happened with your father and the other people, was it more like the waves, or more like something you choose to think? There were five minutes of silence. Then she said: "Like the waves."

Bill thinks that understanding the difference between what she could control and what she couldn't helped Anna to overcome her trauma and get back on the road to health. She no longer felt like a bad little girl, because she understood that she had been a three-year-old child unable to control an adult man. The bad things he did were out of her control. But how she thought about it, in the present, was in her control. Anna didn't slide into drugs or alcoholism. She started to do very well at her classes, and when her IQ was tested again, it came out in the high range, at 128. Knaus says: "Therapy didn't raise her IQ, but it cleared away a lot of the obstacles for her capabilities to emerge. She became an A-grade student, graduated from high school, and went on to university. She recently got married." He concludes: "Anna's example shows that, even after growing up with highly disturbed parents putting you through horrific experiences, you can still learn to develop the rational coping skills that Epictetus first taught." Anna was blaming herself for her father's actions, and getting over it meant accepting this was a situation where she was powerless. She didn't have any control over it. It wasn't her fault. But now, years later, she *did* have control over how she thought about it, and how she chose to move on from it. As Knaus says: "What happens to us may not be our fault, but how we think about it is our responsibility."

NOT USING OTHER PEOPLE AS AN EXCUSE

Another example of someone who showed resilience in the face of terrible parenting is Brett Wheat-Simms, who is a friend and Stoic now living in Ohio. He's thirty-six years old, with a beard and shaved head, and a permanent big grin. When Brett was growing up, his mother was addicted to methamphetamine. Because of her addiction, she lost the hair salon she owned, then their home, their car, and "pretty much everything else." The family moved to Phoenix, where Brett's mother and stepfather had drug connections. Brett tells me:

> For the next four years, I lived in some of the most abject circum-
> stances you can experience. My teenage years were hell — sleeping
> in odd places, being woken up in the middle of the night by drug
> deals happening in the living room where I slept, carrying a .38 pistol
> around for fear of drug deals gone bad. I was shot at by gang mem-
> bers, I caught my parents in bed with strangers, our house was fire-
> bombed, you name it. I would spend nights out in the desert waiting
> for my parents to finish marathon amphetamine sessions so I could
> go back to our trailer in the city. My parents were oblivious to me in
> that period. I didn't exist, except that I was the only one working. I
> worked 10-hour shifts at a grocery store to pay the rent when they
> couldn't, and I'd be the bodyguard when they needed me.

He was, he says, "a very angry young man, which played itself out in me making very poor judgments, in physical altercations, in problems with the police. I went to jail twice for assault and battery and for carry-ing a loaded shotgun in a public park. I was smart enough to see where it was all heading. I was sure I would be dead or in prison by the time I turned twenty-one." One morning, when he was eighteen, he woke up and thought, "That's it, I can't do this anymore." He packed up his belong-ings, walked out the door, and never looked back. He was taken in by a Christian evangelist family, who gave him his first-ever taste of having a stable, loving family. He embraced their faith, and even went to seminary school to train as a preacher. But then he started to have doubts about the Christian faith. After much wandering, and a brief stint as a missionary in the Balkans, he came across Marcus Aurelius's *Meditations* while travelling through Europe in his early twenties. He says: "I didn't know any deep philosophical principles of Stoicism, but I liked the line: 'Vex not thy spirit at the course of things, they heed not thy vexations.' It dawned on me that external things have no control over me if I don't let them, and that the only thing I have control over is myself."

He eventually graduated from Oklahoma University, and invited his mother to the graduation ceremony. His father had by that point died of a heroin overdose:

> We sat on my front porch and, with tears in my eyes, I asked her why they did all the things they did. She told me I was overreacting and couldn't understand why I was making such a big deal of it. I could see in her eyes and by the twitch of her mouth that she had been up several days, high on her drug of choice. That day my relationship with my mother ended. We still talk on the phone, but nothing substantial. She's off drugs now, as is my stepfather (they're no longer together and haven't been for fifteen years), but the damage is done.

Today, Brett is happily married, and has a high-powered job for the catering company Sodexo. Brett could have used his terrible childhood as an alibi to let his own life fall apart. He could have fostered a victim mentality, complaining about all the tough breaks life had thrown him, and all the baggage his parents had left him with. But instead, he learnt that there is much in our life — including our past, and other people's behavior — that is simply out of our control. There's no point making ourselves miserable about other people's issues. At the same time, we can't use other people's behavior as an alibi for what is our responsibility: our thoughts, our behavior, our life choices. Brett recognized he had the power to choose differently from his parents, and he did. He says he still uses Epictetus's lesson in his everyday life. He says: "I can be very stressed-out because I'm a high performer and a high achiever. But I've taught myself to remind myself what is in my control and what isn't. When something doesn't go right, I try not to overreact to the situation, but remind myself that there are limits on what I can control. I'm not a 'sage.' I still have strong emotional reactions to things. I don't think that will ever change. But I will say Stoicism has improved my ability to cope with external situations to a great degree." Both Brett and Anna are, in their different ways, examples of how people can overcome a highly inauspicious start in life by reminding themselves what is in their control and what isn't. It's not a question of saying either "everything is my fault," as Anna initially did, or saying "everything is other people's fault," as Brett could easily have done. Both responses are too simplistic. We have to learn to be discriminating. By insisting that we always have some control over our thoughts, but only limited control over everything else, Epictetus gave us a powerful method for defining and preserving our locus of control even under the most difficult circumstances.

3. Musonius Rufus and the Art of Fieldwork

MICHAEL IS A FORTY-SEVEN-YEAR-OLD major in the US Army Special Forces, or the Green Berets as they are known by outsiders. He joined the Rangers when he was thirty-one, and five years later joined Special Forces. Michael first came across Stoicism while training at the Navy SEALs' SERE (Survival, Evasion, Resistance, and Escape) school in Fort Bragg in 2001. He says:

> We were taught how to survive being tortured, and one of the things we were taught was James Stockdale's experience in Vietnam, and how he'd used ancient philosophy to cope with his seven years in a POW camp [we'll meet Stockdale in chapter seven]. Afterwards, I found out more about him online, and gradually became more and more interested in Stoicism. Eventually, I thought we should change our Special Forces training to simply a course in Hellenic philosophy, because so much of Stoicism is about understanding humans and why they make the decisions they do, which is a crucial part of Special Forces operations.

One of Special Forces' primary missions is training and advising foreign military and political forces. Michael says: "We usually work through other people. That's one of our mottos — 'by, with, and through.' We're force multipliers. We go into a foreign country, and build, train, and lead a force from scratch. Because of that, one of our most critical skills is understanding human beings. That way, hopefully we can stop fighting before it happens. Stoicism has really helped me understand why people make the decisions they make." Michael says:

> Most of our decisions are automatic. We make them because of social convention. We don't really think about them. Now if you know that, and you know the social conventions by which someone is programmed, then you can make them do what you want to do, without them even being aware of it. You can learn about the biases that guide people's decision-making, then use that knowledge to manipulate them. You have to be a trained Stoic to resist that sort of manipulation. Hopefully, I'm now slightly better at resisting it.

Michael has a fairly austere Stoic practice by comparison with other contemporary Stoics. He rises every morning at 4:30 AM, and reads Stoic texts for forty-five minutes — at the moment, he is reading Pierre Hadot's *Philosophy as a Way of Life*. He then embarks on a gruelling bout of circuit training called "CrossFit," in which members of the CrossFit network compete to see how many workout circuits they can complete within a given time. They then post their times on a website. Michael sets the circuit for other members of his local network, and posts it on his blog. Even reading it is painful:

21 X Hang Snatch
21 X Knee to Elbows
21 X Box Jumps 24 inch
20 X Air Squats
1 Mile run
Execute the entire WOD [workout of the day] wearing a 20lb vest

He says: "It's much more than athletics. It also requires skill and integrity. It's a daily test of character, because you can cheat to get a better time or to beat an opponent, but you'll know if you cut corners. What it does is test whether you make good decisions under extreme physical and emotional stress. It gives you practice for unexpected moments, and teaches you how to practice self-control." He does this for an hour or so, on an empty stomach: "I only eat one meal a day, in a four-hour window between 5 PM and 9 PM. I've been doing that for a couple of years. What you learn is that hunger becomes more comfortable. You get a sense of control from it; you learn to manage pleasure and pain. It drives my wife and my friends nuts, though, when I just sit there at lunch watching them eat." He adds: "I like the Stoic philosopher Musonius Rufus on this topic. He says you should see food as nutrients for strength. Look at it from a detached point of view. Why do we eat? We eat because of what the body needs. It's a necessity. But you're in danger of letting it control you when you take too much pleasure in it. It's like Socrates said — eat to live, don't live to eat." Michael is not that impressed with modern America's self-discipline, when he returns from his missions abroad: "The thing I notice most about America, when I come home, is how many people are overweight. Our children are the fattest, most spoilt children in the world. They've never had the 'benefit' of poverty. My father, for example, grew up during the Depression. And he was a very resilient human being. It's remarkable how plentiful our lives are today, and yet we never stop complaining."

PHILOSOPHY AS TRAINING

In the modern world, we tend to think of philosophy as a purely intellectual activity, which we can practice from the comfort of our armchair. For the ancients, by contrast, philosophy was a full-body workout, which was taught and practiced in the gymnasium as much as the classroom. They were celebrated as much for their physical toughness as their mental acumen: Plato was a famous wrestler (his name means "broad-shouldered"), Cleanthes the Stoic was a boxer, Socrates was considered the toughest soldier in the Athenian army, while Diogenes the Cynic was so hardy he was content to live in a barrel. Their physical hardiness was proof that they lived their philosophy rather than just talking it. Wisdom can't be purely theoretical — you need to get off your chair and see how you fare in real-life situations. Epictetus warned his students that they may be proficient in the classroom, "but drag us into practice and you will find us miserably shipwrecked."[1] The philosopher who best emphasized the idea of philosophy as mental and physical training was Epictetus's teacher, Musonius Rufus.

Rufus is not as well known as the rest of our faculty, but he was the most esteemed philosopher of his day, nicknamed the "Socrates of Rome." He was a full-time philosophy teacher, whose most famous student was the slave Epictetus. Like Epictetus, Rufus didn't write any books but some of his lessons were written down by students. He had some quite radical views for his time — he said slaves had the right to defy an unjust order from their master, and suggested women were just as capable of philosophy as men. Such radical thinking got him in trouble with the imperial authorities, and he was twice exiled from Rome, but managed to avoid execution. Rufus was a great champion of street philosophy. He insisted that philosophy was worthless if it wasn't embedded in practical training, or *askesis*. He told his students:

> Virtue is not only a matter of theoretical knowledge, but also practical, just like medicine and music. Just as the doctor and musician have mastered not only the theoretical aspects of their trade but have also practised implementing them, likewise a person who wants to be good should not only thoroughly learn the teachings, but also practise doing them...[For] how could anyone gain self-control, if he only knew theoretically that one should resist pleasure, but had never practised resisting it?[2]

Rufus insists that philosophical training is physical as well as mental. The Stoic student should, Rufus said, be trained to "adapt to cold, heat, thirst, hunger, plain food, a hard bed, abstinence from pleasure, and endurance of strenuous labor. For through these and other things, the body is strengthened and becomes unfeeling, hard and useful for every task, and the soul is strengthened, being made manly through endurance of toil, and learning self-control by abstaining from pleasure." The student has to be conscious of what to eat and drink because "the beginning and foundation of temperance lies in self-control in eating and drinking." Any foods too delicate or luxurious should be shunned — Rufus banned all cookbooks from his students' homes. The aim of our diet should be "health and strength" rather than physical pleasure, which weakens us and makes us the slaves of our stomachs. In fact, "when food performs its proper function...it gives no pleasure at all." Not a great dinner-party host, Rufus, but better than the Pythagoreans, who would strengthen their self-control by holding banquets at which the most succulent dishes would be brought in, held temptingly in front of the guests' faces, only to be taken away and given to the slaves.³ The Stoics, like the Pythagoreans, thought voluntary occasional fasting was a great way to improve self-control — Rufus's student Epictetus suggests we should take some water in our mouths when we're thirsty "spit it out, and tell no one." The point about not telling anyone is that this kind of ascetic training can easily become a spectacle where you prove how tough you are to an admiring public (think of the "endurance artist" David Blaine). Stoics don't practice for the applause of the public. They practice to attain inner freedom and resilience to adversity.

This sort of physical training was taken to an extreme by Sparta, the military city-state to the south of Athens, who put their poor children through the most austere training imaginable to turn them into perfect soldiers. Spartan boys were turned over to the state at the age of seven, to undergo a fourteen-year training process called the *agoge*, or "abduction." They lived in barracks, in groups known as "herds," dressed in simple cloaks, and fed on a broth made of pig's blood. One visitor, on trying this disgusting soup, remarked: "Now I understand why you Spartans are not afraid to die!"⁴ They trained in singing, dancing, and fighting. They showed off their training in public displays known as *gymnopedias*, where the Spartan girls would gather to mock the weaker kids. At twelve, they were forced to undergo the "contest of endurance," where they were brutally whipped, sometimes to death, while trying to steal food from the Temple of Artemis. They were then sent off to live in the wild for a year, dressed only in their cloaks, without shoes. They had to make their own beds from reeds pulled up by hand from the river. They only ate what they could steal or kill. Their ascetic education trained them to deny the self, to cope with physical pain, and survive in the wild, all with the aim of making them the perfect soldier and servant of the state.

The philosophers of Athens were fascinated (and slightly horrified) by Spartan education practices — in fact, the *agoge* was partly designed by a Stoic philosopher, Sphaerus of Borysthenes. Athenians thought Spartans were mindless drones, who simply obeyed orders and lacked Athenians' culture and ability to think for themselves. But the Stoics also admired the Spartans for their toughness, and liked to share the story of the Spartan boy who stole a fox one day, and hid it under his cloak. Rather than be discovered, he kept silent as the fox tore out his innards.[5] This impressed the Stoics greatly.

KEEPING TRACK OF YOUR PROGRESS

How do we know if we're making progress in our philosophical training? The analogy of the gymnasium is useful: we can't tell if we're really making progress in the gym unless we keep track of ourselves, see how far we can run, what weights we can lift, how many calories we've burnt, how fast our pulse rate is, and how we're improving over time. The ancients took the same approach to their philosophical practice, keeping track of themselves, their thoughts, moods, and actions, to see if they were really making progress. Philosophical training takes time. It's not enough to come back from a class feeling like you've really made a breakthrough and are a changed person. That might last for a day or two, then you'll slip back into your old habits. You need to track your progress over time, monitor your habits, and see if you're really making advances or just going round in circles.

One of the ways the ancients did this was to use journals, or *hupomnemata* as they were called in ancient Greek. At the end of each day, the trainee-philosopher writes a brief account of their behavior that day in their journal. They consider how they spent the day, what was done well, and what could have been done better. Seneca writes that every day we must call upon our soul to "give an account of itself. This is what [the Neo-Pythagorean philosopher] Sextius did. When the day was over and he had withdrawn to his room for his nightly rest, he questioned his soul: 'What evils have you cured yourself of today? What vices have you fought? In what sense are you better?'... Is there anything more admirable than this custom of examining a whole day's conduct?"[6] So, for example, if a Stoic student is aware that they have a temper problem, they keep watch over themselves throughout the day, and then at the end of the day, count up any times they've lost their temper that day, record it in their journal, and look to see what progress they're making over time. Epictetus told his students: "If then you wish to free yourself of an angry temper...count the days on which you have not been angry. 'I used to be seized by an irrational emotion every day, now every second day, then every third; then every fourth.'" By counting the days you have managed to give up a bad habit, you strengthen your will and sense of progress. When your progress is visible and quantifiable, it encourages you to carry on the work. Many of us who have given up smoking used this technique, counting the days we have gone without a cigarette, and Epictetus says a similar method can be used for kicking other bad habits. According to him, the magic period for kicking a habit is thirty days. Epictetus said: "If you have omitted [a bad habit] for thirty days, make thanks to God because the habit begins at first to be weakened, before it is destroyed completely."[7] Journals are also places where we can reflect on episodes that gave rise to strong negative emotions during the day, and then drill down to discover what beliefs led to our emotions. Then we can consider that belief, hold it up to the light, see if it makes sense, and if not, challenge it with a more rational and considered response. When we use the journal in this way, we engage ourselves in a Socratic dialogue. We wrestle with our destructive mental habits, trying out new attitudes, and practicing them until they in turn are habitual.

MARCUS AURELIUS'S *MEDITATIONS*

The greatest example of a journal we have from the ancient world is the *Meditations* of Marcus Aurelius. Marcus was emperor of Rome from AD 161 to 180, the last of the "five good emperors" as historians call them, and is generally thought to have done the job well. The eighteenth-century historian Edward Gibbon claimed that the rule of the five good emperors (Nerva, Trajan, Hadrian, Antoninus Pius, and Marcus Aurelius) was "the most happy and prosperous" period in all of human history.[8] In fact, Aurelius's reign was not an easy one. During his rule, Rome was hit by a succession of disasters — floods, earthquakes, plague, and repeated uprisings by tribes on the Empire's northern borders. Aurelius spent the last decade of his life on campaign, fighting the German barbarians in gruelling and vicious winter campaigns. He was old, unwell, he missed his family, he must have longed for release from the endless war. But he stayed at his post. And he kept a journal, in which he kept track of his thoughts, and tried to fortify himself against life's challenges.

The *Meditations* is probably my favorite book of philosophy. Epictetus's *Discourses* are more powerful medicine, but there is a unique poetry and mysticism to Marcus's insights about the universe. Some readers have complained that the *Meditations* are fragmentary and repetitive, and not nearly as coherent and well crafted as, say, one of Cicero's or Seneca's exquisite books. But this is to misunderstand the point of Aurelius's book. He wasn't writing to please an audience. The book's title is literally translated as "thoughts to myself." It's a working book, written for himself alone, in which he tracked and challenged irrational thoughts, and rehearsed wiser attitudes. That's why it can be repetitive or fragmentary: because he was responding to whatever his mind came up with that day, and practicing responses until they became automatic. Aurelius used his journal as a resource, as an inner gymnasium in which he could retreat from the demands of imperial life, go over his thoughts, and rehearse spiritual training. He used writing as a workout. He took a situation that had upset him, and then thought it through, turned it, considered it from different angles. The social psychologist James Pennebaker has studied self-writing, and how people are often profoundly helped by writing about traumatic experiences. He's found those who were most helped by self-writing moved from using mainly the first person pronoun in their writing (I, me, my) to using a variety of different pronouns (you, they, we, it) and causal connecting words (because, therefore, that's why).[9] They de-personalize a difficult situation, hold it at arm's length, and come to terms with it — literally.

This is what we see Marcus doing — seeing difficult situations from multiple perspectives, making his mind flexible, like in a yoga workout, and then rehearsing new attitudes until they're habituated.

FROM GREEK ASKESIS TO CHRISTIAN ASCETICISM

In the last centuries of the ancient world, the Greeks' idea of philosophy as *askesis* was taken up by early Christians, who practiced many of the Greeks' techniques for spiritual training, such as training yourself to be mindful, tracking yourself in a journal, and improving your self-control and hardiness through physical training. However, some Christian practitioners took this training to an extreme — they turned Greek *askesis* into fanatical asceticism, often practiced in the desert alone or in small eremitic communities. Christianity introduced a new dimension to asceticism, with its introduction of a mythology of demons and devils. The Stoics talked of "keeping watch over the enemy of your self," by which they meant watching over your automatic self so it doesn't slip into bad habits. Early Christians took up this language of "guarding against the enemy," but for them, the Enemy was actually a powerful supernatural being constantly plotting to bring you down.[10] The threat of the Devil and of eternal damnation gives Christian asceticism an intensity that often tipped into pathological fanaticism. The most famous example is St. Simeon the Stylite, who stood for years on a pillar in the Syrian Desert. There's some similarity with the Cynics, who we'll meet later, who also left their homes to live in the open. But the Cynics were known for their good humor, while St. Simeon was a humorless misanthrope. And the Cynics had a very easygoing attitude to sex: Diogenes famously masturbated in the open while other Cynics preached free love *al fresco*. Christians, by contrast, thought sex was the principal snare the Devil would use against us, so they went to extremes of flagellation and even emasculation to purge their fallen flesh. The excesses of Christianity gave asceticism a bad name, and many centuries later, when philosophy broke free of the Church in the seventeenth and eighteenth centuries, Enlightenment philosophers ridiculed Christians for their fanatic asceticism, which they viewed as symptoms of a diseased personality.[11] Asceticism, like monasticism, was seen by the Enlightenment as uncivic, impolite, antisocial. The Enlightenment philosopher engaged with the world of commerce and letters, they enjoyed their coffee and wine, and some of them, like the Scottish philosopher David Hume, even knew how to cook. But unfortunately, in rejecting the extremes of Christian asceticism, Western philosophy lost sight of the idea of philosophy as mental and physical training.

THE RETURN OF PHILOSOPHY AS *ASKESIS*?

But perhaps academic philosophy is slowly coming back to the idea of philosophy as training, and if so, it's mainly thanks to the French academic Pierre Hadot, who insisted that philosophy was originally a set of spiritual exercises to be practiced repeatedly. His contemporary Michel Foucault drew on Hadot's work and brought it to a wider audience in books like *The Care of the Self*. But the shift within philosophy has been slow — you'd still be hard pressed to find an academic philosopher who thinks self-training is a worthwhile area of study, let alone something to practice oneself. However, the idea of training ourselves to improve our self-control *has* become a focus of research for modern psychology. Particularly interesting, on the topic of asceticism, is the work of Walter Mischel of Columbia University. In the late 1960s and early 1970s, Mischel conducted a series of famous "marshmallow experiments": children were put in a room with a plate of marshmallows in front of them, and were told they could have a marshmallow immediately, or they could wait for fifteen minutes, and then be given two marshmallows. Around a third of the children managed to hold out for fifteen minutes. Twenty years later, Mischel happened to notice a correlation between how long a child had resisted the marshmallow, and how well they flourished in later life. The longer the children deferred marshmallow gratification, the less behavioral problems they had later in school, and the better they did academically.[12] Since then, self-control has become one of the main focuses of interest for psychology, and several studies have suggested it is a better predictor of academic success than IQ. It also predicts our financial stability, our job stability, even our marriage stability.[13]

Self-control appears to be the key character-strength. This insight has started to be integrated into schools, like the KIPP academies across the US, where the academy shops sell T-shirts bearing the slogan "Don't eat the marshmallow!"

The question is, can our ability to resist the marshmallow be improved by training, as the Stoics believed, or are the weak-willed among us always condemned to reach out and eat it? Psychologists are increasingly coming round to Rufus's idea that we can improve our self-control through training. As the Stoics suggested, psychologists have discovered that self-monitoring is essential to this training. The pioneer of this field is the psychologist Albert Bandura, Professor Emeritus at Stanford University. In 1983, Bandura and his colleague Daniel Cervone tried out an experiment with a group of ninety cyclists on cycling machines. They divided them into four groups — one group were given no goals or feedback; another group were given goals, but no feedback; a third group were given feedback, but no goals; and the final group received both goals *and* feedback. The final group performed significantly better than the other groups. Setting ourselves goals, and watching our progress toward those goals, motivates us to carry on the struggle.[14] The neuroscientist David Eagleman has recently taken this idea further, developing a brain-scan machine that can show when a person successfully resists the impulse to, say, have a cigarette. You can see, on a brain scan, when the cognitive parts of the brain successfully regulate an automatic habitual desire. Using this visual feedback, Eagleman believes we can train people to develop their powers of self-regulation, and he's suggested we introduce this technology into prisons to help inmates develop self-control and the ability to resist impulses.[15]

A simpler and cheaper technology might simply be to use the journal, as the ancients did. Roy F. Baumeister of Florida State University, who is one of the leading experts on the psychology of self-control, has experimented with getting people to keep a food diary for a few weeks, in which they keep track of what they eat. He's found that this simple form of self-tracking improves their self-control, and this self-control then spills out into other areas of their life, making them better able to manage their finances for example.[16] I tracked down Baumeister at a social psychology conference in Texas, and asked him why this sort of training works. He replied:

> Self-control works like a muscle: repeated exercise develops it. So, for example, we've found that a simple exercise like using your left hand more than your right (if you're right-handed) for three weeks increases people's self-control. They're practicing exerting their conscious will against their automatic habits. And this self-control can then be used in other tasks. The self-control they built up from that regime carried over into other areas of their life — they became more self-disciplined in general.

QUANTIFYING THE SELF

Self-tracking has now become the inspiration for a whole movement, called the Quantified Self, which has the very Socratic motto: "Self-knowledge Through Numbers." Members of the Quantified Self movement have invented bio-digital devices to track their daily calorie intake, alcohol intake, heart-rate, blood sugar levels, exercise regimes, social life, sex life, emotions, finances — there's even a digital rosary app to keep track of how many prayers you've said. The movement now has forty-five meet-up groups around the world, where practitioners present their wacky inventions for self-tracking, some of which are commercially viable, some less so.[17] The idea behind this craze is simple: if you want to improve yourself, you need to take a rational, scientific approach to self-improvement, which means keeping account of yourself, so that you can see what progress you're making, which interventions are really working, and which are a waste of time. And self-quantifiers, unlike the secretive Stoics, love to share the results of their training with others. They've found that when they publish their progress toward goals like weight loss, they are more likely to stick to their regimes, and to elicit support from others. They take a socially networked approach to asceticism, which is quite different from the Stoics or early Christians (Michael's cross-fit training, in fact, is an example of this socially networked asceticism).

One man who has taken the self-quantified life to an extreme is Tim

Ferriss, the author of the *4-Hour Workweek* and the *4-Hour Body*. Tim is a self-improvement nut, and also a big fan of the Stoics: his Google talk on Seneca has brought Stoicism to thousands of people. Tim describes himself as a "life-hacker": he wants to work out how to get the maximum improvement in his life from the smallest changes. For example, he wanted to be as fit as possible, with the minimum wasted effort. So he started tracking himself, to self-experiment and find out what interventions would make him sleep better, run better, heal better, even make love better. He writes: "I've recorded every workout I've done since age eighteen. I've had more than 1,000 blood tests performed since 2004, sometimes as often as every two weeks, tracking everything from complete lipid panels, insulin, and hemoglobin A1c to IGF-1 and free testosterone...I have pulse oximeters, ultrasound machines, and medical devices for measuring everything from galvanic skin response to REM sleep. The kitchen and bathroom look like an ER."[18] This may sound somewhat fanatical, but all this self-tracking has allowed Ferriss to self-experiment, to see what interventions really work, and to measure his progress toward his goals. Such self-tracking is in the spirit of Socrates, the original life-hacker, who once said the best occupation for a man is "effective action," or "doing a thing well after learning and practicing how to do it."[19]

Of course, there's the important question of what end you are serving with your training. You might be putting yourself through rigorous training purely to look good, to get rich, to win the admiration of the world or other external goals, which would be quite different from the Stoics' goal of training to attain inner freedom from external attachments and aversions. But you can equally use self-tracking techniques for internal moral goals, such as giving up smoking or improving your temper. Many self-tracking devices are designed to help people overcome emotional problems. For example, Margaret Morris, a clinical psychologist who works at Intel, has designed a smartphone app called Mood Mapper, which allows users to keep track of their moods using a colored circle that represents the emotional spectrum. Throughout the day, the app asks users how they're feeling, and if the user enters a particularly negative mood, the app suggests alternative ways of looking at the situation. Morris tells me: "If you are measured as feeling particularly depressed, Mood Mapper might ask you to consider if you're catastrophizing, or it might ask if there's another way you can view the situation that's upsetting you." The app is sort of a pocket Socrates, which you can carry around with you to examine your inner states.

Less sophisticated but no less effective is the use of the journal by cognitive therapy. If you go to a cognitive therapist in order to overcome depression or anxiety, the chances are they will ask you to keep a journal in which you can track your automatic thoughts, emotions, and acts, to see how you're progressing, and to give yourself a place to challenge automatic habits and try to ingrain new habits — just like Marcus Aurelius did two thousand years ago. You might have the depressive habit of always focusing on the bad things in your life. The journal would let you become aware of this unconscious habit, and then challenge it by, for example, writing down three things that you have to be grateful for each day (a technique psychologists call the "gratitude journal"). Aurelius himself used this technique — the entire first book of the *Meditations* is taken up with the emperor reminding himself what blessings he owes to other people. There are now several apps where you can keep CBT journals or gratitude journals on your smartphone (some apps also allow you to share your life-logging directly with your therapist). You can also use mood-mapping apps to track your emotions and correlate them with other data, to show, for example, how your mood correlates with your sleep patterns, or your alcohol intake, or your social activities. So if your mood plummets, you can look at your personal well-being dashboard and see that it's probably because you're not getting enough sleep, or drinking too much, then you can correct your course without crashing.

The self-tracking movement, it seems to me, is an interesting fusion of ancient philosophy with modern technology. Socrates's student Xenophon tells us that Socrates "strongly encouraged his companions...to study their own constitutions throughout life, to see what food or drink or what kind of exercise was good for them individually...He said that anyone who observed themselves in this way would find it hard to find a doctor who could recognise what was good for their health better than they could themselves."[20] Ancient philosophy, as Cicero put it, trains us all to be doctors to ourselves, and self-tracking technologies put the power in our hands. We don't need to simply trust the experts: we can all become experts in our own self-improvement.

STOICISM AND SPORT

Stoics often used the metaphor of philosophy as a training for the Olympics. God sends adversity your way like a boxing coach sending you a sparring partner, to see how well your training has progressed, how far you have advanced physically, mentally, and spiritually. And if you look for this sort of Stoic attitude in modern life, the place you're most likely to find it, besides the services, is in sport. As the historian Darrin McMahon has commented, sports coaches are now, in a strange way, filling the role in our schools once filled by philosophers or chaplains. "The only people teaching values in schools seem to be sports coaches," he says (in fact, the study of ethics in sport is a growing field in academic philosophy).[21] Take the film *Coach Carter*. It seems quite a traditional Hollywood movie in which a dysfunctional school team is inspired by a coach to eventually win the state championships. Except, in the final, they lose by one point (sorry for giving it away). But, in the closing scene, the coach comes into their changing room, and gives a very Stoic speech. He tells them: "What you achieved goes way beyond the win-loss column or what's gonna be written on the front page of the sports section tomorrow. You've achieved something that some people spend their whole lives trying to find. What you achieved is that ever-elusive victory within." That's a very Stoic idea: sport doesn't simply train and develop our bodies. It trains our characters, trains us to push through pain, to resist discomfort, to serve our team, to face setbacks with dignity, and to maintain a steady resolve in the high moments and the low moments. Sport trains us, in the words of Rudyard Kipling that are inscribed over Wimbledon's center court, to "meet with triumph and disaster, and treat those two imposters just the same."[22] It teaches us Stoicism. Today, if you type "stoic" into Google News, you are more likely to find the word in the sports pages than the arts or politics sections.

SCOUTING AND SPARTA

Outside academia, there's also been a return to the Spartan idea that young people should be initiated into adult society through outdoor endurance challenges. Look, for example, at the Scouts movement, which was started by Robert Baden Powell at the beginning of the twentieth century. Powell, a committed imperialist, worried that the British Empire was going the way of Rome, which had declined, he believed, because of "the growth of luxury and idleness." The way to strengthen Britain's spiritual resources was to follow the advice of the Spartan king Lycurgus, who said, in Powell's words, "that the wealth of a state lay . . . not so much in money as in men who were sound in body and mind, with a body fit for endurance, and with a mind well disciplined and seeing things in their proper proportion."[23] The best method to train up young citizens' bodies and minds was to do what the Spartans did — take youngsters out of the comforts of civilization, and throw them onto their own resources in the wild. Baden Powell wrote: "Character is a difficult thing to develop in the boy within the school walls, however good the system, since it cannot be taught in class."[24] Within the bounds of the school, we have become too obsessed with "Safety First," he complained, when character can only properly be developed in the proximity of risk and danger. Scouting, like the Spartan *agoge*, took young boys away from their parents, organized them into "gangs" under the leadership of older boys, and then taught them how to survive in the wild, how to make shelters, how to make fires, how to trap animals, and also how to help other people through skills like first aid, firemanship, and bridge-building. The goal of this was very Stoic: to "help the boy become self-reliant, resourceful, to 'paddle his own canoe' — that is, to look ahead and shape his own course in life."[25]

Of course, it's easy to mock Powell today, for his imperialism and his personal peculiarities. Still, scouting remains undeniably popular with young people, and by 2007 the worldwide scouting and guiding movement had 41 million members in 216 countries. For millions of young boys, scouting is their "first major step towards the most important goal of all: becoming a good man," as the former US Defense Secretary Robert Gates put it in a speech to the Annual Scout Jamboree in 2010. Gates said: "We live in an America today where the young are increasingly physically unfit and society as a whole languishes in ignoble moral ease. An America where in public and private life we see daily what the famous news columnist Walter Lippmann once called 'the disaster of the character of men...the catastrophe of the soul.' But not in scouting."[26]

SAM'S STORY

The Spartan ethos could be taken too far — it could lead to a fascist intolerance of mental or physical imperfection, in you or anyone else (the Nazis taught Spartan history in their schools, and seemed to have been inspired by its practice of infanticide in their own eugenics program). You could be too fundamentalist in your interpretation of the Olympic motto "Better, faster, stronger," and become obsessed with creating the "perfect body," using whatever technological or chemical enhancements you can get. The Stoics were certainly admired for their physical strength, but it was their *moral* strength that was really admired, and you can develop that even if, like me, you're not exactly Charles Atlas. A good example of this second sort of strength is Sam Sullivan.

At the age of nineteen, Sam, a lanky, athletic teenager from Vancouver, broke his spine in a skiing accident, and lost the use of his arms, legs, and body. For six years, he battled with depression and suicidal impulses. Then he managed to get a philosophical perspective on what had happened to him, so that his spirit wouldn't be crushed along with his body. He says: "I played many different mind games to get a perspective on what had happened to me — I don't mean games in a frivolous sense, but in the philosophical sense. For example, I imagined I was Job [the character in the Old Testament], and God was looking down on me and saying, 'Anyone can maneuver through modern society with two good arms and two good legs, but let's take away the use of his arms, legs, and body — *now* let's see what the guy's made of.' "

Sam turned to Stoicism to give him the moral strength to cope with his body's disabilities, and used its philosophy of endurance to help him through the slow and painful work of recovering the use of his arms. Then, it inspired him to re-engage with society, and start fighting for better conditions for the disabled in his native Vancouver. He tells me: "One of the things that most attracts me to Stoicism is the commitment to public life. Think of Zeno, the founder of Stoicism, hanging out under the painted porch, right in the center of the action." Sam campaigned for better access for the disabled on Vancouver's streets, public transport, and public services. He helped design sailing boats that could be used by the disabled, and campaigned for public funding for their introduction. He helped introduce disabled rock-climbing to Vancouver. He won a seat on Vancouver's City Council, and then, in 2004, he was elected mayor of the city.

One of his earliest international responsibilities as mayor of Vancouver was to travel to Turin for the closing ceremony of the 2006 Winter Olympics, to accept the Olympic flag in preparation for the 2010 Winter Olympics in Vancouver. He joked that it was strange that Vancouver was sending the city's worst skier to the event. Sullivan accepted the enormous Olympic flag from the mayor of Turin, placed it in a special holder on his wheelchair, and then rotated his wheelchair to twirl the flag. He says he had practiced the maneuver in parking lots at night in Vancouver. The occasion was seen by millions of viewers (you can still see it on YouTube) and Sam was subsequently flooded with over five thousand emails, letters, and phone calls, a lot of them from disabled people saying they had been inspired by the moment. Sam says: "Really, I don't consider accepting a flag as one of the great achievements of my mayoralty." Maybe not — but it's still a pretty cool moment. It reminds me of the lines of Epictetus: "when a difficulty falls upon you, remember that God, like a trainer of wrestlers, has matched you with a rough young man. 'For what purpose?' you may say. Why, that you may become an Olympic conqueror."[27]

4. Seneca and the Art of Managing Expectations

"I GREW UP ON THE NORTH SIDE OF CHICAGO in the early eighties," says Jesse, a thirty-seven-year-old law enforcement officer. "It was a pretty rough neighborhood." The north of Chicago in the 1980s was where and when the modern street gang first appeared. It was here that gangs like the Latin Kings, the Vice-Lords, and the Gangsta Disciples first coalesced, and grew until their numbers ran into the tens of thousands. Jesse says: "My local high school was gang-ridden. There were constant stabbings and shootings. I never joined a gang so I was picked on a lot. I didn't fight because it would bring more trouble. I learnt to avoid trouble, to spot the gangs by their markings." Eventually, Jesse's mother took him out of public school and borrowed money to send him to a Catholic private school. But the violence and stress of his early environment stayed with him, in a volatile temper that he struggles with to this day. His family upbringing was also tempestuous — he was born out of wedlock, to an alcoholic dad who was a "terrible father," who disappeared for several years at a time.

After graduating, Jesse joined the sheriff's office in Cook County, Illinois. He was eventually put in charge of the lock-up, which brought him face to face with many of the gangsters he had spent his childhood trying to avoid. He says: "In the street, it's about your pride, about whether you're getting respect. If you look at me the wrong way, you're disrespecting me. Then if I don't get violent and step to you, I'm a wimp." This street code was still, to some extent, inside him. "I've had a bad temper all my life," he says. He would lose his temper if a gangster dissed him in lock-up, if one of his subordinates in the sheriff's office was disrespectful, even if someone cut him off on the road. That old law of the street, that if someone disrespects you then you must step to them or you're a wimp, was still in his head.

When he turned thirty, he came across Stoicism. His first encounter was with Seneca, in a book on humanism given to him by his father. "His words stuck in my heart. He was ethical, upright, he did the right thing. And his ideas didn't insult my reason with some magical story I had to believe in." He developed his practice through a Stoic training course taught by a former Green Beret called Major Thomas Jarrett, who became Jesse's mentor or Jedi master, teaching him Stoic philosophy combined with the techniques of CBT. When something in his external environment triggered Jesse's temper, he would ring up Jarrett, and talk it out with him over the phone until he could reach a rational interpretation of the situation. When Jarrett was called up to serve in Iraq, Jesse carried on his practice on his own: "I try to read the texts regularly. If I have a spare ten minutes during the day, I'll pick up and read Seneca, Aurelius or Epictetus. I still take notes. And if something happens that triggers a negative emotion, I'll go home and have a rational talk with myself until I find some peace."

Gradually, Jesse started to make some progress in his anger management:

There was a situation where I was working in lock-up, and there was a gentleman in there. I'd taken pains to treat him with respect, to give him the benefit of the doubt like Stoic ethics teaches us to do. "Our job is to do others good and to put up with them," as Marcus Aurelius writes. But when I was searching this man, I saw him trying to hide things that didn't belong to him. It really enraged me that I had gone out of my way to give him the benefit of the doubt and yet he tried to do something so underhanded to me. So I took two steps towards him, and then I stopped myself. I remembered a passage I had read in Marcus Aurelius that morning: "When you wake up in the morning, tell yourself: The people I deal with today will be meddling, ungrateful, arrogant, dishonest, jealous, and surly. They are like this because they can't tell good from evil." And I caught myself. I realized, "This guy doesn't know any better. It's the culture he's raised in, or it's his false thinking. And the tragedy is he'll probably always be like this." So I didn't rise to it. I let it go.

Sometimes, Jesse says, his own colleagues can be just as exasperating as the gangsters. He says:

I overheard one of my deputies making jokes about me. We were fuelling up the cop cars, and he gave me this grin, like I was a big idiot, and it made me very angry. I wanted to grab him by the neck. But instead, I went home at the end of the day, and I sat down and tried to think it through logically. I thought about this guy, how he talks about his friends, and I thought "This isn't to do with me, this is typical of this guy, this is how he always behaves." And it actually worked.

Through Stoic practice, Jesse has managed, to some extent, to rise above the street code of respect and revenge that he grew up surrounded by, and to reach a higher code. He says: "I've learnt that no one can impede us or frustrate us. No one can hurt me or implement me in ugliness. What stands in the way becomes the Way. I'm getting better at realizing that. But I still find it difficult to this day. I'm still practicing. That's why I have a hard time with academic Stoics, people who see it just as an intellectual pursuit. I am not by nature a calm person, so I have to work really hard to be a Stoic."

SENECA, POLITICIAN, BANKER, SELF-HELP GURU

One of the first works of anger management in Western culture was written by Lucius Annaeus Seneca, who lived in the Roman Empire from around 4 BC until AD 65. Seneca was born into a rich and powerful Iberian family, and from an early age his family prepared him for political office. But he discovered how insecure life could be even for a Roman aristocrat. He was chronically ill for much of his life, plagued by asthma and suicidal bouts of depression. And being a prominent politician was extremely dangerous in an empire ruled by mad dictators like Caligula and Nero. After making a particularly brilliant speech that aroused the emperor Caligula's jealousy, Seneca was exiled from Rome, and it's said his life was only spared because he was so ill that Caligula expected him to die soon anyway. In the last decade of his life, Seneca returned to Rome, became tutor to the young emperor Nero, amassed a fortune as a moneylender, and for a while was one of the most powerful and wealthy men in Rome. But he eventually fell out with Nero, was accused of plotting against him, and was forced to commit suicide.

Throughout his life, and when facing death, Seneca turned to Stoic philosophy for strength and consolation. It was typical for Roman aristocrats to be taught some Stoicism, but Seneca seems to have embraced it with particular zeal, and used it to cope with his physical illnesses and political setbacks. He wrote that philosophy "molds and constructs the soul; it orders our life, guides our conduct, shows us what we should do and what we should leave undone... Countless things that happen every hour call for advice; and such advice is to be sought in philosophy."[1] Seneca was not embarrassed to dish out Stoic advice as well. He never set up a philosophy school — he was raised a politician, and wanted to be in "the thick of it," as he put it. But he did write Stoic letters to friends and acquaintances, to provide consolation if they'd been exiled, lost a child, or faced some other misfortune. It must have been a rather strange experience to receive one of Seneca's long, florid, and rather rhetorical letters after a personal tragedy, particularly when they seemed to be written more for the general reader than for the particular recipient. Nonetheless, even if we might not hire him as a therapist, we can admire him as a writer. His letters, essays, and tragedies are literary masterpieces, and exerted a great influence on later periods, particularly the Elizabethan Age: T. S. Eliot suggested that Seneca's Stoicism was the main influence on Shakespeare's worldview, and you hear echoes of Seneca in some of Shakespeare's finest speeches.[2]

SENECA'S TIPS FOR ANGER MANAGEMENT

Seneca wasn't just a great writer — he was also an excellent psychologist, and his insights into the emotions, and particularly into anger, are a main influence on the modern field of "anger management," as we'll see. Seneca wrote one of the first works of anger management, called *On Anger*, which he penned as a letter to his bad-tempered brother Novatus (history does not relate if Novatus thanked him for the advice). The first question it asks is: Is anger manageable? Can we control our passions, or do they arise involuntarily, irrationally, and uncontrollably? Our passions certainly *feel* out of our control. Once they've got hold of our bodies, we can't just flick a switch in our heads and become perfectly calm and rational. But Seneca insists that there is a moment, right at the beginning of an emotional episode, when we have a choice. Anger arises from a judgment we make about a situation. Seneca says the judgment is typically "I have been injured by someone or something, and it is appropriate that I revenge myself upon them." This judgment might have become habitual and ingrained, so that we're not even conscious that it *is* a judgment and not an objective fact. But, if we examine our minds like Socrates taught us to, we can see the beliefs that create our passions, and decide if we want to accept those beliefs or not.

Seneca suggests short-term and long-term anger management techniques. Among the short-term fixes, first of all, know your triggers: "Let us take note of what it is that particularly provokes us...Not all men are wounded in the same place; and so you ought to know what part of you is weak, so you can give it the most protection." Secondly, when you feel the red mist descending, take a "time out," as anger management specialists put it: "The greatest cure for anger is to wait," Seneca writes, "so that the initial passion it engenders may die down, and the fog that shrouds the mind may subside." Third, try smiling rather than frowning: "let the expression on our faces be relaxed, our voices gentler, our steps more measured; little by little, outer features mould inner ones."

Then there are longer-term structural issues to be addressed. Some of them are social and behavioral. Social psychologists talk about "social contagion" — how we pick up good and bad habits from those around us.[3] Seneca likewise writes: "vices move stealthily, and swiftly pass to all those nearest. Accordingly, just as in times of plague we must take care not to sit besides those bodies that have already been infected and burn with the disease... so in selecting friends we must pay attention to their characters." So if you have an anger problem, don't surround yourself with angry people (though of course, if you're a cop, soldier, or prison inmate, your situation forces you to interact with some angry people). Longer-term, we also need to dig down and deconstruct the cognitive causes of our anger. Seneca writes: "We shall prevent ourselves from becoming angry if we repeatedly place before our eyes all anger's faults and form a proper judgment of it." The key word is "repeatedly." We need to *repeatedly* challenge the core beliefs that lead to anger, because those core beliefs have become ingrained and habitual. The old habits need to be replaced with new habits.

One of the core habitual beliefs we need to challenge is the belief "it is appropriate to become angry," or even "it is *good* to become angry." We might think it's manly, brave, and effective to be angry. So we need to put anger in the dock and consider what it's really like. First of all, what does it look like? It looks horrific:

> ...one moment rough and fierce, then pale when the blood has flowed back and been dispersed, then flushed and, it seems, gorged with blood... with swollen veins, with eyes now restless and protruding, now fastened and rooted in one fixed stare; note also the sound of gnashing teeth, as if the owners were eager to eat up someone... notice the cracking of joints... the repeated beating of the breast, the fast breathing and deep groans, the shaking body, the broken speech with sudden outcries, the lips quivering... Wild beasts, believe me, present a less ghastly sight than a man on fire with anger...[4]

Not only are such outbursts profoundly unattractive, they're also deeply damaging. They damage your relationships, your friendships, your home life, your business, even your society. Our emotions aren't private affairs — we're all connected to each other, so our bad temper can infect the body politic, particularly if we're a senior politician or emperor (Nero murdered many of those closest to him, including his mother, while the mad emperor Caligula once had an entire section of the Colosseum audience thrown into the arena to be eaten by wild animals). Whole societies can be consumed by rage, to their detriment. Seneca notes how a "madness beyond words" sometimes seizes societies, so that they launch into reckless and ill-conceived military campaigns, "with no time to let public tumult subside... until a great disaster makes them atone for the rash boldness of their anger." There are instances of this in our own time too.

OVERLY OPTIMISTIC EXPECTATIONS

Seneca suggests that perhaps the main fallacy that leads to anger is an excessively optimistic expectation of how things will turn out. He writes:

> We are mightily stirred by all that happens contrary to hope and expectation, and this is the only reason why in domestic affairs we are vexed by trifles, why in the case of friends we call neglect a wrong. "Why, then," you query, "do the wrongs done by our enemies stir us?" Because we did not expect them, or at any rate not wrongs so serious. This is due to excessive self-love. We decide that we ought not to be harmed even by our enemies; each one in his heart has the king's point of view, and is willing to use license, but unwilling to suffer from it.[5]

There is something spoilt, infantile, and ungrateful about anger. We kick and scream like a child when the world does not immediately adopt our "king's point of view." We think of what the world owes us, rather than what we are lucky to have. Seneca tells his brother, rather unsparingly: "You ask what is the greatest failing in you? You keep accounts badly: you rate high what you have paid out, but low what you have been paid." The angry person is acutely sensitive to all they are owed by the world, and blind to all they have received.

If overoptimistic expectations are one of the main causes of anger, then the cure is to lower our expectations, to try to bring them more in line with reality, so that we're not constantly feeling let down by the world. The Stoic tries to see the world as it really is, rather than demanding that it fit their expectations. They practice reminding themselves what this world is like, and what we can expect to encounter in it. Seneca writes that the wise person "will ensure that none of what happens to him will come unexpectedly. For by looking ahead to all that may happen as though it were going to happen, he will soften the attacks of all ills, which bring nothing unforeseen to those who are prepared and expectant, but come as a serious blow to those who show no concern and expect only blessings."[6]

Stoics try to make a clear-eyed appraisal of the world we live in so its blows are not unexpected. We live, Seneca writes, in the realm of Fortune, and "her rule is harsh and unconquerable, and at her whim we will endure suffering deserved and undeserved. She will waste our bodies by violent, cruel and insulting means: some she will burn with fire...some she will put in chains...some she will toss naked onto the shifting seas..."[7] She will bring down cities, drink up seas, divert rivers...in fact, she destroys whole planets and galaxies, sucked up into black holes then spat forth again, until eventually, the whole universe will be consumed in one great conflagration (so the Stoics believed anyway), only to be born again, so that the whole fraught process can be gone through again. And in the middle of this chaos stands man. "What is man? A weak and fragile body, naked, in its natural state without defense, in need of another's assistance, exposed to all the insults of Fortune, and once it has given its muscles a good exercise, food for the first wild beast."

If this doesn't sound very enticing, too bad. This is simply the way things are, say the Stoics, and getting furious about it is as pointless as losing your temper with the rain. Rage stems from an overestimation of our power to get what we want. And it personalizes something that is impersonal. We rage at the weather and say, "How dare this happen to *me!*" But it's not happening to you. It's just happening. What about when someone is rude to us? Surely that is a "personal" insult? Not necessarily. Think back to Jesse's colleague who was rude to him. Jesse thinks about the person's character and decides that, actually, he's just a rude person. He's always rude. So to expect him to behave other than rudely is, frankly, overoptimistic.

And the same goes, unfortunately, for the rest of the human race. You might get angry when people are thoughtless, rude, incompetent, selfish, inconsiderate, and so on. But the fact is, people *are* all of those things, often and sometimes chronically. So expect it. You could also remind yourself of all the times *you've* been surly, ungrateful, rude, and selfish. Then, suggests Seneca, perhaps you'll have more tolerance for others' faults. We need to recognize how limited our reason and control is, and how hard it is to develop into a mature adult. Seneca writes: "Why do you tolerate a sick man's lunatic behavior, a madman's crazed words, or children's petulant blows? Because, of course, they appear not to know what they're doing… [Therefore] let us show greater kindness to one another."[8]

STOIC OPTIMISM

The Stoic worldview might seem rather tragic. And in one way, of course, it is. Seneca was Rome's greatest tragic playwright, and the brutal and chaotic world he describes in his plays and prose is close to the world that Shakespeare would later paint in plays like *King Lear* and *Hamlet*. Watching tragedies was for Seneca, as for Aristotle, a form of mass therapy, a reminder to the audience of the worst that can happen in this world, so that when they leave the theater and go back to their pampered lives, their complacency and petulance are shaken, and they learn to be grateful for what they have. We tell ourselves stories of catastrophe to prepare ourselves for adversity.

On the other hand, Stoicism has a very *optimistic* worldview, because Stoics, like the other schools of the Socratic tradition, believe that nature has blessed us with consciousness, reason, and free will, and these blessings mean we can adapt ourselves to *any* circumstance to achieve happiness here on earth. Where the angry person is inflexible and dogmatic in their demands, the philosopher is flexible. They know how to shrug, how to bend with the wind. Stoics believed in the *Logos*, a religious idea that we'll explore more deeply in Heraclitus's lesson. The *Logos*, which the Stoics sometimes called God or Zeus, is a divine cosmic intelligence that permeates, connects, and directs all things. It is the "great conductor" of the universe, and thanks to it everything turns out for the best. To serve the *Logos*, the Stoic simply has to develop their reason and moral consciousness, which is a fragment of God, and use it to adapt to whatever circumstances the *Logos* sends them. Nothing can ever get in the way of this mission without our permission. Obstacles only add fuel to the flame of the Stoic's virtue. They "regard all adversity as a training exercise," as Seneca puts it.[9] Fortune can only damage externals, and the Stoic puts no moral value on externals, but rather seeks happiness and fulfilment in rising above Fortune and doing the right thing. They do this not for the sake of a good reincarnation (Stoics, unlike Platonists, are oddly reticent on the question of the afterlife) but because they believe virtue is its own reward. Tortoise-like, they withdraw from externals, and find their happiness in what Marcus Aurelius called the "inner citadel" of their soul. And because what is really valuable is not their house or their career or their reputation but their soul, nothing in the outside world can really do them injury. If someone insults their honor, they haven't really been damaged: the Stoic philosopher Cleanthes had such a thick skin and benevolent disposition, his disciples nicknamed him "the Ass." The Stoic puts up with any insults because they know nothing can harm their soul except their own vices, like anger. And Stoics believed that the *Logos* connects us all, because we all have rational souls. The universe is one interconnected city, a *cosmopolis*, and we're all citizens of it, so we have a moral duty to try to put up with each other, no matter what particular gang, ethnicity, or nationality we're from. But, importantly, this reverence for the *Logos* doesn't mean that Stoics passively accept the political circumstances of their time. The *Logos* makes sure everything turns out for the best in the end, but that cosmic process might involve you fighting and even dying for justice.

Socrates Café, Baghdad

We saw in Epictetus's lesson how the US Army is drawing on Stoic-inspired CBT techniques to teach resilience to every soldier. In fact, before the Comprehensive Soldier Fitness program was introduced in November 2009, the army was already teaching Stoicism directly to some soldiers to help them with resilience and anger-management issues, through the work of Major Thomas Jarrett, Jesse's mentor. Jarrett, a former Green Beret, left the army in 1993, and went to train as a counsellor under Albert Ellis. Through Ellis, Jarrett encountered Stoicism and found it more appealing than CBT, which used Stoic techniques while dropping any mention of virtue, honor, duty, and other Stoic values.

When the Second Iraq War started in 2003, Jarrett returned to the army and travelled to Iraq, where he taught a course called Warrior Resilience and Thriving.[10] Jarrett would fly out to teach the course to units stationed around Iraq, or in a corner of Camp Liberty in Baghdad that Jarrett nicknamed "Socrates Café." He taught Warrior Resilience to fourteen thousand soldiers, teaching them cognitive techniques from CBT combined with insights from Epictetus, Marcus Aurelius, and Seneca. Jarrett spoke to me of his work, though he was careful to say his opinions are his own rather than that of the US Army. He says: "The Stoic philosophers were men of the world, just like the soldiers who did the Warrior Resilience course. I found that soldiers respond to the Stoic language of virtue and duty, which CBT had left out. Most soldiers I know joined the army out of a sense of service rather than for commercial reasons. And they like the idea of an ancient warrior ethos. They might not know what Stoicism means, but they've all seen 300, they'd all seen *Gladiator*..." (Jarrett himself seems to embrace the idea of an ancient warrior philosophy — he has a tattoo of the Roman army's insignia on his right arm).

Jarrett tried to train soldiers to battle with the "internal insurgents" of their negative beliefs and irrational expectations. For example, a soldier came to see him in Baghdad, angry with the behavior of his sergeant, and feeling that he didn't treat him fairly. "This might very well have been the case," says Jarrett. "But this guy kept repeating, 'It's *just not fair*.' He even brought in the NCO creed and slapped it down on the table, and said, 'I'm upset he's not living up to it...he *should* live up to it.' I told him that's like saying every Christian *should* be holy, or every car *must* work. We might prefer it to be so, but it's simply not the case. So you have to expect that, prepare for it, deal with it." Jarrett would try to teach his soldiers to "expect and prepare for adversity and hardship by developing resilience and character strengths." He says:

> *Expect* suffering. *Expect* pain. To be a soldier is to be in a certain measure of pain. In training, we inflict pain on soldiers to help them be ready for battle. A friend of mine was in Spetsnaz [Russian special forces]. They did their assault courses in the middle of the night when they were very tired, and when they reached up to the top of the obstacle course, they reached into entrails and pigs' blood, then they had to crawl through a trough of intestines. Then when they were in Chechnya and saw the carnage, their minds could stay focused. There's a time to be very emotional and grieve, and there's a time to be fairly nonemotional. You have to have your emotions in check when you're seeing people suffer around you, or when you have the ability to make people suffer and you need to observe the rules of engagement.

Jarrett says: "Soldiers need a philosophy that enables them to suffer, and not even to see it as suffering, but instead as a form of service. I have to think that my life is not as important as preserving the country. I *have* to believe that, and if I don't, I'm playing at being soldier. If your philosophy doesn't work in the most dire circumstances, then abandon it now, because it's a Starbucks philosophy."

CHRIS'S STORY

Another of Major Jarrett's Stoic padawans is Chris Brennan, a thirty-four-year-old firefighter living in Chicago, who teaches Stoic resilience in the US Fire Service. He says Stoicism has helped him carry on working in some fairly traumatic situations:

> One of the first things they teach you in the Fire Service is, when you go into a fire-ground, remember that you didn't create this problem, you're there to fix it. Sometimes you'll see some awful things, you have to deal with the broken, the burnt, the dying, the dead, things that have an intense emotional impact on your sympathetic nervous

system. That's natural. If you have no sense of sorrow when you pull a dead seven-year-old from a building, you're probably maladaptive. The key is not to be without emotion, it's to recognize you don't have any control over what has already happened to that boy, only over what happens now. So keep focused on the task in hand and the choices you're making, because those choices can mean the difference between other people living or dying.

Part of keeping on top of your emotional responses, Chris says, lies in managing your expectations. You need to expect to encounter death during your work: "We have accepted the luxury and prosperity of our time as normal, and no longer recognize that death and privation are normal for most of the world. Most Americans will never see a child die, because of the wealth and technological advancement of our society. We don't think it's in the natural order of things. We don't imagine that we will die either. We disregard that fact. We put it out of our minds." Chris suggests that some people join the Fire Service without fully facing how dangerous the job is. The US Fire Service has fifty thousand fire-ground injuries every year — more than have been injured in the US Army during the whole of the Iraq and Afghanistan campaigns. Chris says: "This is a dangerous job, and if you choose it, at some point you will end up in a hospital bed. If you don't want to face that likelihood, there's nothing dishonorable in saying, 'This job isn't for me.' But if you choose this life, then you should stand by that choice, even when it means putting your life at risk."

The Fire Service has, Chris suggests, been in a state of shock ever since it lost 343 firemen on 9/11, and has responded with a new motto of "Everyone Goes Home," to try to prevent any unnecessary deaths among firemen. "Everyone Goes Home" is also the name of a new computer-training simulation the Fire Service has introduced, to train new firemen without actually putting them at risk. But Chris says:

You can never totally take away the risks of the job. We have around one hundred firemen die on average each year. You can and should always try to reduce that number, but you will never reduce it to zero,

short of not sending firemen and firewomen into burning buildings.
Why embrace a mission statement that's doomed to failure? We have
a tendency these days to call deaths tragic. But if someone chooses to
put their life at risk, knowing the risks, in order to help other people,
then that's not a tragic death, it's a heroic death. Those 343 firemen
died heroically. We just had a fatality in our team, a twenty-eight-
year-old called Bryan, who went into a burning building to rescue
an old man in a wheelchair. The building flashed over after he went
in [a flashover is when gas builds up in a room or floor and then suddenly ignites]. He knew it could flash over at any time. But he made
a choice to go in, in my opinion the right choice. To me, that is not a
tragic death, it's a heroic death. I guess it's about accepting the inevi-
tability of death getting you at some point. That doesn't mean being
reckless, it doesn't mean having no goals or objectives. On the contrary, it means living each day in the awareness that something could
happen to you today, tomorrow, in a year. So don't put off doing the
things you want to do. Don't put off playing ball with your kid.

STOICISM FOR SOCIETY

This, then, is Stoicism, in all its gritty realism, and for many of us, perhaps,
it's a little *too* gritty as a way of life (hang in there, it's the Epicureans
next). We might wonder if such a demanding and individualist philosophy could ever be the foundation for a community. In fact, a Stoic community *has* begun to grow in the last few years, online and offline. This is
quite a new phenomenon in the history of Stoicism: in the ancient world,
there was very little Stoic community, beyond a few schools and a network
of friends who communicated with each other through philosophical letters. The modern Stoic community has the advantage of the internet. In
1999, a former parole officer in San Diego called Erik Wiegardt started a
website called the Stoic Registry, which eventually became NewStoa.com,
encouraging hundreds of Stoics from around the world to emerge from
the closet and declare their Stoicism to the world. He also set up a Stoic
Yahoo group, which is still going, and an online Stoic school. Others set up
Stoic Facebook pages, chat rooms, YouTube videos, podcasts, and blogs,

and a few benevolent Stoics made all the surviving Stoic texts available as free e-books. This online renaissance started to spread offline — some of us travelled to Erik's home in San Diego in April 2010, to discuss modern Stoicism and celebrate Marcus Aurelius's birthday.[11] Building a Stoic community hasn't proved easy, because your typical Stoic is male, argumentative, and fiercely individualistic, and never misses an opportunity to assert their autonomy by leaving a group rather than finding a way to stay in it. This has long been a problem with Stoics — as long as they're true to their conscience, they don't mind seeing the rest of the world burn. In the first century AD, Cato the Younger, a Roman senator who was fiercely Stoic, could perhaps have saved the Roman Republic from civil war if he'd just agreed to a politically expedient marriage between his niece and Pompey. But he wouldn't, because it went against his principles. One obstacle to building a Stoic community is that some Stoics are theists and others are atheists, and heaven forbid they should compromise their principles to find some common ground. In the run up to that inaugural gathering in San Diego, the fledgling Stoic movement had its first schism, with members falling out over whether Stoics had to believe in the *Logos* or not.

Could Stoicism ever be a philosophy for a whole society? To some extent, it's already a profound part of Western culture, giving us ideas like natural law, the brotherhood of man, and the idea that we're all interconnected citizens of the cosmos (which is where the modern word "cosmopolitan" comes from). Stoicism was particularly popular with the Victorian ruling class as they served the Empire in Afghanistan and elsewhere, and it's popular now with the US Army as they follow in the British Empire's footsteps. But it's unlikely Stoicism could ever become a mass religion: it's a highly rational philosophy, which lacks any rituals, festivals, songs, symbols, or myths. It speaks to the intellect rather than also appealing to the emotions like Christianity, which is why the Victorian thinker Matthew Arnold thought it was only suitable for the elite, while the masses needed something more emotional.[12] Stoicism has often appealed to the political elite — from Cato to Seneca to Marcus Aurelius all the way to Frederick the Great, Bill Clinton (I know, sounds unlikely), and Prime Minister

Wen Jiabao of China, who says he has read the *Meditations* over a hundred times.[13] But it's noticeable that none of these political leaders ever attempted to instill Stoicism in their citizens. Marcus Aurelius, the most powerful man of his day, knew how hard it was for a freely consenting individual to practice Stoicism, so he accepted that you could never force it on an unwilling public.

We have talked in this lesson about the virtue of Stoic acceptance and adaptation to life's ills. That can certainly be useful and healthy. But we could also make an argument for maladjustment: many of the great advances of civilization, such as the huge drop in infant mortality, come from a stubborn refusal to accept "the way things are."

And yet, for all their fatalism and grim-faced puritanism, the Stoics do have a lot to offer us. Despite the modern meaning of "stoic" as "someone who represses their emotions," actually the Stoics had a profound understanding of how emotions arise and how we can, not repress them, but transform them. As the philosopher Martha Nussbaum has written, Stoic analyses of emotions "have a subtlety and cogency unsurpassed by anything on that topic in the history of western philosophy."[14] Thanks to Stoicism's influence on CBT, millions of people like me have now experienced the benefit of Stoic ideas and techniques for transforming the emotions. We might not embrace the Stoic goal of attaining a completely dispassionate detachment from externals, and no government-financed therapy like CBT could ever promote such an extreme therapy, but we've still benefited from understanding how emotions arise and how we can change them. Only a few hardcore Stoics today pursue the goal of becoming entirely without passions. More common today is the Aristotelian position that measured emotional reactions to the world are appropriate and useful, as long as we don't allow them to become fixed into chronic emotional disturbances. Most philosophers and psychologists also disagree with the Stoic belief that inner virtue is entirely sufficient for happiness. They prefer the Aristotelian position that *some* externals are usually necessary for a happy life, such as a loving family, a network of friends, a decent home, a fulfilling career, and a free society. So if we lose these things, we really have been damaged, according to Aristotle. What this means is that humanity is fragile — we can lose our goodness through accidents of fortune. We can be destroyed by catastrophe, not just materially, but even morally and spiritually. This is the argument that Martha Nussbaum puts forward in her book *The Fragility of Goodness*. And of course she's right. Poverty can destroy our characters. Trauma can destroy our characters. Insult, neglect, war, and unremitting brutality can destroy our characters. And yet I also admire the Stoics, who insist not on humanity's moral fragility, but on its resilience, its inner strength, its ability to face the worst with dignity and defiance. It's an attitude summed up best, perhaps, by William Ernest Henley's nineteenth-century poem "Invictus," which inspired Nelson Mandela through his long years in prison:

> Out of the night that covers me,
> Black as the Pit from pole to pole,
> I thank whatever gods may be
> For my unconquerable soul.

> In the fell clutch of circumstance
> I have not winced nor cried aloud.
> Under the bludgeonings of chance
> My head is bloody, but unbowed.

> Beyond this place of wrath and tears
> Looms but the Horror of the shade,
> And yet the menace of the years
> Finds, and shall find, me unafraid.

> It matters not how strait the gate,
> How charged with punishments the scroll.
> I am the master of my fate:
> I am the captain of my soul.

LUNCH

Philosophy Buffet

EPICUREANS:*
Milk, olives, cheese

PYTHAGOREANS:
Bread, honey (no beans)

HERACLITEANS:
Grass

PLATONISTS:
Shared mezze

PLUTARCHIANS:
Caesar salad

ARISTOTELIANS:
Dissected octopus

STOICS:
Stoics are asked to do without lunch, and not make a fuss

---

* Students of Horace are allowed one glass of wine

5. Lunchtime Lesson:
Epicurus and the Art of Savoring the Moment

I ENTER THE IDLER ACADEMY in Westbourne Grove, and browse the bookshelves, while a young shop assistant offers me a cup of tea and a biscuit. Shortly afterward, a slightly rumpled figure in a blue suit and plimsolls emerges blinking from the basement. "Oh, hi," says Tom Hodgkinson, the forty-three-year-old founder of the Academy. "I was just having a nap." As part of the recent revival of ancient philosophy in modern life, some enterprising thinkers have tried to establish philosophy schools in the ancient mold, where ordinary people can gather, eat, drink, and learn about the art of life, just as they used to do in Athens, Rome, Alexandria, and elsewhere. One such school is the Idler Academy, which Tom set up in West London in 2011. He wants his Academy to combine the buzz of an eighteenth-century coffeehouse with the sort of leisurely philosophical enquiry practiced in the ancient schools of Plato, Aristotle, Epicurus, and the Stoics. It's still early days, and the Academy is slightly chaotic — in a good way. Last week, the sewers burst. This week, the boiler is on the fritz. A customer's order has gone missing (the Academy includes a bookstore), and everything still needs to be set up for this evening's philosophy workshop. Setting up a small business is hard work — "It's stressful!" sighs Tom — but the local businesses are, on the whole, friendly and helpful to this unusual venture set up in their midst.

Tom's new philosophy school is the latest experiment in a defiantly unconventional career. In fact, "career" is probably the wrong word.

"Career is a try-hard notion," Tom has written. "It's a middle class afflic-
tion."[1] After studying philosophy at Cambridge, Tom's misadventures
began with a job at a Sunday newspaper magazine in London. He hated it.
He went from a student life of leisure, partying, and punk rock to having
to get out of bed at 7:30, commuting to work, and spending most of the
day in (what seemed to him) a joyless and soulless office where the workers
were forbidden to talk to each other. Looking back on it, he realizes he was
perhaps "a bit puffed up" after university and that his new employers were
simply trying to take him down a peg or two. But he nonetheless found the
experience traumatic. "I remember going round to my parents and bursting into tears," he says. "Your early twenties are a weird time. Everyone
is terrified of failing or not fitting in. Even the parties have this horrible
competitive edge: 'What are you doing at the moment?' Back then, all my
friends seemed to be more successful than I was." He and his friends tried
to escape the horrors of office life by raving at the weekend, but the ecstasy
comedowns "only heightened the misery on Mondays." Eventually the
Mirror fired him, but rather than be crushed by this setback, Tom decided
to strike out on his own path. In 1995, at the age of twenty-six, he set up an
alternative magazine, the *Idler*, which celebrated the Generation X ethos
of leaving the rat race and pursuing a life of pleasure, creativity, and political apathy.

  The *Idler* ethos was anarchistic, but it was the sort of anarchy that
didn't threaten anyone with violence. The magazine had headlines like
"How to Save the World Without Really Trying," and "Lie Back and Protest." "The best way to smash the state," Tom wrote, "is to take no notice
of it and hope it goes away."[2] He advocated not voting, paying as little tax
as possible, and opting out of the financial slavery of mortgage and pen-
sion plans. They were all part of capitalism's conspiracy to make us defer
the pleasures of the present moment for the distant prospect of some future
felicity. "The future is a capitalist construct," Tom declared. "We are kept
quiet by means of the idea that, at some point in the future, things are going
to get better. But rather than waiting for the glory days of retirement, let
us take our pleasures now." We should do as little work as possible, skive
as much as we can off the state and the aristocracy, and drink as deep as

possible from the cup of life — without, however, allowing any pleasure to become an addiction. "The key is not to renounce pleasures, but to master them," Tom wrote. The *Idler* philosophy was, from the start, a strange combination of lifestyle journalism and self-help. It was, Tom argued, a cure for the needless stress and anxiety of the rat race: "Idleness, doing nothing — *literally* nothing — can help fight anxiety," he assured his readers.

Quite quickly, the magazine did well. Tom's *Idler* manifesto struck a chord with the libertine ethos of 1990s London, and from the start he showed a genius for getting interviews and guest articles, from the likes of Damien Hirst, Will Self, Louis Theroux, Alain de Botton, Alex James of Blur, Bill Drummond of the KLF, and others. "We were interested in interviewing anyone who had managed to get through life without a proper job." The *Idler* diversified into books, producing works glorifying the *Idler* lifestyle such as *How to Be Free*, *How to Be Idle*, and *The Book of Idle Pleasures*, and other books attacking the rat race, such as *Crap Jobs*. For one who openly extolled the pleasures of the slacker life, Tom was surprisingly busy, and successful.

And then there were the parties: "We used to throw a party every new issue of the magazine, so that was five or six a year. We held them in a semi-illegal squat in Farringdon. It was a real bohemian hangout, full of criminals and drug dealers. They were really wild parties, with three hundred people or so, cabaret, comedy, bands like Zodiac Mindwarp." I went to one of these parties myself, and remember a cabaret performer being suspended from the ceiling by wires attached to her nipples. In his early thirties, however, Tom and his wife, Victoria, decided to leave the wild London nights behind them and move to Devon, where they rented a ramshackle old house without central heating, and devoted themselves to the bucolic dream of growing your own vegetables, raising livestock (including some ferrets), making your own beer ("That particular experiment was a disaster," Tom confesses), and having long, leisurely lunches. "I can make a living working three to four hours a day on writing and journalism, and the rest I can spend hanging out with my kids, reading, going for walks, doing whatever I want really." He and his wife organized occasional weekend workshops on rural self-sufficiency, in partnership with Alain de

Botton's School of Life. After organizing philosophy workshops at the Port Eliot festival and other festivals around the UK, Tom decided to set up his own Academy in 2011. It teaches a three-part curriculum: "philosophy, husbandry, and merriment."

EPICURUS AND THE PHILOSOPHY OF PLEASURE

Tom's *Idler* philosophy is a strange farrago of anarchism, slackerism, nostalgia for Merrie England, and hedonist libertarianism, but one of the defining influences is Epicurus, an idol of the *Idler* movement. Epicurus was born around 341 BC on the Aegean island of Samos, which was also the birthplace of Pythagoras. He served in the Athenian army for two years, then devoted himself to studying and teaching philosophy. He had an early experience of the trouble philosophers could find themselves in when he was kicked out of the city of Mytilene, on the island of Lesbos. Epicurus lived during an unsettled period of Greek history, in the late fourth and early third century BC (the same period that Stoicism arose), when the Greek city-states were under the cosh of the Macedonian empire. Rather than opposing the empire, Epicurus's response was to advocate a philosophical withdrawal from society. He told his followers: "When tolerable security against our fellow humans is attained...[the philosopher should seek] a quiet private life withdrawn from the multitude."[3] Intellectuals should strive to "live unnoticed." So he and a handful of his friends pooled their resources, and bought a house on the outskirts of Athens, near a river, set among some olive groves, and established a philosophical commune which they called "The Garden." A sign above The Garden's entrance read: "Strangers, here you will do well to tarry; here, our highest good is pleasure."

Pleasure, Epicurus taught, is the "alpha and omega of existence." There's no absolute good or evil, only thoughts and acts that lead to pleasure, and those that lead to pain. Epicurus believed in the gods, sort of, but thought they were idle beings who existed in a state of languid self-sufficiency in some far-off corner of the universe, entirely untroubled by human affairs. And we should strive to become as untroubled and apathetic as the gods. Likewise, Epicurus was convinced there was no afterlife where we might be rapped on the knuckles for following a life of pleasure. An important part of his philosophy was the study of physics, particularly astrophysics. Epicurus followed the fifth-century philosopher Democritus, known as the "laughing philosopher," in asserting an atomistic physics: the universe is a collection of atoms swirling around according to mechanical laws, and when humans die we simply dissolve back into this celestial stew of atoms. And yet, while we're alive, through some incredible good fortune, we have consciousness, and reason, and free will, and this means we have everything we need to follow a life of happiness and pleasure. As Richard Dawkins put it in an ad on the side of London buses: "There's probably no God. Now stop worrying and enjoy life."

Epicurus tells us that we're only on this planet for a few years before we disappear, and while we're here there's nothing we *have* to do. There's no one we *have* to please. There are no commandments we *have* to follow. We can choose simply to enjoy ourselves, rather than finding reasons to be miserable. We can make the radical choice of happiness. This was, and remains, a rather scandalous suggestion. Without fear of the afterlife and divine retribution, what's to stop the masses from enjoying themselves any way they please? There'd be raves, riots, orgies in the streets. The other philosophical schools — the Stoics, the Platonists, the Aristotelians, and later the Christians — looked on Epicurus's philosophy of pleasure with deep suspicion, and threw all sorts of accusations against it. It was claimed that Epicurus indulged himself in feasting and boozing until he was sick. It was said he wrote erotic literature. It was rumored he and his followers indulged in all-night sex parties. These calumnies last until today, when the dictionary tells us that the definition of Epicurean is "one devoted to the pursuit of sensual pleasure, particularly fine food and wine." Today, if you search for Epicurean schools on the internet, you will be directed to the Epicurean School of Culinary Arts, which offers courses in "pro-baking," "cake decoration," and "mastering chocolate."

Rational Hedonism

But the popular image of Epicureans is probably untrue — at least of the original commune. If Epicurus was a hedonist, he was a very austere and rational one. He had few possessions, and kept to a simple diet of bread, olives, and water. On particularly festive days, he might have a bit of cheese. "Mastering chocolate" for him would probably mean resisting it, or confining himself to a very small piece. He wrote:

> When we say that pleasure is the end and aim of life, we do not mean the pleasures of the prodigal or the pleasures of sensuality, as are understood by some through ignorance, prejudice or wilful misrepresentation. By pleasure we mean the absence of pain in the body and disturbance in the soul. It is not an unbroken succession of drinking-bouts and of merrymaking, not sexual love, not the enjoyment of fish and other delicacies of a luxurious table, which produce a pleasant life; it is sober reasoning, searching out the grounds of every choice and avoidance, and banishing those beliefs through which the greatest disturbances take possession of the soul.

His Roman disciples were a bit closer to what we think of today as epicures — they liked their wine, feasts, and dancing girls, and would meet on the twentieth of every month to celebrate Epicurus's birthday with a philosophical banquet. Horace, who was this kind of Epicurean, wrote many beautiful odes celebrating his idler existence of poetry and wine. The Stoics would have deeply disapproved.

For all their enmity and rivalry with the Stoics, the Epicureans shared with them a conception of philosophy as therapy. Both schools believed philosophy can make us happier, by helping us remove the false beliefs which lead to emotional disturbances, leaving us free to live a life of self-sufficiency and tranquillity. Epicureanism might not be quite as strenuous as Stoicism. It might not involve so many wrestling metaphors. But it still requires us to work. "We must exercise ourselves in the things which bring happiness," Epicurus wrote. It takes effort to achieve a life of pleasure, because we often seek pleasure in the wrong places. We make bad choices, and this leaves us emotionally agitated. So we must become rational hedonists, not out of any grim sense of "virtue" or "duty," but simply out of rational self-interest. "No pleasure is in itself evil," Epicurus assured his followers, "but the things which produce certain pleasures entail annoyances many times greater than the pleasures themselves."

Epicurus drew up a classification of human desires. "Of desires, some are natural, others are groundless. And of the natural, some are necessary as well as natural, and some natural only." To achieve a life of tranquillity, the Epicurean has to examine his or her desires, and ask if they're really natural and necessary, or not. They have to consider the pleasure it will lead to, and the pain and inconvenience, and "measure the one against the other." Take smoking. Nicotine makes you think cigarettes are to die for — the addiction curls around your brain and into your thinking, so your first thought in the morning, and every second thought throughout the day, is: "I can't wait to have a cigarette." Sometimes, even while smoking a cigarette, you're thinking, "I can't wait to have another cigarette." And yet how pleasurable is smoking, really? Is it really worth all the expense, bad health, and curtailed activity that comes with it? We have to measure the pleasure against the pain. Or we might have a taste for champagne. But if we consume too much, we'll be sick, and if we get habituated to it, we'll either have to work really hard to pay our credit card bills, or suck up to rich patrons so they'll buy it for us. Either way, we've become enslaved by our taste for the high life. And there's always the fear that we'll lose our access to the Dom Pérignon and end up drinking Special Brew in an alley. To achieve more unbroken tranquillity, the rational hedonist learns to limit their desires to what is easy to achieve. "To habituate oneself...to a simple and inexpensive diet supplies all that is needful for health, and enables a person to meet the necessary requirements of life without shrinking...and renders us fearless of fortune," Epicurus wrote.

The fewer and simpler your desires, the easier it is to meet them, the less you have to work, and the more time you have for hanging out with your friends. In fact, all you need for the good life is some basic security, your health, your reason, and your friends. Epicurus put friendship at the very heart of the good life: "Of the means which are procured by wisdom to ensure happiness throughout the whole of life," Epicurus said, "by far the most important is the acquisition of friends." It was far more important to him than sexual love, which led to jealousy and all kinds of emotional disturbances; or the family (he never married); or the state. Epicureans rejected the corrupt city-state, and made their own little societies of friends. "Friendship dances around the world," Epicurus declared, "bidding us all awaken to the recognition of happiness."

ENJOYING THE PRESENT MOMENT

I have my reservations about Epicurean philosophy, but there is something wonderful in it. Epicurus grasped how incredibly bad we are at being happy, and how talented we are at making up reasons to be miserable. We might put off our happiness, telling ourselves as we squeeze onto the Tube to go to our spirit-crushing job that at some point in the future we'll be happy, when we're promoted, when we're rich, when we're retired. Meanwhile the present moment flows by, unnoticed and unenjoyed. In the words of an Epicurean saying: "Why do you keep putting off your joy?" Or we might say we can't be happy because of the past. We can't be happy now because we were bullied at school, or our parents were mean to us. But is the bully still there, teasing you today? Are your parents still in control of your life now? They're not the ones being mean to you in the present: that's you. You're the one making yourself miserable. So why not give yourself a break, and allow yourself to be happy? Seneca, who admired this aspect of Epicureanism, wrote: "What's the good of dragging up sufferings which are over, of being unhappy now just because you were then?"[4] This is the difference between cognitive therapies like Epicureanism, and psychoanalysis: psychoanalysis encourages us to dive into the past to discover all the culprits for our misery. Epicureanism, like Stoicism and Buddhism, brings us back to the present moment, and our beliefs in the here-and-now. The Zen teacher Alan Watts once said: "Things are not explained by the past, they are explained by now. That's the birth of responsibility. Otherwise you can always look over your shoulder and say 'I'm neurotic because my mother dropped me, and she's neurotic because her mother dropped her,' and so on, all the way back to Adam and Eve. You have to face the fact that you're doing all this. There's no alibi."⁵

Or we might ruin our happiness with anxieties about the future. "What if I'm a failure? What if my wife leaves me? What if I fall ill? What if I die?" Epicureans look at these "what ifs" and shrug. So what if you do? Why ruin the present worrying about possible futures? The Epicurean poet Horace put it well: "Let the soul which is happy with the present learn to hate to worry about what lies ahead." If something bad happens to us in the future, philosophy gives us the means to cope with it, and if we die, we won't exist anymore so it's not really a problem. "But if I died, I'd lose all the possibility of future happiness." Well, life isn't always an unmitigated good. Perhaps nonexistence is preferable to being very, very old or sick. "But what if I'm punished in the afterlife for enjoying myself too much?"

THE UNIVERSE DOESN'T CARE WHAT WE DO

In our own secular times, fear of divine punishment is not a major concern — until, perhaps, we're finally on our deathbed. But it used to be a huge source of anxiety. The human imagination was plagued with nightmarish visions of what would happen after death. That's why the message of Epicureanism — enjoy this life, don't worry about the afterlife — was radical and, for some, truly liberating. As one Epicurean gravestone puts it: "I was not, I have been, I am not, I do not care."

One person who recognized the power of Epicurus's message was his most famous follower, Titus Lucretius Carus, a Roman poet who lived in the first century BC. We hardly know anything about Lucretius's life, except for the calumnies that later Christian writers heaped upon him, such as St. Jerome's suggestion he was driven mad by lovesickness. What we do have, thankfully, is his wonderfully weird poem *On the Nature of Things*. This was Lucretius's attempt to put Epicurean philosophy into verse, and thereby to "light brilliant lanterns" in the superstitious minds of his readers. For Lucretius, as for other followers, Epicurus was a godlike figure, a guru, whose cosmic revelations provoke "shivers" of "divine delight." Like a true evangelist, Lucretius felt he had to spread the word of

Epicureanism. As he put it, his poetry was a way of sweetening the cup of philosophy, to make the medicine go down easier. His poem was, and still is, a very unusual creation, as Lucretius recognized at the time. Before him, poets had sung of gods and warriors. Suddenly, he used poetry to describe the atomistic nature of the universe, and to sing the joys of philosophy. He boasted:

> I joy to pluck strange fruits from a glorious wreath, the first
> Whose brow the Muses ever crowned with blossoms from this spot.

Lucretius understood that if people were to be freed from religious super-stitions, they needed to be given new myths, new stories, new songs. Humanists are beginning to understand that today, as writers like A. C. Grayling and Richard Dawkins try to create secular stories, myths, and poems.[6] Yet no one has surpassed Lucretius's original effort, over two thousand years ago, to sing the life atomic. He describes the atomistic nature of the universe — how elements come together and then come apart, how everything is "riddled with nothingness," how the universe fol-lows mechanical laws and doesn't care anything about us — to try to free us from the irrationality of fearing death and divine punishment. And yet we insist on ruining our life through such fears:

> Sometimes the phobia of death can grip a man so tight
> He comes to loathe his very life and looking on the light,
> And in his mournful heart resolves to die by his own hand,
> Oblivious this fear's the source of what he cannot stand.[7]

"Death is nothing to us," Lucretius insists. After we die, we will not be. Nonexistence is nothing to be afraid of. So enjoy life, pursue pleasure wisely, and avoid getting hung up on anything like wealth or religion or sexual love (Lucretius is very wary of falling in love, which he thinks causes more pain than pleasure). It's a really wonderful poem, and still helps people today: the Renaissance scholar Stephen Greenblatt, for exam-ple, says reading the poem when he was a teenager helped him get over the crippling fear of death that his neurotic mother did her best to instill in him.[8] But how adequate is the philosophy of pleasure when you're really ill, and genuinely facing the end?

HAVI'S STORY

Havi Carel had everything going for her. At thirty-five, she had recently met the love of her life, she'd just brought out her first book, and she was about to start her dream job, teaching philosophy at the University of the West of England in Bristol. The future looked rosy. Then, she started to notice she lost her breath very easily. She had always been fit and healthy, yet suddenly she couldn't keep up with her aerobics class, or walk up a hill while talking on her mobile. She thought she might be getting asthma. On a visit to her parents in Israel in 2006, her father, a doctor, suggested she have a CT scan of her lungs. The evening after the scan, she and her father stopped off at the radiology clinic so he could pick up the results. Havi tells me:

> I sat in the car and waited for him to come back. And waited. After half an hour, I knew something was wrong, so I went into the center. I walked into the lab, where my father and the radiologist were staring at a CT scan of my lungs. My father looked in shock. The radiologist looked surprised and embarrassed to see me there. He said to me: "Do you know what you've got?" I said I didn't. "Have a read," he said, and handed me this enormous diagnostic manual, opened at an illness called Lymphangioleiomyomatosis (LAM). It was full of dense terminology, but at the bottom it said "Prognosis: ten years." I felt this deep, physical shock, and just kept thinking, I'm going to be dead by forty-five.

At first Havi thought it must be some mistake. Then she was furious. She was an atheist, but she still found herself railing against fate.

> I didn't smoke, I didn't drink, I didn't take drugs, I'd always been good, and now I get this incredibly rare illness? It seemed deeply

unfair. Why me? Then I wondered if I was somehow being pun-ished. I'd just finished my first book, about death. I wondered if writ-ing about that subject had somehow caused the illness. It took me a long time to accept this was simply something random — a one in a million piece of very bad luck. Then I had to cope with the social reality of having a life-threatening illness: first of all, you're often treated by medical staff just as a malfunctioning body, rather than a person experiencing an illness. And then many of your friends and acquaintances don't know what to say. So they leave you alone, when in fact, I was terrified of being alone. The first few nights after the diagnosis, I slept in the same room as my sister, with the light on.

Then, after a few months, Havi decided to use one resource she had: phi-losophy. "I thought, how will philosophy help me now? If it couldn't help, there was no justification in carrying on with it." She found Epicurus to be her most helpful mentor. She says: "I knew my future had been curtailed, but I could still find happiness even within illness, by using Epicurus's technique of focusing on the present moment. I tried to really enjoy what-ever I was doing at that moment: yoga exercises, say, or going for a walk, or talking with my husband. Epicurus is right: we don't need that much to be happy." And yet, Havi is less sure about the Epicurean claim that "what is painful is easy to endure." In fact, as her condition deteriorated, she found it harder and harder to endure. "You get used to a stage of the illness, and then suddenly it gets worse, and your world shrinks further. I found that really hard."

Luckily, in 2007, a new drug treatment stabilized her condition. The clouds have lifted, and her prognosis is much more positive. Havi says she's incredibly relieved to have come through the experience. Yet she also says: "You think that you will never forget not to worry about the small stuff and to enjoy each moment like it's your last. The sad thing is, you do forget. You get caught back up in the small stuff." Nonetheless, Havi seems to have been transformed by the experience — not least, her concept of philosophy has changed. She's no longer so interested in it as an "aca-demic, highly specialized" subject that is cut off from ordinary people's concerns, and is now organizing a pilot program to provide a "philosophical toolkit" in the National Health Service for people confronting serious illness.

EPICUREANISM FOR LIFE?

Could we set up Epicurean communes today? There have been some efforts in this direction. The School of Life, which Alain De Botton and friends established in Bloomsbury in 2008, was set up in conscious imitation of Epicurus's Garden. De Botton wrote in the *Idler*: "The example of the Garden has haunted me ever since I read about it at university. I too have longed to live in a philosophical community rather than simply read about wisdom and truth in a lonely study...So that's how I and a few other philosophically minded friends came to start our own version of the Garden in autumn 2008."[9] The School of Life, like the Idler Academy, has a bookshop and a classroom where workshops and talks take place. It also holds "secular sermons" at Conway Hall every Sunday, the first of which was given by Tom Hodgkinson back in 2008. The shop has tree trunks in it "in honor of Epicurus," and a bust of Epicurus looks over the bookshop. De Botton says that the School, like the Garden, "gathers a regular contingent of people, and together we eat, hear lectures, go on journeys and, most importantly, attempt to live philosophically." Tom's Idler Academy is also set up in the mold of Epicurus's Garden, and a bust of Epicurus overlooks the shop. In fact, there is a bit of rivalry between the schools. Tom says: "It's like the Beatles and the Stones. Friendly rivalry is good for creative people. I think there's room enough for both of us, and for more such places. I'd like there to be philosophy schools in North London, South London, in other cities, in the countryside. Epicureans established philosophical communes across the whole of the Roman Empire. This is just the beginning."

Both these schools are wonderful additions to London's cultural and philosophical life. Though of course, they're both a long way from a school in the ancient conception. For one thing, neither school gathers "a regular contingent of people" who eat together, philosophize together, and live together. Neither school expects members to sell their possessions and pool their financial resources. Nor are they expected to worship the godlike founder of the school, as Epicurus's followers did. Rather, various members of the public come in, pay around £30 to listen to a talk, have a glass of wine and a discussion, and then go back to their private lives. The schools aren't really philosophical communities, in the sense of expecting their members to commit to a particular way of life. Nothing is demanded of attendees except the entrance fee (perhaps if they demanded more than that they'd be accused of being cults). But both schools succeed, brilliantly, in expanding the audience of philosophy and taking it beyond the academy and into the heart of the city.

ACTION FOR HAPPINESS

Could Epicureanism ever be a political philosophy for the whole of society? That was never Epicurus's intention. Epicureans see politics as a source of pointless anxiety and insecurity. They have no confidence that the masses will ever take to philosophy, so they opt out of politics, and retire behind their gated communities of pleasure. That could be a risky strategy: unless you have your own private security guards and a basement full of guns, it helps to have the protection of a well-ordered state. And it's a rather self-ish and un-civic solution. The Epicureans declare themselves free of any responsibility for those poor fools who are still suffering from ignorance and deprivation: Lucretius describes the pleasure of looking down on the suffering masses from his ivory tower of wisdom. A few Epicureans in the ancient world tried outreach programs: one Epicurean, Diogenes of Oenoanda, built an eighty-meter wall next to a main road, carved with several Epicurean texts, to "show the remedies of salvation by means of this porch." But on the whole, Epicureans have followed the opt-out, don't vote, Idler philosophy once put forward by Tom Hodgkinson (although Tom tells me he has since moved to a more Aristotelian belief that political engagement is an important part of the good life).

There have, since the collapse of the Roman Empire, been Epicureans of a more political and civic orientation. Thomas More's *Utopia* put forward a half-joking blueprint for an ideal society devoted to pleasure — although More also insisted everyone in Utopia should believe in the afterlife, in case people misbehaved too much. Karl Marx wrote his dissertation on Epicurus, and other socialists have embraced radical hedonism rather than the Protestant-capitalist deferral of pleasure. Thomas Jefferson called himself an Epicurean,[10] and managed to get "the pursuit of happiness" into the Declaration of Independence. However, his revolutionary idea that humans possess "inalienable human rights" which their governments must protect is not something you'd find in the relativist Epicurean philosophy, and instead owes more to the Stoic or Aristotelian conception of natural law. Christopher Hitchens also declared himself an Epicurean,[11] while dedicating his life to campaigning for global justice. But why should an Epicurean care about global justice? Why should an Epicurean cause themselves any pain or suffering for the sake of some unknown barbarians in a foreign land? We might admire Hitchens for his indefatigable indignation, but it's not Epicurean.

The Utilitarians of the eighteenth century, led by Jeremy Bentham, tried to turn Epicureanism into a genuinely political philosophy, by suggesting that we and our governments should be guided by the principle of "the greatest happiness of the greatest number."[12] Bentham, like Epicurus, was a materialist who insisted the goal of life was feeling good. If we could just work out a way to measure pain and pleasure scientifically, then we could use this "happiness calculator" to add up the moral value of every action and government policy. Bentham was wonderfully anti-elitist. He famously declared that "push-pin is better than poetry," because it made more people happy. So government policy should promote push-pin, and leave poetry to the poets. Whatever makes the most people happy, is good.[13] In the twenty-first century, Utilitarianism has been ably revived by Lord Richard Layard and his political movement, Action for Happiness. Layard gave a "sermon on happiness" at the School of Life, in which he suggested that the philosophy of happiness could become a "new secular spirituality" to fill the hole left by the decline of Christianity.[14] Since being set up in 2011, Action for Happiness has amassed over 20,000 supporters globally. They campaign for happiness lessons to be introduced in schools, disseminate advice on how to maximize our good feelings, and take to the streets to give out free hugs.

The happiness movement has already won some notable policy successes, like getting the British government to start measuring national happiness, which it started to do in 2010. Layard has argued that happiness scientists like Daniel Gilbert and Ed Diener can now accurately measure how happy individuals are, and even how happy whole societies are, therefore governments should use this data to guide policy, just as Bentham once dreamed. Modern Epicureanism has a political edge that its ancient ancestor lacked, and is now influencing the highest levels of politics.

WHAT'S WRONG WITH THE IDEOLOGY OF HAPPINESS?

There's a lot to applaud in Action for Happiness. I like the way they spread simple well-being techniques, including some from Stoicism, such as Epictetus's technique of focusing on what we can control and relaxing about what we can't. I'm also very impressed by Layard's success in getting two British governments to commit over half a billion pounds to train six thousand new cognitive behavioral therapists. That's a huge achievement. And I admire the way Layard and his happy army have got us thinking about the meaning of life, and whether "feeling good" is enough of an answer. However, I don't think it *is* enough of an answer, and I wouldn't want my children to be taught rational hedonism in schools, unless they were also taught the criticisms you can make of it.

What are those criticisms? Firstly, fixating on happiness as the ultimate goal of life may paradoxically make us less happy and more neurotic, as some psychological research has found.[15] I put this to Layard, who told me: "No one is saying we should ask ourselves constantly if we're happy. If you want to be happy, don't think about it all the time."[16] That would be easier if Action for Happiness wasn't constantly telling us to be happy. Secondly, Action for Happiness puts happiness on a moral pedestal when it is, to a large extent, a personality disposition. Some people, particularly extroverts, are naturally happier than others. That doesn't make them morally superior to introverted or depressive people. Yet the Action for

Happiness movement insists that happy people *are* morally superior: more likely to give to charity, more likely to volunteer. The happiest person in the world, it claims, is a Buddhist monk. If you're unhappy, you're a loser, a heretic, and a bad influence on your environment, because unhappiness spreads like a virus. I think there's a risk such a philosophy will just make gloomy personalities feel even worse about themselves: they're not just morose, they're a moral failure.

Is Hedonism Selfish?

You can also criticize Epicureanism as being egotistic, selfish, and atomized. Aren't we all already selfishly striving for our personal happiness? Isn't that the philosophy of personal gratification we've been following since the 1960s, with disastrous results for our families, our societies, and our planet? Layard disagrees. He thinks we need to be persuaded that the best way to find personal happiness is through altruism and civic engagement. Layard says: "All the evidence shows that the best way to be happy is to work for other people's happiness."[17] He hopes his movement for happiness will encourage people to be more altruistic and other-oriented. But doing good to increase your own pleasure does not seem to me a sufficiently durable motivation for altruistic behavior. Some rather easy forms of altruism give you a warm glow, like giving someone a hug or donating money to charity. But they don't require much time or genuine sacrifice. Harder forms of self-sacrifice, like tending to a disabled child or parent, or fighting for your country, can be really stressful and demanding, and you need a stronger motive to stick with them than pleasure — like love or duty.[18] Rational hedonists may put a great emphasis on friendship, but arguably theirs is a fair-weather friendship. As long as your company is pleasant, they'll happily hang out with you. But if your company is in any way painful, demanding, or discomforting they're gone (because the scientific evidence tells them that unhappiness is infectious).

Is There More to Life Than Happiness?

One might also criticize the happiness movement for having a simplistic or naive conception of happiness. Layard, like Epicurus and Bentham, is adamant that happiness is simply the presence of pleasant feelings and the absence of painful feelings. He firmly disagrees with the idea in Aristotle and John Stuart Mill that some forms of happiness are "higher" or "better" than others. That's elitist nonsense, he says. I asked him if he thought that meant that XBox was better than poetry, because XBox makes more people happier than poetry. He agreed that XBox was better than poetry.[19] So, according to Layard, the government should drop the literature classes and let the kids play Grand Theft Auto to their hearts' content. I enjoy Grand Theft Auto as much as the next man, but any philosophy which rates it above Shakespeare or Tolstoy shows "a deficiency of imagination," as John Stuart Mill described Bentham.[20] The value of these writers is that they show us the complexity of human experience, and the beauty of other colors beyond the shiny yellow of happiness. Human fulfillment is more complicated than simply feeling good, in my opinion. Most of us want more than that: knowledge, freedom, creativity, achievement, transcendence — even if our longing for these "higher goods" makes us restless and discontented.[21] On the other hand, positive emotion is surely *some* part of the good life. If your life is one long round of painful duty and cheerless virtue, you're probably doing it wrong.

How Useful Are Happiness Measurements?

It's fairly easy to measure people's pleasant feelings, simply by asking people how happy they feel on a scale of one to ten. And such measurements at the individual level tell us interesting and counterintuitive things about what really makes us happy, as Daniel Gilbert's 2006 book, *Stumbling on Happiness*, ably explores. But national happiness measurements aren't the best guide to how governments are doing, because of something called "hedonic adaptation": humans adapt to different situations, so national happiness levels tend to stay flat over time, no matter what's happening politically or economically. Our national happiness levels have stayed flat through the sexual revolution; the spread of yoga, meditation, and therapy; the mass production of antidepressants. They've stayed flat through Keynesianism and Thatcherism, through several economic booms and busts. More recently, after a brief dip in 2010, Americans' reported levels of happiness returned to their pre-Credit Crunch levels by 2011, even though unemployment was still double what it was before the crisis.[22] It seems we forget how happy or sad we were in the past and adapt to the present, and when people ask us how happy we are on a scale of one to ten, most of us say "oh, about a seven." What do happiness economists expect? Do they think that, if our government just pulls the right levers, the national happiness level will suddenly rise from a seven to an eight, then a nine, until finally the entire nation shouts "Ten!" before ascending in orgasmic rapture unto heaven? They seem to have a Utopian faith in the power of state intervention.

Besides the practical limitations of national happiness measurements, there are moral objections to relying too heavily on happiness science. It would be an odd sort of person who, when faced with major ethical life decisions, immediately consulted the latest data to discover what, on average, made people happier. At some point, you have to find your own answers to ethical challenges, beyond the statistical happiness average. I'm not convinced that pleasant sensations are the best ethical compass in life: the most pleasant sensations I ever felt was when I was on Ecstasy, when I was a teenager. Unfortunately, the comedown was rather unpleasant, but let's say scientists invent a new drug which has all the fun of Ecstasy and none of the side effects. Why not take that all the time? Why doesn't the government provide us all with a weekly supply of MDMA, like the government in *Brave New World* dosing its population with "soma"? That would certainly give national happiness levels a boost. We might reject this idea because, unlike Epicurus, we think there's more to life than simply feeling good. We might hope that our lives have some higher meaning beyond pleasant sensations. Layard dismisses what he calls "the ridiculous soma argument."[23] But it's a serious concern, because pleasant sensations are increasingly easy to engineer artificially. In a world of smart drugs, the "happiness machine" that the philosopher Robert Nozick imagined is no longer science fiction.[24] So we need to think seriously whether we want to embrace such a materialist and mechanistic philosophy.

To consider whether our lives have any real cosmic significance, we need to ponder the universe, and our place in it. Now that we've finished lunch, sit back, recline your seats, look up, and you'll see the classroom roof pull back to reveal an exact reproduction of the night sky. That red light moving on the left is the *Apollo 14* spacecraft, where an astronaut, Edgar Mitchell, is about to have an unusual experience.

Mystics and Skeptics

6. Heraclitus and the Art of Cosmic Contemplation

EDGAR MITCHELL WAS ON HIS WAY back from the moon when the ecstasy overwhelmed him. Mitchell was one of the three-man *Apollo 14* space mission, which left Earth on January 31, 1971, and landed on the moon five days later. He was responsible for the lunar module, and spent nine hours on the surface of the moon. He was the sixth human ever to walk there. On the way home, with his lunar responsibilities fulfilled, Mitchell had "more time to look out of the window" than his fellow astronauts. He tells me:

> We were orbiting perpendicular to the ecliptic — that's the plain that contains the Earth, moon and sun, and were rotating the shuttle to maintain thermal balance. Every two minutes, a picture of the Earth, moon and sun, and a 360-degree panorama of the heavens appeared in the spacecraft window as I looked. And from my training in astronomy at Harvard and MIT, I realized that the matter in our universe was created in star systems, and thus the molecules in my body, and in the spacecraft, and in my partners' bodies were prototyped or manufactured in some ancient generation of stars. And I had the recognition that we're all part of the same stuff, we're all one. Now in modern quantum physics you'd call that interconnectedness. It triggered this experience of saying wow, those are my stars, my body is connected to those stars. And it was accompanied by a deep ecstatic

experience, which continued every time I looked out of the window, all the way home. It was a whole-body experience.

Mitchell didn't speak to his fellow astronauts about his ecstatic experience — "it was rather private" — but when the shuttle landed back on Earth, he tried to find out what had happened to him.

I started digging through the science literature, and I couldn't find anything, so I appealed to some anthropologists over at Rice University near the space center, and said "Please help me try and understand what was going on." They came back to me a short time later, and pointed out to me the Sanskrit term "Samadhi," an experience of seeing things in their separateness, but experiencing them as a unity, accompanied by ecstasy. And I said, yes, that's exactly the type of experience I had.

As Mitchell continued his research, he discovered that

in virtually every culture in the world, notably in ancient Greek culture, there's some similar type of experience. I call it the Big Picture Effect. In other words, you see things in a larger context than you saw them before. I do believe that that's the beginning of all religions — some mystic in the past had such an experience, and started trying to make sense of it and put a story around it. Now, it's different in every culture, but it starts in kind of the same place, with seeing things in a larger perspective than you ever saw them before.

Two years after the *Apollo 14* mission, Mitchell established the Institute of Noetic Sciences, an institution dedicated to exploring and promoting the expansion of human consciousness — the word "noetic" comes from the ancient Greek *nous*, meaning intuition or understanding. He says he feels transformed by that experience on the way home from the moon. "I became a die-hard peacenik. I think war, and the fact we kill each other over border disputes and who's got the best god, is an absolute abomination. It's not civilized behavior at all. It's an outgrowth of the old 'big fish eat the little fish' primitive existence, and we humans have to grow past that." He says other astronauts have also been spiritually transformed by the Big Picture Effect:

> Other astronauts have had comparable experiences — a "wow" at seeing Earth in the larger scheme of things. We have talked about it over the years, and there's even been a book written about it by Frank White, called *The Overview Effect*, which describes all our experiences. We have all said over the years, if we could get our political leaders to have a summit meeting in space, life on Earth would be markedly different, because you can't continue living that way once you have seen the bigger picture.[1]

THE IONIAN SCHOOL AND THE BIRTH OF PHYSICS

For the ancient Greeks, ethics — or the exploration of how to live — was intricately connected to physics — or the exploration of the nature of the universe. You can't separate practical questions about how to live from questions about the nature of the universe in which you find yourself. In this early-afternoon session, we're going to consider some of the ancient Greek philosophers' theories about the nature of the universe, and how they informed their sense of what we should do here on Earth. And we'll explore a tension within ancient philosophy between mystical and Skeptical explanations of nature.

The earliest Greek philosophers are known today as the "Ionian school," because they all lived on the Ionian peninsula on the western coast of what is today Turkey, in the sixth and fifth centuries BC. They weren't exactly a school, as they put forward quite varied theories of ethics and physics, but they shared a desire to explore the nature of the universe. Aristotle called them *physiologoi*, or "those who discourse on nature." They are credited, by the astronomer Carl Sagan, as being the first practitioners of what would become the scientific discipline of physics.[2] Rather than relying on supernatural explanations of natural phenomena, the Ionian philosophers looked instead for natural, materialist explanations of the universe. Thales of Miletus, for example, who lived from the end of the seventh to the middle of the sixth century BC, and who is credited by Aristotle as being the father of Greek philosophy, postulated that the fundamental element of the universe, out of which everything else grew, was water. His disciple, Anaximander, was the first person to claim that humans emerged from more primitive life-forms, who in turn evolved from earth and water. His student Anaximenes speculated that the fundamental element of the universe is air. We are still, in fact, engaged in the search for the fundamental elements of the universe which these philosophers began 2,500 years ago, as we search for the elusive "God particle" with the help of the Large Hadron Collider.

HERACLITUS AND THE CONSCIOUS COSMOS

As soon as the first philosophers started to replace supernatural explanations of nature with materialist explanations, it raised ethical questions. If the cosmos obeys natural laws rather than the will of the gods, then how should humans behave? What is the good life in a cosmos where the gods either don't exist, or don't obviously intervene? We're still grappling with this question. And one of the first philosophers to attempt an answer was the strange, rhapsodical, and mystical philosopher Heraclitus. He was born of a wealthy aristocratic family in Ephesus, a city on the Ionian peninsula, in the late sixth century BC. He was a renowned misanthrope, and had an aristocratic contempt for the masses, who he thought cared only for food and sex, and took no notice of philosophy. He so despaired of the human race that he is said to have abandoned political office to wander the fields outside Ephesus, even eating grass like a cow, while weeping bitterly all the time (this legend earned him the nickname "the weeping philosopher," and he is shown in Raphael's *School of Athens* looking distinctly morose). It is said that he fell sick with an eye infection, which he attempted to heal with a homemade remedy made from a cow pat. Sadly, it didn't work, and Heraclitus died.

He left behind him a work called *On Nature*, which he is said to have left in the Temple of Artemis before leaving the city to live in the wild.

Heraclitus's attitude to nature is more mystical than most of his fellow Ionian philosophers. He wrote that "nature loves to hide," and he seemed to think that the best way to reveal the paradoxical secrets of the universe was through cryptic epigrams rather than dry scientific discourse. Alas only fragments remain, making his philosophy even more obscure, and philosophers from Aristotle to Heidegger have pondered his utterances ever since. His most famous saying is: "One cannot step twice into the same river, for other waters are ever flowing onto you." Where other philosophers searched for the stable element that underlay the universe, Heraclitus saw ceaseless flux and transformation. He is also quoted by Plato as saying: "Everything flows. Nothing stands still." Nothing exists separately and permanently in itself, but everything is part of the interconnected flow of nature. The universe is a dance of opposites, each thing turning into something else: "Cold things become hot; hot things, cold. Wet things dry, dry things wet." Or again: "To live is to die, to be awake is to sleep, to be young is to be old, for the one thing flows into the other."

What Heraclitus bequeathed us was a very dynamic picture of the universe, in which nothing stands still, and everything is constantly changing. This is in contrast to other Greek philosophers, like Pythagoras and Plato, who thought the cosmos was perfectly harmonious and stable. The Stoics preferred Heraclitus's dynamic cosmology, and they added the idea that the cosmos was rapidly expanding, until it would finally be consumed in flames. Then the whole cosmic process would begin again, from Big Bang to cosmic expansion to eventual conflagration. This dynamic theory of the universe only returned to astrophysics in the last hundred years, after the astronomer Edwin Hubble gazed out of his telescope and discovered, to his shock, that the universe was far bigger than we imagined, and getting bigger all the time. Today, astronomy suggests Heraclitus was right that the universe is an incessant flux of creation and destruction, with black holes consuming galaxies, and then vomiting them out again as new stars. "We must know that war is common to all," Heraclitus said, "and all things come into being through strife."

THE *LOGOS*

But beneath this cosmic conflict and flux, Heraclitus perceived a deeper harmony, a unity of opposites: "The unseen design of things is more harmonious than the seen," he declared. "Opposites cooperate. The beautifulest harmonies come from opposition." Beneath the apparent chaos, the universe is unified and guided by a cosmic intelligence, which Heraclitus called the *Logos*. He wrote, in words that recall the Taoist sage Lao Tzu or the Gospel of St. John:

> The *Logos* is eternal
> but men have not heard of it
> and men have heard it and not understood.
> Through the *Logos* all things come into being,
> yet men do not understand...

This *Logos*, or Universal Law, which Heraclitus seemed to believe was made of fire, coordinates and brings into harmony the play of opposing forces: "God is day night winter summer war peace enough too little, but disguised in each and known in each by a separate flavor." In the place of the personal gods of Olympus, Heraclitus deified this Universal Law of Nature. And he built an ethical theory on the foundation of his cosmology: humans partake of the *Logos*, because they possess rational consciousness, which is made of the same fiery matter as the *Logos*. Humans are the *Logos* made flesh. Our rational nature is connected to the nature of the universe. This means that the self is really a fragment of God, and to "discover one's true self" is to discover the cosmos in one's own nature. The "meaning of life," the reason we're apparently on this planet, according to Heraclitus, is to develop the flame of our consciousness so that we "know the thought by which all things are steered through all things." We need to raise our awareness from our own narrow and egotistic concerns and attain what the French academic and mystic Pierre Hadot has called "cosmic consciousness."

Attaining "cosmic consciousness" means overcoming egotistic attachments and aversions, which divide nature into good and bad experiences.

From a cosmic perspective, everything is good, everything is as it should be, everything is beautiful. "To God," Heraclitus wrote, "all is beautiful, good, and as it should be. Man must see things as either good or bad." The ignorant masses divide the ever-changing phenomena of existence into "good" and "bad," while the wise person sees through such conventional labels and perceives the beauty of all manifestations of the *Logos*. Heraclitus wrote: "Listening not to me, but to the *Logos*, it is wise to agree that all is one." We can attain a cosmic perspective on nature, Heraclitus believed, by cultivating our reason, controlling our passions, and purging ourselves of bad habits like drunkenness or gluttony which darken the flame of our consciousness and drag us down from a cosmic perspective. When we give in to our "heart's desires," we dim our consciousness. If we follow a life of reason and temperance, then we "dry out" our soul and let the fire of consciousness burn brightly, so that it can comprehend and illuminate the *Logos*, and bring itself into harmony with it.[3]

Heraclitus was certainly an unusual fellow, even among philosophers, and yet his answer to the big question of the meaning of life is shared by most ancient Greek philosophers. The Stoics, for example, embraced Heraclitus's idea that human consciousness is a fragment of the divine intelligence that guides the universe, which they also thought was made of fire. Like Edgar Mitchell, the Stoics believed the universe was a unified intelligence, in which "all things are interwoven with one another; a sacred bond unites them; there is scarcely one thing that is isolated from another" (in the words of Marcus Aurelius). The *Logos* of divine intelligence vibrates in all matter, the Stoics believed, but it vibrates in human consciousness at a particularly high frequency. When we develop our consciousness using philosophy, its flame burns brightly within us, so that we can see through egotistic attachments and aversions, and reattain oneness with the cosmos, as perhaps Mitchell briefly did on *Apollo 14*. We can know the *Logos*, and unite with it. And this, somehow, is the aim of the universe. "God has introduced man to be a spectator of his works," as Epictetus puts it, "and not just a spectator, but an interpreter."[4] Plato also thought the meaning or goal of human existence was to develop our consciousness so that it frees itself from earthly attachments and perceives divine reality.

Even Aristotle, the great biologist and pragmatist, believed the ultimate goal of human existence was to contemplate God.

THE VIEW FROM ABOVE

Ancient philosophers tried to cultivate "cosmic consciousness" by sending themselves off on imaginary flights into the cosmos, using a visualization technique that the French classicist Pierre Hadot has called the "View from Above."[5] Rather like the superheroes of popular culture, philosophers would imagine themselves rising up into space, looking down on their street, then their city, then their country, and finally at the whole planet from the perspective of space. This flight of imagination would expand their minds, lifting them from their particular personal and tribal attachments, and turning them into cosmopolitans — citizens of the universe. Contemplating the universe was a form of therapy for the ancients. Seeing the Big Picture puts our own troubles and anxieties into a cosmic perspective, so that our anxious egos become stilled with wonder and awe. Aurelius tells himself: "Survey the circling stars, as though yourself were in mid-course with them. Often picture the changing and re-changing dance of the elements. Visions of this kind purge away the dross of our earth-bound life."[6] Contemplating the stars elevates our spirit, and makes our day-to-day concerns seem insignificant. Aurelius writes: "Many of the anxieties that harass you are superfluous: being but creatures of your own fancy, you can rid yourself of them and expand into an ampler region, letting your thought sweep over the entire universe, contemplating the illimitable tracts of eternity."

The View from Above is what psychologists call a distancing or minimization technique. It's a method of zooming out from your life, placing it in a cosmic perspective, and thereby gaining a measure of detachment. We say that anxious or depressed people "make a mountain out of a molehill," zooming in on their problems until each little obstacle seems of enormous and terrible proportions. We can practice doing the opposite, zooming out, widening our perspective to cosmic dimensions so that we make a molehill of every mountain. This is what Aurelius does, whenever he takes himself and his problems too seriously: "In the universe," he tells himself, "Asia and Europe are but two small corners, all ocean's waters a drop, Athos a puny lump of earth, the vastness of time a pin's point in eternity. All is petty, inconstant and perishable."

We can practice the technique whether we believe in God or not — Epicureans also practiced the View from Above, they also sent their minds out on flights of imagination across the universe, to still their passions and sharpen their sense of wonder. We can practice the technique simply by opening a book of astronomy, logging on to the Hubble or NASA websites, or watching one of Carl Sagan's or Brian Cox's beautiful documentaries. Much of the popularity of modern astronomy today stems, I suggest, from its ability to widen our perspective and soothe our emotions. Watching Sagan's *Cosmos* is an emotional as much as an intellectual experience. It is a meditation, comparable to Aurelius's *Meditations*, in which we stand before immense vistas of time and space, and find our anxieties calmed and our spirits quietened with awe. One of the roles of philosophy and religion is to give us a sense of the infinite. Today, that role is fulfilled by astronomers like Sagan, who makes our minds spin with his descriptions of the billion billion *billion* stars in the universe.

Yet it's possible we could overuse this zooming-out technique. We could become *over*distanced from terrestrial affairs, so accustomed to zooming out and seeing the Big Picture that life on Earth seems meaningless and unworthy of concern. What does one life matter, in a cosmic perspective? What do even a billion lives matter? Overdistancing ourselves could make us a sociopath like Harry Lime in the film *The Third Man*, who looks down on the masses from the top of a Big Wheel, and asks: "Look down there. Tell me. Would you really feel any pity if one of those dots stopped moving for ever?" Or we could become like Doctor Manhattan, a superhero in the graphic novel *The Watchmen*, who looks down on Earth from Mars, and struggles to feel any concern for humanity's plight. We might look on the vast wastes of the universe and feel an overwhelming sense of nausea and meaninglessness. What's the point in human existence? What significance can any human life possibly have in such a vast universe? The mystics' response — by which I mean the response of Heraclitus, Pythagoras, the Stoics, and Plato — is that human consciousness is the flower of the cosmos. It is woven into the fabric of the cosmos, and the evolution of self-awareness in sentient beings is the universe's goal. But that doesn't really answer the question: *Why?* Why should the universe *need* us to become self-aware? Why should God *need* a spectator for His works?

CAN PHYSICS TELL US THE MEANING OF LIFE?

A modern physicist would also complain that the mystics' basic physics is wrong. It uses esoteric terms like *"Logos," "world-soul," "divine intelligence," "spirit,"* or *"consciousness."* The mystics' physics seems to be dualist — it insists the universe has two quite distinct things in it, "spirit" and "matter" (in fact, Heraclitus and the Stoics are materialists of a peculiar kind). So far, scientists have been unable to find any of this mysterious stuff called "spirit," and in the past few years, physicists have lost patience with priests and philosophers who insist on using folk concepts like "spirit," "soul," or "consciousness" and have taken the battle to them. Stephen Hawking, for example, recently announced that philosophy was "dead." Philosophers, he says, "have not kept up with modern developments in physics and biology, and their discussions seem increasingly irrelevant and outdated." It falls to physicists and biologists, therefore, to answer the big question: why are we here? And there's a growing confidence that science can in fact explain both the nature of the universe *and* the meaning of human life, without any need for philosophers or God. Hawking says: "Almost all of us wonder 'Why are we here? Where do we come from?'" Now that philosophy is dead, he says, "scientists have become the bearers of the torch of discovery."[7]

So what, according to Hawking, is the meaning of life? Why are we here? Hawking says: "We should seek the greatest value of our actions." But that's not the most convincing answer. It begs the question: how and to what do we allocate value? "We assign higher value...[to] those societies most likely to survive," he says. So Hawking seems to suggest that the meaning of life was best discovered by Charles Darwin, and the meaning is basically "survive and reproduce." But should we understand this

Darwinian imperative as individuals, as families, as nation-states, as ethnicities, as a species, as a planet, or even as a galaxy or universe? And is "surviving" really a satisfactory meaning to life? Is there no cosmic significance to human existence? Hawking gazes into the cosmos and comes back with the answer: no, there's no cosmic significance to human existence. There's no "why." Modern physics can perhaps tell us *how* we got here, but not *why* we're here. It's as if we came home one day and discovered a man standing in our kitchen. We ask him, "Why are you here?" He explains that he walked out of his house, walked to his car, put the key in the ignition, started the engine, drove down his street, parked outside our house, and then climbed through the window. We might stand there patiently listening to his story, before asking: "Yes, but *why* are you here?"

THE HARD PROBLEM OF CONSCIOUSNESS

Many modern scientists have a materialist view of the universe (a view first articulated by ancient philosophers like Epicurus and Democritus), and a Darwinian view of the goals of life on Earth. But that worldview still has to grapple with two questions related to human consciousness: *how*, and why. First of all, what philosophers call the "hard problem": How can consciousness arise from inanimate matter? How can something with free will and self-awareness emerge in a universe determined by physical and mechanical laws? How can there be a ghost in the machine? And, secondly, *why* should human consciousness exist? Why should humans have this capacity and desire to reflect on the universe and our own place in it? What's the point?

There are four common responses to the questions of how and why we have consciousness. Firstly, a hardcore physicalist might reply that consciousness and free will are illusions. They're physically impossible. You can't have some ghostly phenomenon called free will hiding in the machinery of the universe, so we have to accept it doesn't exist — and eventually science will prove it. We may have some fleeting consciousness, but it's an epiphenomenon, a helpless spectator, powerless to intervene. Some scientists and philosophers take this position: Thomas Huxley did, the biologist Anthony Cashmore does, so did Francis Crick, one of the discoverers of DNA.[8] I personally don't find this view convincing, because the scientific evidence and my own experience suggests that humans are capable of consciously reflecting on our mental habits and changing them. Our consciousness and reason are certainly weak, but we're capable of focusing them, and using them to reprogram ourselves to overcome emotional disorders like depression, rather than being locked in dysfunctional responses our whole lives. Considering the amount of energy required by our "conscious-reflective system," it would be a strange thing if it didn't actually do anything.

The second explanation of the how and why of consciousness is functionalist. Consciousness is a physical process which we don't yet fully understand, but which evolved through natural selection, because it serves the genetic goals of survival and reproduction.[9] But that explanation seems to me like using a copy of Shakespeare's complete works to hammer in a nail, or using a Ferrari to drive to the shops once a week to pick up the groceries. Why do we have such a powerful operating system for such a basic task? Ants survive and reproduce very well without the capacity for poetry or philosophy. Why is our reasoning capacity so much greater than every other species? And what's the evolutionary function of our endless self-questioning as to the meaning of life? We consider Hamlet one of the most interesting human characters ever created. But from an evolutionary perspective, he's a complete dud. He wanders around asking metaphysical questions, then shuffles off before he's reproduced. Roger Penrose, the great physicist and one-time colleague of Stephen Hawking's, writes: "Of course there would be no problem about programming a computer to seem to behave in this ridiculous way (for example, it could be programmed to go about muttering 'Oh dear, what is the meaning of life, why am I here, what on earth is this self that I feel?'). But why should natural selection bother to fashion such a race of individuals, when surely the relentless free market of the jungle should have rooted out such useless nonsense long ago!"[10]

As Penrose suggests, consciousness seems more than mere survival-aiding computation, as functionalists believe it to be. If that was all it was "for," then we will soon have designed computers than can fulfill that function far better than we can, without any of our pointless soul-searching. And yet programmers have so far failed to create a "Turing machine" that can convince us of its consciousness or humanness. Computers can't fake consciousness (not yet anyway), because consciousness seems to be something more than an algorithm.

A third theory, which has been particularly well expressed by Richard Dawkins and Stephen Jay Gould, suggests that consciousness is a by-product of some adaptive features of our brain. Our thinking powers developed to make us better able to survive, but as a side effect we also became capable of imagining our death, and started to ponder the meaning of life. This led to religion, philosophy, and much deep soul-searching, which might be satisfying for us, but is of no consequence to the universe. Human consciousness is really a fluke.[11] The Darwinian universe gave rise to it purely by chance, like a monkey banging at a typewriter who happens to write *King Lear*. This fluke gives us the unique ability to rise above our genetic programming, challenge the tyranny of our selfish genes, and to reason freely about our goals and the meaning of life.[12] So there is a human point to philosophy — it allows us to resist our evolutionary programming and to find earthly happiness in wiser and better ways. But there's no *cosmic* point to philosophy. On the contrary, humans are a small capsule of meaning adrift in a vast black ocean of meaninglessness. This view of consciousness is plausible, but to me it's unconvincing. If natural selection designs most things with an adaptive purpose, is it probable that human consciousness — the most complex phenomenon in nature — should have arisen as an evolutionary by-product, like the male nipple? Dawkins suggests that human consciousness was a radical leap into something new and unique in nature, and it happened completely by chance: we accidentally tripped into consciousness. To me, it's too improbable.

Another way of approaching the "how" of consciousness is that it is some form of matter, force, or even dimension that quantum physics doesn't yet fully comprehend, but which will turn out to be of central importance. Perhaps consciousness will eventually be integrated into a genuine "theory of everything" along with space, time, gravity, mass, and energy. But at present, our physics is simply not adequate to the task. Heraclitus's view that consciousness is somehow contained in all matter may not be as far-fetched as it sounds. In fact, the general theory of "panpsychism" (the idea that consciousness or the potential for consciousness exists in all matter) has attracted cautious support from some credible thinkers, such as the nineteenth-century philosopher Alfred North Whitehead, the contemporary philosophers David Chalmers, Galen Strawson, and Thomas Nagel, the psychologist William James, the physicist Roger Penrose, the astronomer Bernard Carr, and the astronaut Edgar Mitchell (although the theory also attracts many less credible voices looking to flog their own brand of "quantum-tantric-shamanic law of attraction" — some of whom we'll meet in the next chapter).[13]

As to the "why" of consciousness, it is conceivable that Heraclitus, Plato, Aristotle, and the Stoics were right, and that human consciousness arose because the animate universe intended it to, not merely to help humans survive and reproduce, but to enable them to reflect on the cosmos and reveal its truths. This is close to the "anthropic principle" supported by Roger Penrose, who suggests that we live in a "Platonic universe," guided by eternal mathematical laws, and that humans were fitted with minds capable of comprehending those laws. Human consciousness, then, is perhaps not some freak accident in an inanimate and meaningless universe. Rather, it could be the offspring of what Penrose calls the universe's "intelligent groping" (which sounds like a Mensa Christmas party, but I think we get what he means). Perhaps the microcosm of the human mind is connected to the macrocosm of the universe, as some Greek philosophers believed.

But the Greeks made a mistake, I would suggest, in defining consciousness only in its highest-known manifestation, as the ability to reflect on the universe and on our own thinking and meaning through language. By that definition, only humans seem to possess consciousness. That could be used as a justification to treat all nonhumans as disposable matter — and in fact, hardly any Greek philosophers showed a concern for animal welfare, with the exception of Plutarch, a vegetarian, who suggested animals possess consciousness.[14] To me, other species (particularly mammals) clearly possess higher states of consciousness, in the sense of emotions, empathy, some self-awareness, and a sense of play, and those species are the ones with whom we feel a strong kinship. One of the capacities of conscious animals is to play and celebrate existence, and I don't think that capacity is unique to humans. It seems to me that dolphins and whales play and celebrate existence, so do dogs, cats, monkeys, elephants, horses. Birds celebrate existence every morning. They don't sing merely to attract mates or mark their territory. Sometimes they just sing. Children have barely learnt to walk before they are dancing. You could explain dancing in Darwinian terms, as a way to attract mates, but that's a rather dull and narrow explanation. Sometimes we just dance, to celebrate life. There is a joy, humor, play, and celebration of existence that moves through consciousness. Computers can't joke, because they don't have consciousness, which is filled with laughter.[15]

Or perhaps not. Perhaps the physicalists will prove to be right, and consciousness will turn out to be an amusing sideshow rather than the main event. At the very least, the debates and arguments about consciousness that have burst into flames over the last twenty years are proof that Hawking is wrong: philosophy is not dead. In fact, philosophers like Daniel Dennett, David Chalmers, or John Searle are right in the thick of it, engaged in fascinating dialogues with physicists, neuroscientists, astrophysicists, and even the occasional Buddhist monk. The young field of consciousness studies is a wonderful model for how the sciences and humanities can engage and come together, and how, contrary to reports, there's some life in philosophy yet.

ARE WE ALONE IN THE UNIVERSE?

If evolution leads to consciousness, then perhaps it has arisen on other planets and in other life-forms. Modern astronomy has brought home to us the sheer size of the universe. As Carl Sagan put it: "There are a hundred *billion* galaxies, each of which contain around a hundred *billion* stars. Think how many kinds of life there may be in this vast and awesome universe."[16] Philosophers haven't often considered the possibility of extraterrestrial life or its implications for philosophy. Yet if you look to popular culture, and to our fantasies about extraterrestrial life, you see two main philosophies of existence represented. I call them the Predator and ET schools of thought.

According to the Predator school, we must assume that other life in the cosmos has arisen according to the same Darwinian law of "survival of the fittest" as exists here on Earth. Darwin's theory of evolution must hold true not just for this planet, but for the entire cosmos. This raises the uncomfortable possibility that there are other life-forms out there in space that may lack humans' consciousness and moral awareness, while being even more advanced killers. These advanced killers might one day visit Earth, and colonize us, use us for food or as beasts of burden, as we have used other species. This view of life is represented in films like *Aliens*, *Predator*, *Species*, *Starship Troopers*, and *The Matrix*. The other school of thought, however, imagines aliens as morally advanced beings who possess human-like consciousness and moral awareness, evolved to a greater degree. This school is represented by films like *ET*, *Close Encounters of the Third Kind*, and *Contact*, which was written by Carl Sagan. The suggestion of such films is that consciousness is not a fluke, but rather that nature somehow points toward it — therefore it will arise not just on Earth, but on other planets too. So perhaps Heraclitus was right, and the *Logos*, the universal law of consciousness, is literally universal, connecting not just sentient beings on Earth, but all beings in the entire cosmos under one moral law. In which case there might one day be an intergalactic parliament of cosmopolitans, each representing their own planet, each agreeing to a common moral law. A far-fetched idea, of course, and yet I love that Carl Sagan seemed to consider this possibility, and acted as a sort of first ambassador for Earth, sending out messages to describe our way of life to other intelligent life-forms. He was a true cosmopolitan, a true citizen of the universe, waiting patiently by his radio-transmitter for a helpful alien to explain why we're here.

Now we're going to float back to Earth from these cosmic speculations, in the company of Pythagoras, another member of the Ionian school, who was as much a magician as a philosopher, but who nonetheless has some useful advice on how to practice philosophy in our own time.

7. Pythagoras and the
Art of Memorization and Incantation

JAMES STOCKDALE WAS A YOUNG FIGHTER PILOT flying bombing missions over North Vietnam, when his A-4E Skyhawk aeroplane was hit by antiaircraft fire. Stockdale ejected from his aircraft and parachuted down to the village below. When he landed, angry villagers attacked him and broke his leg so badly he walked with a limp for the rest of his life. He was then taken to Hoa Lo prison, where he spent the next seven years. As the senior naval officer in the prison, he was in charge of organizing the other inmates' tactics and their escape bids. He was also first in line for torture, and was tortured fifteen times, put in solitary confinement for over four years, and kept in leg irons for two years. Within this extreme and disorientating environment, the teachings of ancient philosophy were his survival kit. He had come across the Greeks when he was studying philosophy at Stanford University, and his philosophy professor had handed him a copy of Epictetus's *Handbook*. Stockdale had felt an immediate kinship with the ancient Greek worldview, and kept the *Handbook* on his bedside throughout his three seven-month tours on aircraft carriers off the coast of Vietnam. Because he had read and memorized certain key passages of these books, he had them "at hand" to deal with life in the POW prison. He remembered many of the ancients' "attitude-shaping remarks" (as he puts it), and they helped him cope with his adverse circumstances. He remembered, above all, the first sentence of the *Handbook*: "Some things are up to us, and others are not." He accepted that most of his life was out of his control, but that his own character, dignity, and self-respect was in his control, and no one could take it away from him.

Through his memorization and absorption of philosophical maxims, Stockdale was able to maintain his sense of autonomy and dignity. He was not broken by fear, or shame, or guilt, as his North Vietnamese interrogators were hoping he would be. He was not brainwashed. He refused ever to bow to his guards, or to be paraded to foreign visitors to show how well POWs were treated, or to go on Vietnamese state television saying he accepted the principles of Marxism–Leninism. He declared his spiritual independence.

KEEPING THE MAXIMS AT HAND

Ancient philosophy was designed to be memorized, so that it could be "at hand" when we are confronted with tumultuous situations like the one Stockdale found himself in. The teachings of Stoics, Epicureans, Cynics, Pythagoreans, and Platonists were often condensed into short, pithy maxims designed to be easily remembered, so that they would pop up in our heads when we are in stressful situations. Many of these maxims have come down to us today: "know thyself"; "life is but what you deem it"; "nothing to excess"; "it's not what happens to you but what you do about it"; "be the captain of your soul"; "no one can harm you without your permission"; "difficulties are what show men's characters," and so on. The students wrote these maxims down in their handbook, memorized them, repeated them to themselves, and carried them around — that's the point of a handbook, so the teachings are *procheiron*, or "close at hand." The student reminded themselves of them as often as possible, because "it is not easy [for a man] to come to a judgment," according to Epictetus, "unless he should state and hear the same principles every day, and at the same time apply them to all his life."[1] Maxims were like neural shortcuts, like icons on a desktop that instantly connect you to a body of information. They helped turn a conscious philosophical principle into an automatic habit of thinking. The student repeated the maxims until "through daily meditation [they] reach the point where these wholesome maxims occur of their own accord," as Seneca put it.[2] They assimilated them into their inner dialogue, and made them a "part of oneself." Plutarch says we should "meditate on coping remedies before trouble comes, so that they are more powerful from practice. For just as savage dogs…are only soothed by a familiar voice, so too it is not easy to quiet the wild passions of the soul, unless familiar and well-known arguments are at hand to check its excitement."[3]

These short principles, maxims, or persuasive arguments could be marshalled in an instant, like the "weapons in an armory," as the sixteenth-century neo-Stoic Justius Lipsius puts it,[4] or like a first-aid kit kept "handy for emergencies," in Marcus Aurelius's phrase. Students of philosophy put maxims on walls, paintings, pendants, pieces of furniture, anywhere where they could remind them of the teachings throughout the day. Some students, today, even get philosophical maxims tattooed onto their body, taking Seneca's words literally that the teachings should merge with their "tissue and blood," and become part of their body until the *Logos* becomes flesh.[5] The point of maxims is that humans are incredibly forgetful animals, therefore, like the amnesiac hero of *Memento*, we need constant little reminders if we are to steer a rational course through life.

PYTHAGORAS, THE MAGICIAN-PHILOSOPHER

The philosopher who invented this technique of compacting philosophy into memorable bite-size maxims was Pythagoras, an unusual and magical figure from the Ionian school, who lived and taught in Greece and Italy in the sixth century BC. His teachings were a major influence on Plato, and because of this Bertrand Russell called him the most influential philosopher in the history of Western philosophy.[6] In fact, Pythagoras was as much a magician as a philosopher, and would have felt more at home in Hogwarts than in any modern academic department. Ancient philosophy grew out of shamanism, and sometimes retained aspects of the magical or supernatural. Pythagoras, for example, was said to have been descended from Apollo Pythius, the snake-god — hence his python-like name. Some legends suggest he was himself an incarnation of Apollo, which he is said to have proved to his followers by revealing that his thigh was made of gold (he was the first philosopher of bling). He taught his followers to believe in reincarnation, and claimed he could remember his past lives and those of his students. In accordance with this belief, his followers refused to eat meat, asserting that "all animated beings are kin, belonging to one family." He could predict the future, appear in two places at once, talk to animals and rivers, hear the music of the spheres. His disciples were a fairly magical bunch as well: one of them, Aburis the Sky-Walker, could fly through the air on his magical arrow.

All these stories can be taken with a large pinch of salt (scholars are unsure if Pythagoras even existed), but whether as myth or historical figure Pythagoras certainly inspired a school of followers, who practiced his philosophy as a way of life. His school was based in southern Italy, and the entrance process was very demanding. Applicants would automatically be refused entry, and then secretly observed for several years to see how they conducted themselves. Those accepted would have to keep a vow of silence for five years, and give up all their possessions. The few deemed worthy would, finally, be initiated into the esoteric secrets of the cult, which involved an unusual mixture of geometry, music, and magical incantations. Like later cults, the chosen were not allowed to reveal its higher teachings, and if you left the cult or revealed its secrets, the other members ignored you as if you had died, and even erected a tomb to you.

Pythagoreans lived in a sort of monastic fraternity, in which they shared all possessions, followed a vegetarian diet, wore white robes, and spent each day according to a specific philosophical program, or rule of life. The aim of this rule was to develop the divine part of them — their psyche, or reasoning soul — and free it from their animal passions, to ensure a good reincarnation in the next life. All aspects of their life were designed to serve this goal. Initiates rose in the morning, put on their white robes, and sang songs to prepare them for the day. Music had a central place in the Pythagorean care of the soul. Pythagoras was supposed to have discovered the chromatic, diatonic, and enharmonic scales, which he thought reflected the divine mathematical order inherent in the universe. Music connects our souls to the divine cosmos, Pythagoreans believed. It can either agitate us and cause our passions to swell, or purge us of passions and agitations, making our souls a calm reflection of the cosmos.

After their morning chorus, the Pythagoreans practiced memory exercises, trying to bring to mind exactly what they did the day before, and also committing to memory key Pythagorean maxims. Then they set off on a solitary morning walk, somewhere quiet and peaceful to bring their souls into a state of inner serenity. After that, they met up with fellow initiates for philosophical discussion and incantation of the maxims. Newer initiates simply listened, while the more advanced initiates might retire for the secret practice of mystical geometry. Then the initiates took part in some gymnastics, particularly wrestling and running. Lunch was a simple meal of bread and honey. (Alcohol and meat were strictly prohibited. So were beans, for some reason.) Then another stroll, this time in company with two or three other initiates. This rather pleasant schedule ended with evening prayers, songs, sacrifices, and incantations, to prepare the soul for sleep and make sure it had good dreams.

Memory exercises and incantations had a central place in the Pythagorean way of life. Pythagoras and his followers had a profound understanding of the irrationality of the human psyche. It's not enough to try to transform the personality through abstract philosophical reasoning, although that has its place. You need to speak to the irrational part of the psyche using maxims, songs, symbols, and imagery, so that your philosophical insights really sink into the brain and become part of your nervous system. Pythagorean maxims were short, cryptic sayings which packed together more complex thinking. For example, "Eat not the heart" is thought to have meant "don't wallow in unnecessary melancholy or self-pity"; "Tear not to pieces the crown" supposedly meant "don't be a joy-killer"; "Never sing without the harp" meant "try to live life as a whole." The initiate would say these maxims repeatedly to themselves, or even sing them. They became incantations — short phrases that were spoken or sung repeatedly, to magically charm the soul. The most famous magic spell in Western culture — abracadabra — was a similar sort of philosophical incantation — it supposedly healed the soul of various illnesses. Pythagoras is said to have declared: "God the Father, deliver them [humanity] from their sufferings, and show them what supernatural power is at their call." What he seems to have meant is that humans, uniquely among the animal kingdom, possess speech, the *Logos*, the Word, which has a magical charm over our souls. Philosophy, for Pythagoras, was supposed to be memorized, repeated, and sung so that it imprinted the magical words of the *Logos* into our flesh, blood, and nervous system.

PYTHAGORAS AND THE LAW OF ATTRACTION

Pythagoras's techniques of memorization and incantation have had a rather colorful renaissance in modern self-help. His incantation techniques were "rediscovered" by Emile Coué, a French psychologist working at the beginning of the twentieth century at the same time as Sigmund Freud, who made his own discoveries and theories about hypnosis and autosuggestion. Coué declared that the mind could make whatever it thought into a reality — it could think itself into health, wealth, and happiness, or think itself into misery, sickness, and destitution, simply by repeating phrases to itself. This secret, Coué said, had been discovered by Pythagoras:

> Is it not clear that by means of thought we are the absolute masters of our physical organism and that, as the Ancients showed centuries ago, thought — or suggestion — can and does produce diseases or cure it? Pythagoras taught the principle of autosuggestion to his disciples... The Ancients well knew the power — often the terrible power — contained in the repetition of a phrase or formula. The secret of the undeniable influence they exercised through the old Oracles resided probably, nay, certainly, in the force of suggestion.[7]

Therefore, in order to make oneself happy, healthy, and rich, it is only necessary to endlessly repeat to oneself positive affirmations. Coué suggested we repeat to ourselves, each morning: "Every day, and in every way, I'm getting better and better." A similar idea is found in the New Thought movement, which blossomed in the United States in the 1910s and 1920s, and which promoted the idea that thoughts and words "make" reality. If you want to be successful, just think and repeat successful self-affirming statements. You can do or be anything you want to be, the New Thought movement insisted. Just say the magic words, and it will be so. And, in keeping with the boom years that preceded the Great Crash of 1929, the dominant thought of the New Thought movement was how to become rich. Its most famous publication was *The Science of Getting Rich*, published in 1910 by Wallace D. Wattles. The book begins with the wonderfully brash opening: "Whatever may be said in praise of poverty, the fact remains that it is not possible to live a really complete or successful life unless one is rich." The way to be rich is simply to think rich, to feel rich, to repeat self-affirming statements of richness until the money magically rolls in. For "a thought produces the thing that is imaged by the thought." So one simply has to repeat statements like "I am successful in whatever I do" or "Everything is getting better every day" until one *really believes them*, and, abracadabra, it will be so. The New Thought movement used the techniques of ancient philosophy for the profane goal of personal enrichment. Wattles declared, in a degraded parody of Pythagoras: "You must dwell upon this [the belief that money is coming your way] until it is fixed in your mind, and has become your habitual thought. Read these creed statements over and over again, fix every word upon your memory and meditate upon them until you firmly believe them."

The New Thought movement has enjoyed an enormous revival in the past twenty years, particularly through the sensational success of Australian filmmaker Rhonda Byrne's book and film *The Secret*. The secret Byrne reveals to us is the New Thought idea that we attract to us whatever we think or say. The universe, in this vision of existence, becomes a giant supermarket, and all we have to do is place our order. Marketing guru Joe Vitali, who features prominently in the movie, sums it up well: "It is like having the universe as your catalogue. You flip through it and say, 'I'd like to have this experience and I'd like to have that product, and I'd like to have a person like that.' It is you placing your order with the universe. It's really that easy." We see this cosmic consumerism at work in Byrne's film. In one scene, a girl looks longingly at a necklace in the window of a jewelry shop. Then she closes her eyes in prayer and — presto! — the necklace magically appears round her neck.

One of the many smart marketing devices Byrne uses is that she creates the impression that the greatest minds in history have all known this "secret." She traces it all the way back to Pythagoras, thereby lending her trashy ideas the air of historical legitimacy. I'm not convinced that Byrne actually read any books about Pythagoras, but if she has, I think she has dangerously misinterpreted his ideas. First of all, nowhere does Pythagoras (or any other ancient philosopher worth their salt) claim that philosophy will make you rich and powerful. In fact, the Pythagoreans were an ascetic community who gave up all their possessions and worked to conquer the passion for wealth and fame. The same is true of later philosophers, like Plato or the Stoics, who are sometimes invoked by self-help gurus. None of them claimed that philosophy would make you rich or powerful. Epictetus told his students: "Land, wealth, reputation — philosophy promises none of these things."[8] Philosophers suggested it could bring you inner wealth — not external riches.

Pythagoras and his followers knew the limits of philosophy, and they knew that one of the most important lessons it had to teach was the first lesson we learnt: recognizing the limits of our control over the universe. We read that "the thought which afforded [Pythagoreans] the greatest support in endurance was the conviction that no human adversity should be unexpected by men of intellect — so they must resign themselves to all vicissitudes beyond human control."[9] Philosophy gives us power — extraordinary power — to transform our own natures and heal our emotions. But there's still a rough, violent world out there which we can't control. In fact, Pythagoras and his followers fell out with the local community where they lived, and ended up being massacred. According to Byrne's Law of Attraction, that would mean that Pythagoras — supposedly one of the pioneers of the Secret — had allowed himself to think negative thoughts. Bad things only happen to us if we think bad thoughts, according to Byrne. But that's obviously nonsense. In fact, many of the greatest minds and wisest souls of our species died violent deaths — think of Pythagoras, Socrates, Seneca, Cicero, Hypatia, Jesus, Boethius, Gandhi, Martin Luther King Jr. Philosophy can give you inner strength and control over yourself, but it can't protect you from all the vicissitudes of the outside world. The idea that we can protect ourselves from all adversity by repeating magic words is simply wishful thinking.

MAKING THE CONSCIOUS AUTOMATIC

So is Pythagoras a crazy magician who is unworthy for inclusion in our dream faculty? I don't think so. There's a core of common sense and psychological insight to his techniques of memorization and incantation. He recognized something that cognitive therapy has since proven: our minds listen to everything we think and say, and absorb it. This, in fact, was one of the great discoveries of Aaron Beck, one of the two inventors of CBT. Beck discovered that emotional disorders like depression are, to a great extent, caused by "self-talk": by the running monologue that we keep up with ourselves throughout the day, usually unconsciously. We're constantly talking to ourselves subvocally, interpreting the world and our own actions in it. If you stop and listen to yourself, you can hear this running commentary going on in your head. You might find yourself humming a song, and if you tune in and listen, the song is sometimes an unconscious commentary on how you're feeling. This unconscious self-talk directly impacts our emotions and our experience of reality. Philosophical therapy brings this unconscious self-talk into consciousness, using techniques like the journal or the Socratic dialogue. Then we have to take our new philosophical insights and repeat them until they soak into our mind and become part of our automatic self-talk.

Similar techniques of memorization and repetition exist in all the great religious traditions. Eastern religions and philosophies use the *mantra*, for example, a short phrase repeated or sung for hours until the trainee is in a trance state. The repetition of the mantra imprints the principles of a religion or philosophy onto the trainee's mind, and also supposedly creates certain energies through its noise and vibration — which is a very Pythagorean concept. In Islam the holy names of Allah are repeated or sung to transform the soul. In Judaism and Christianity, we see a similar use of short, easily remembered phrases; in the Book of Proverbs, for example, which is full of memorable sayings like "A man who is kind benefits himself, while a cruel man harms himself," or "A man without self-control is like a city broken into and left without walls." Again and again, the author(s) of Proverbs tells the reader to pay heed, to listen, to remember, until the teachings become inscribed on our mind and absorbed into our body, as in these lines from Proverbs 7:1:

> My son, keep my words
> And treasure up my commandments with you;
> Keep my teachings as the apple of your eye;
> Bind them to your fingers
> Write them on the tablet of your heart.

When I practiced CBT to overcome social anxiety, the therapy course asked me to read various handouts to myself every evening, out loud. They were filled with solemn, incantatory phrases like "Acceptance is an active experience," "What you resist persists," "I refuse to give my negative thoughts power over me," "In the present moment is peace and happiness," and so on. Each of these maxims compacted one of the ideas in the therapy into a neural shortcut. Feeling unbearably cheesy, I would read these handouts every evening, and even listened to recordings of them while travelling on the bus or Tube, so that they really soaked into my brain and became part of my automatic self-talk. I also carried around a little handbook, like the ancients used to do, in which I'd written some of the "power phrases" from the therapy course. When I felt really stressed, I would retreat to a private space, pull out the handbook, and repeat a "power phrase." Naturally, I felt ridiculous, but it worked. It was not enough just to have a one-off epiphany into how my thinking habits were causing me suffering. I had to take a systematic approach to creating new thinking habits — and the art of memorizing and repeating maxims was crucial to that process, however ridiculous it felt. Another person who found this technique very useful is the CEO of a mental health trust in the UK, who suffers from bipolar disorder. He's managed to conquer the disorder, and hasn't taken a day off work for fifteen years, thanks to the little handbook that he carries around with him, which he has filled with the ideas and quotations that he finds most useful in challenging his old habits of thinking and feeling. Whenever the bad old habits come back, he turns to the relevant page, and arms himself with a useful quotation or two. Like me, he's found this technique a lifesaver.[10]

BRAINWASHING?

But perhaps we should consider this technique more carefully before we practice it. First of all, can philosophy really be simplified into bite-size chunks and bumper-sticker catchphrases? Isn't the whole point of philosophy that it trains us to go beyond such clichés, to think more deeply? And secondly, isn't there something a little sinister about this endless repetition of catchphrases until they become automatic habits of thinking? The psychoanalyst Darian Leader, one of the chief critics of the British government's support of CBT, has gone so far as to suggest that CBT is equivalent to the brainwashing techniques of China's Maoists. Didn't Chairman Mao also insist that everyone carry around a little handbook filled with his quotations, as part of his program of mass indoctrination?[11]

In answer to the first concern, yes, of course, philosophy is designed to develop our powers of conscious deliberation and skeptical enquiry so that we can think beyond the clichés of our culture. But if philosophy is really going to transform our psyches and be an effective therapy for our emotional habits, then it also has to speak to the irrational and automatic parts of our psyche. It has to become absorbed into our automatic habits of thinking, feeling, and behaving. Otherwise, your prefrontal cortex may be very wise and philosophical, while the other 95 percent of your personality is just as incorrigible as ever. If you think about it, you have been brainwashed already, without necessarily consenting to it. From birth, you have been soaked in messages, from your parents, your friends, your colleagues, advertising, the media, all of which have embedded certain values, beliefs, and habits of thinking and feeling in your nervous system. Perhaps you are lucky and were instilled with entirely wise and enlightened principles. But it's unlikely. The reason people practice philosophy is because they suspect that some of the beliefs they have been carrying around are not that wise, and not that conducive to their flourishing. But your new philosophy will only ever be skin-deep if you don't really soak yourself in it, surround yourself with it, use every method you can to remind yourself of it, and imprint it on your psyche. As the emperor Marcus Aurelius told himself: "Your mind will be like its habitual thoughts; for the soul becomes dyed with the color of its thoughts. Soak it then in [wise] trains of thought."[12] There is, I hope, an important ethical distinction between voluntary, conscious brainwashing — which is what Aurelius is suggesting — and unconscious, involuntary brainwashing. Pythagoras's memorization technique is useful while you are wrestling with powerful old habits of thinking and feeling. But there is a danger that your new automatic habits of thinking could in turn become ossified, dogmatic, and overly rigid. So there's a necessary balancing act between creating automatic habits of thinking, and maintaining the ability to question those habits and consider their adaptability and usefulness.

The second concern about this technique, raised by Darian Leader, is that it is cultish. It could be a method for an individual or a group of individuals to exert their power over others, in order to brainwash them and turn them into zombies. That's what the Chinese government reportedly tried to do to American captives in the Korean War, priming them to denounce the United States on television. More recently, it's what some cults do to the unfortunate people who wander into their clutches. They use the same terminology over and over, attaching them to very powerful emotional experiences, until their initiates absorb their way of thinking and it becomes part of their automatic self-talk. When you control someone's inner self-talk, you control their selves. The concern that Leader and other critics of CBT have is that government-sponsored CBT involves this kind of forced brainwashing. It forces the depressed and anxious to think "positive thoughts," to see the world through rose-colored spectacles, turning them into happy zombies of the state. So the argument goes.

This is a popular misconception of cognitive therapy, which often gets confused with Positive Psychology, a younger school of psychology which developed from it. Positive Psychology does indeed try to teach people, including children, certain habits of "optimistic thinking." But this is not what CBT teaches. Albert Ellis, in particular, tried to get people to accept that the world is a rough, unfair, and often immoral place. He didn't pretend you could think the world into whatever shape you wanted. That's wishful thinking. He was explicitly critical of the "positive autosuggestion" theories of Emile Coué. Ellis wrote: "You can positively tell yourself, 'I can accomplish anything I want!' But, of course, you can't. You can enthusiastically think, 'Everything will happen for the best.' But alas, it won't... Accentuating the positive is itself a false system of belief, since there is no scientific truth to the statements that 'Day by day in every way I'm getting better and better.' In fact, this kind of Pollyannaism can be as pernicious as the negative claptrap which clients tell themselves to bring about neurotic conditions."[13] James Stockdale, who we met at the beginning of this chapter, had a view of his situation that was anything but rose-tinted. He was once asked which prisoners found captivity the hardest to endure. He replied: "Oh, that's easy, the optimists. Oh, they were the ones who said, 'We're going to be out by Christmas.' And Christmas would come, and Christmas would go. Then they'd say, 'We're going to be out by Easter.' And Easter would come, and Easter would go. And then Thanksgiving, and then it would be Christmas again. And they died of a broken heart." Stockdale says: "This is a very important lesson. You must never confuse faith that you will prevail in the end — which you can never afford to lose — with the discipline to confront the most brutal facts of your current reality, whatever they might be."[14]

The Vietcong tried to brainwash Stockdale, but failed — because they had no leverage over him. He had made an inner choice to stand by his principles even if they cost him his life. His torturers could break his bones and even kill him, but they couldn't force him to accept a belief that he chose not to accept. As Epictetus put it: "The robber of your free will does not exist." So was Stockdale's memorization of ancient philosophy an example of "brainwashing"? Only in the best sense. His story is an example of how we can choose our guiding principles, and then ingrain them in our psyches to enable us to withstand external pressures. In fact, the Navy SEALs SERE school in San Diego, where American soldiers learn how to resist torture and brainwashing techniques, is named after him.

8. Skeptics and the Art of Cultivating Doubt

I'M IN A CONFERENCE ROOM in Las Vegas, above a vast sea of flashing lights, ringing bells, and spinning wheels, where gamblers slump by fruit machines, like participants at an orgy that has become repetitive. Here, in the middle of the Nevada Desert, the Skeptics have gathered to hold their annual conference on the art of rational living. Las Vegas is an odd place to celebrate human rationality, but the Skeptics seem serenely untroubled by the temptations of the city of sin. "We're far too rational to be tempted by gambling," says James "The Amazing" Randi, the organizer of the event, which is named after him: The Amazing Meeting, or TAM. This is the ninth Amazing Meeting — "TAM 9 from outer space" — and it's the biggest yet. There are 1,600 Skeptics here, from all over the world, gathered together by their belief in science and critical reasoning, and their dislike of organized religion.

There have always been people who suspected religion was a load of old codswallop, but unlike the faithful such people didn't always have places to congregate and share their views. Now, the internet has created a space. Today, the global Skeptic movement has several million followers. There are two Skeptic magazines; a whole host of Skeptical podcasts, such as The Skeptics' Guide to the Universe, Skeptoid, Skepticality, and the Pod Delusion; and even more Skeptic chat rooms, email lists, and blogs, where Skeptics ferociously debunk their own and other people's beliefs. There are also offline Skeptic groups around Europe, Australasia, and in most American states, where unbelievers can come together, eat, drink, watch movies, and share stories of other people's gullibility. The Skeptic movement has its own Washington lobby group, its own student groups on many campuses, even its own summer camps for children. "The kids come to Camp Inquiry for friendship, fun, and free thinking," says Conrad Hudson, who helps to organize Skeptic summer camps in states across America. How do the camps encourage free thinking? "We tell the children that the camp is home to an invisible dragon called Percy, and offer a prize for anyone who can prove Percy exists. The younger children really want to find him. The older ones start to realize he doesn't exist…"

Like any movement, Skepticism has its rock stars. There's even a Skeptics Top Trumps pack, with cartoon caricatures depicting the leading personalities in the movement, along with an assessment of their Skeptic superpowers. One of the movement's biggest icons is Richard Dawkins (his Top Trump card says his superpower is "hoofing the enemies of reason in the logical goolies"), who stalks in sunglasses through the South-point casino, flanked by a bodyguard, before being mobbed by fans like an atheist Elvis. His keynote address receives a standing ovation before he's even said a word. Afterward, the queue of Skeptics waiting for him to sign their books stretches all the way down the corridor. "I had a passage from his last book read at my wedding," one flushed delegate whispers in the queue. "I'd just like half an hour alone with him in a hot tub," murmurs another.

TEAM RANDI

The warm heart of the Skeptic family is James "The Amazing" Randi, a tiny, frail figure with a long white beard, ever-present, ever-approachable for a conversation and a hug. "I'm an inveterate hugger," he tells the audience. Delegates wear T-shirts with his face on it and the legend "Team Randi" or "I'm with Randi." They even wear fake white beards in homage to the man. And, to be fair, Randi is pretty amazing. He was a child prodigy at school, so smart he was excused from attending classes, and given a special card to show to police who accused him of truancy. He tells me: "I was rather lonely as a child, because I had no peer group to mix with." Instead of attending school, he spent most of his time in museums and libraries. He also started to attend theaters, and was particularly fascinated by a magician called Harry Blackstone, who made a woman levitate during his show. After the show, the young Randi went backstage to meet Blackstone, who took a liking to him, and explained how some of his tricks worked. Randi went home determined to become a magician, and he became a very good one. He started off as an escape artist, working the clubs around North America. He made a name for himself in Quebec, when he was arrested by the local police after showing how easy it was to escape from their handcuffs. They put him in jail, and he escaped from that too. He escaped from a straitjacket over Niagara Falls. He escaped from an iron coffin at the bottom of a river. He beheaded Alice Cooper, onstage, several nights in a row. And he also, like the Great Houdini before him, started to expose those charlatans who used illusion to claim they genuinely possessed magical or religious powers.

The most famous instance of this was when he helped Johnny Carson expose Uri Geller. In the early 1970s, Geller had recently arrived in the United States, and was causing a sensation with his mind-reading and spoon-bending powers. He was booked to appear on Johnny Carson's *The Tonight Show*, and Carson rang Randi, who often appeared on his show, to ask how they could make sure Geller didn't fix the act. Randi gave the show's producers careful instructions, and when Geller appeared, his powers mysteriously failed him (you can watch it on YouTube). Randi says: "I felt pretty cocky after that, and thought it would be the end of Geller. But I was very wrong — he was on TV again just a few nights later. Now I realize the media doesn't care about telling the truth, as long as it gets people's attention." When he turned sixty, Randi decided it was "time to hang up the straitjacket" and devote himself full-time to the fledgling Skeptic movement. He set up the James Randi Educational Foundation, which works tirelessly to expose frauds, charlatans, and hucksters in the religious, New Age, and paranormal communities. Randi's foundation has, for the past few years, offered a million-dollar prize to any person who can prove they have paranormal powers. No one has ever won the prize.

The Skeptic movement has many such paranormal investigators, or "debunkers," within its ranks. At the conference, I met one member of the Independent Investigations Group, a paranormal investigation agency in Hollywood (kind of like the Scooby Doo gang), who tells me: "We're all geeks. We love investigating stuff like ghosts and psychics, and a part of us hopes their claims turn out to be true. We had a guy come into the office last month who claimed he could create an energy vortex, right there in the office. We thought, 'Wow, *cool*!' But it turned out he couldn't." Many of the Skeptics I meet are also conjurers and illusionists, who have dedicated themselves to exposing all the tricks that charlatans use. Religion, they believe, is just another illusion show. "Look at the Roman Catholic Church," Randi tells me. "It's as silly and theatrical as you can get." How often, I wonder, over the course of human history, have unscrupulous "wonder-workers" used conjuring tricks to gain wealth, sex, and power from the gullible? How often does it still happen today?

THE ANCIENT SKEPTICS

Skepticism as a philosophical movement has existed for several hundred years and, like most other Greek philosophical schools, it traces its origins back to Socrates. The Skeptics insisted Socrates was the first Skeptic, because he was honest about how little he or anyone else really knew for sure. Skeptics decided that this acceptance of the limits of our knowledge is the essence of philosophy. They called themselves *skeptikoi*, meaning investigators, or enquirers. The first Skeptic, it is said, was Pyrrho of Elis, a contemporary of Epicurus and the first Stoics in the late fourth and early third century BC. Pyrrho is said to have travelled to India with the army of Alexander the Great. There, he came across some "naked philosophers" — presumably Indian yogis — and was inspired by their philosophy and way of life. When he came back to Greece, he introduced "the doctrine of incomprehensibility, and the necessity of suspending one's judgment." Pyrrho and his followers declared that we can never know for sure if something is true or not. We can know, for example, that honey tastes sweet to us, but we can never know if it really *is* sweet, in its essence, or if this is just how it appears to us. It might taste quite different to, say, a sick person, or to another species. We might even be dreaming that we're eating honey. Other philosophical schools, such as the Stoics, rashly claim to be able to go beyond appearances and opinions, and to actually "know" reality. They end up claiming they can even know divine reality, as if human reason can ever know what's going on in God's mind — or even if there's a God in the first place.

It is precisely this kind of dogmatism, the ancient Skeptics insisted, that is the chief cause of emotional suffering. We jump to conclusions, are overconfident in our beliefs, and this makes us either overly depressed or overly euphoric. We are sure God is on our side, and nothing will ever go wrong; or we are certain the universe is against us, and nothing will ever go right. Even if we're Epicurean, and don't believe in divine intervention, we still dogmatically insist that pleasure is the only good, and then become depressed when we're in pain. For all these dogmatic ills, ancient Skepticism offered its followers a form of therapy. It trained them to let go of their certainty and accept how little they knew. It offered specific argumentative devices to oppose any belief with an alternative belief, to show that, seeing as you could believe everything, you might as well not believe anything. One famous Skeptic, Carneades, publicly exhibited this technique in Rome, arguing in favor of justice one day, and then returning to argue against justice the next day. This rather shocked the Romans, who threw Carneades out of the city.

Just as the Zen Buddhist, after pondering a *koan*, reaches a moment where they suddenly let go of reason and logic and achieve *satori*, so the Skeptic, having opposed one argument with another, will suddenly reach a moment where they stop thinking so much, and achieve tranquillity. This untroubled tranquillity is, in fact, the end or goal of the Skeptic's existence, according to Sextus Empiricus, a Skeptical doctor and philosopher who lived in the second century AD. Other philosophical schools, startled by this guerrilla campaign against their theories, hit back. Both Aristotle and the Stoics made the point that if you genuinely suspended all belief about good and bad, you'd be rendered completely inactive. After all, every action involves an implicit belief that something is worth doing. You get out of bed because you think it is worth getting out of bed. Likewise, you philosophize because you think it is worth philosophizing. Otherwise why do it? Why do anything? A Skeptic who genuinely suspended all opinions as to good and bad would be lucky to make it through the week. If a bus drove toward them, for example, why should they bother stepping out of the way? And, in fact, one account says that Pyrrho had to be constantly pulled out of the way of wagons by his disciples. Another story relates that he and a disciple were walking along one day, and the disciple fell into a ditch. Pyrrho kept on walking, serenely untroubled, while other followers pulled the poor disciple out — apparently, the incident only deepened the disciple's admiration for Pyrrho's complete indifference to external events.

The Skeptics marshaled several defenses to the criticism that their philosophy made any action impossible. The most convincing defense is that the Skeptic acts according to what he takes to be probable. This defense was made by the Academic Skeptics, so called because, for a century or so, Skeptics like Carneades were in charge of Plato's Academy in Athens. Academic Skeptics were, typically, a bit more establishment and less gung ho than Pyrrhonian Skeptics. Carneades and other Academic Skeptics argued that, while we can never "know" reality, we can at least construct tentative hypotheses about it. The best we can hope for is an educated and provisional guess that a belief is accurate, unless proven otherwise. We can act according to our tentative hypotheses about reality, while continuously doubting those hypotheses, thereby resisting the foolish dogmatism of the Stoics, Pythagoreans, Epicureans, and other schools.

This less extreme form of Skepticism enjoyed a lot of influence in modern philosophy from Descartes on, as philosophy used Skepticism to criticize Catholic dogma and break free of the influence of the Church. Through the influence of empiricists like John Locke, Skepticism gradually combined with empiricism and the experimental method, which suggests that we can only know reality through hypotheses based on observations which may be proved wrong in the future. All our knowledge, then, is tentative. As David Hume, the great Skeptic of the eighteenth century, pointed out, just because the sun has risen every day for our entire life, that doesn't mean we can be absolutely certain it will rise tomorrow. This

Skeptical attitude would help protect us from "enthusiasm," which is what the Enlightenment called fanaticism in all its forms, particularly religious fanaticism. Why had Europeans spent most of the eighteenth century killing each other over religious differences when, if they were honest, they would admit that none of them could really be sure whether God was a Catholic or a Protestant, or even if God existed? Much wiser to refrain from overconfident and intolerant dogmatic assertions. But Hume's polite Skepticism had some strange children in the nineteenth century. Philosophers like Søren Kierkegaard and Friedrich Nietzsche decided Hume was right: we can't really be certain about anything. Beneath all human theories and values yawns an abyss of nothingness, and this nothingness means that what counts is not reason or logic, but power and faith. We have to assert ourselves as creations of pure will in a meaningless universe. We have to have the courage to be laws unto ourselves. This, at least, is the radical philosophy behind a contemporary self-help school called the Landmark Forum.

THE INVENTION OF WERNER ERHARD
AND THE LANDMARK EDUCATION FORUM

Landmark was invented by an American used car salesman called John Paul Rosenberg. One day, Rosenberg left his wife and four children and moved to St. Louis with another woman. He became a salesman for the *Encyclopedia Britannica*'s Great Books program, and in his free time intently studied some of the leading self-help gurus of his age: Dale Carnegie, Napoleon Hill, existentialist philosophy, Zen, even a smattering of L. Ron Hubbard. He synthesized these into his own intensive coaching technique, which he claimed could completely free people from their hang-ups and give them the possibility to "reinvent themselves." He called it Erhard Seminars Training, or "est." Like the Stoics and CBT, Rosenberg suggested that what causes suffering is not events, but our opinions or "stories" about events. We tell ourselves false stories about reality, then mistake these stories for reality itself. The Stoics believed that, behind all our false stories, there is a true God, and a "right" way to live. Rosenberg is much more

Skeptical than that. Like the ancient Skeptics, he insists that *all* ethical narratives are just "stories." None of them are true. Rosenberg told the BBC's Adam Curtis:

> The real point to the est training was to go down through layer after layer after layer after layer [of the self], until you got to the last layer and peeled it off, where the recognition was that it's really all meaningless and empty. That's existentialism's endpoint. Est went a step further, in that people began to recognize that it was not only meaningless and empty, but it was empty and meaningless that it was empty and meaningless. And in that there's an enormous freedom. All the constrictions, all of the rules you've placed on yourself are gone, and what you're left with is nothing. Nothing is an extraordinarily powerful place to stand…from this nothing, people were able to invent a life.[1]

Out of the nothingness of extreme Skepticism, Rosenberg hoped to empower people to create new selves, to become Nietzschean supermen of pure will in a meaningless world. He had reinvented himself in just this way, giving himself the very Aryan new name, Werner Hans Erhard. Est was a huge success and made Erhard a famous and wealthy man in the 1970s and early 1980s.[2] In 1991, Erhard sold the business to family members and other employees, and it was renamed the Landmark Education Forum. It's continued to do very well since then, with over one million people taking its introductory course. It has centers all over the world, including a four-story building in north London, where I took their introductory course in October 2011.

SHOCK SOCRATIC PHILOSOPHY

The participants gather in a large hall, with rows of chairs facing a stage. On the stage sits the workshop Leader, an Australian called David Ure. He says we are about to experience something radically new in human history: "Humans were messed up for one hundred thousand years, and now Landmark is here to make things work." He admits one intellectual antecedent for Landmark, saying: "The closest thing to what we do at Landmark is Socrates. He didn't have a philosophy to teach. He didn't write anything down. He asked his followers questions. And at the end of the conversation, they knew less than they did at the beginning."

Of course, Socrates didn't charge his students anything, while Landmark's introductory course costs a hefty £365. "It's like poker," says David. "You're not interested in the next card unless you have some money on the table." The cost doesn't put people off: there must be two hundred people gathered in the hall, shivering under giant air-conditioning machines, waiting to be transformed. And these two hundred people go through what is, in essence, a three-day session of intensive life coaching. The sessions are tightly orchestrated by the leader, who follows a careful script. Initially, audience members shout things out or make comments from the floor, but we are told the only way to participate is to go up to one of the three microphones in the room, where we can engage in a "Socratic dialogue" with the leader. The leader insists we move from intellectual concepts to concrete situations in our life. We are exhorted to "share." A great emphasis is put on being "authentic" — though it's not explained why authenticity should be a particularly important moral value in a meaningless universe. Nonetheless, we are told we cannot get the benefit of Landmark unless we publicly share our inner dramas, our secrets, our lies. And people queue up to share their stories. They can't wait to reveal the secrets and traumas they've been carrying around for decades: Daddy never loved me, my uncle sexually abused me, my girlfriend doesn't take me seriously. There's a mass orgy of self-disclosure. This is deeply gratifying in itself: it taps into our liberal narcissistic urge to talk about ourselves,[3] but also our yearning to break out of our liberal isolation and express our feelings with a large group, like people used to do in churches. And it's also great theater, like a three-day Jerry Springer show.

Then, after you've shared your story, the leader rips it apart. Now, confrontational Socratic dialogues are nothing new. Epictetus would really tear into his students, Diogenes pissed on passersby, Albert Ellis would publicly ridicule people at his free Friday night workshops. But in the est sessions, and in some Landmark sessions, the public ridicule could be quite brutal. The leader attacks your "racket," mocks your self-pity, belittles your drama, to show you the emptiness of the story you've been carrying around all these years. In my course, participants were told, "you're a lie from top to bottom," "you're sleazy and completely lack integrity." The participant's ego-narrative is publicly deconstructed by the all-powerful leader — the Big Daddy or Big Mummy sitting on the stage in their director's chair. The participants, standing in front of them like naughty children, naturally feel stressed, humiliated, and vulnerable, but also somehow gratified ("I *am* a lying, cheating scumbag, I deserve this!"). And then, when their story's been publicly taken apart, the leader offers them the prospect of a shining new dawn. If they accept their story is a lie, and accept the possibility of true freedom through Landmark, they can step into a "miraculous new realm of possibility." "You got that?" asks the leader. "I got it," mumbles the participant, like a repentant schoolboy. "Okay, thanks for sharing." Then all two hundred people in the room applaud the participant, and, having felt the intense humiliation of being publicly ridiculed, the participant feels the intense relief of being accepted and celebrated by the whole group, and an intense admiration and even love for the leader who has ridiculed them. "For two days you're going to hate me," David tells us. "By the third day you'll want to marry me."

Landmark's "technology" (as it calls it) has a startling effect on some participants. Traditional therapy is wary of telling people what to do — but not Landmark. One person in my group "shared" with us that he had hidden his homosexuality from his parents. The leader told him to call his mother *at the very next break*. And he did. We were all urged, one break, to phone up a family member and share with them, and everyone rushed out and shared (one participant came back, slightly downcast, and told us his mother had responded: "Oh, sweetie, it's not all about you!"). And, importantly, we were told exactly how to be "authentic" in these communications. We should say that we are at the Landmark. And we should invite the person to our Landmark "graduation" and enroll them in our Landmark experience. "Wouldn't your mother benefit from all this too?" David asked us. "Wouldn't your partner? Wouldn't your children?" We were all primed to spread the meme of Landmark to our friends and family members, like spambots. People were sending out texts to all the contacts in their phone, as if they were email systems infected with a virus. This is part of the genius of Landmark, as a marketing strategy (Landmark was after all started by a salesman, and still has sister companies in marketing and brand design). If you want your product or idea to spread, turn your consumers into advocates. This is where Stoicism failed and Christianity succeeded.

Landmark understands how people long for freedom, but also for approval, for submission to authority, for a common terminology we can share with hundreds of others. We're liberal narcissists, but we're also conformists at a deep level. Landmark "gets" this, and works with it. You'd be amazed how quickly participants absorb and parrot the terminology of Landmark, describing their inner lives in terms of "rackets," "drama," "stories," and so on. The leader repeatedly says: "Anyone else understand that? If you do, raise your hand." And everyone raises their hand.

Joe's Story

Some people find the Landmark experience really useful and transformative. But it's quite a radical and full-on form of coaching. This much is acknowledged by the waiver form everyone has to sign at the start of the course, which tells us that, while Landmark is completely safe, there is an extremely small risk of "mild psychotic behavior" (I love the idea of "mild" psychosis), and that in "less than 1 / 1000 of 1 percent of participants, there have been reports of unexplained suicide." We're "strongly advised" not to do the course if we suffer from bipolar disorder, depression, or insomnia, or are unsure of our mental health, and warned that Landmark officials are not trained in therapy. Despite these clear warnings, I still worried about some people in the group, like one man from India who cried as he told us he'd been sexually abused as a child. He barely spoke English. Did he understand what was being said to him? Did he understand why the whole group was laughing, that they weren't laughing at him, but at something the leader said? No time to find out — the show must go on.[4]

For a few vulnerable people, the experience of having their "ego-racket" publicly deconstructed can be traumatic. It was for Joe, anyway. When Joe left university in the early Noughties, he was depressed, his self-esteem was at a low ebb, and he was stuck in an administrative job he hated. He heard about Landmark, and signed up. The leader of the London session that Joe attended was called Alain Roth. Throughout the weekend, various participants stood up and shared with the group their personal traumas. "People had been raped, abused, one person had killed his father," says Joe. Rather than sympathize with these revelations, the leader would ridicule the person's self-pity and insist they take responsibility for what happened to them. For example, one girl told how she'd been raped. The leader insisted she had "created a clearing" for that to happen. When people went up to her to console her, the leader insisted they too were "creating a clearing" for her self-pity.

Joe was the first to stand up and challenge the leader's authority.

I remember, I was absolutely terrified. My hands were shaking. I was standing up in front of all these people, challenging the leader's authority, but I felt I had to do it. I said: "What if the one thing you want is that everyone in the world admits that not everything is possible?" And the leader just sneered at me: "The thing about you is you like to play clever little games." I felt crushed. I suddenly wondered if it was true, if I was really a worthless person clinging on to my intellect. I sat back down. It wasn't that I'd had a breakthrough...I just didn't have the guts to leave.

For the next three days, Joe became more and more stressed, yet he felt he had to carry on to get the benefits of the course. After the course, Joe was unable to make sense of the world. He suffered from an extreme stress reaction, and his nervous system was flooded with adrenalin, as if he was in mortal danger — after all, his ego *was* in mortal danger. "My self-belief was undermined, but nothing had been put in its place," he suggests. The extreme stress scrambled his cognitive processes and made him suffer from advanced paranoia and psychotic delusions: he thought everyone was speaking in code about him, even the TV news, and that some sort of global cataclysm was about to happen. He ended up being put in a mental home for six weeks, as he tried to figure out where he was and what was happening to him. "For a while, I thought that we were all patients with mad cow disease, except some of us didn't have it, and the game was to figure out who had it and who didn't."

Joe gradually came back to reality, through antipsychotic medication, and through the Skeptic technique of checking for evidence, to see what stories were probably true and which probably weren't. His experience had left him in a pit of deep epistemological doubt, which he pulled himself out of by constructing and testing hypotheses. For example, he was convinced that everyone was looking at him, thinking about him, or talking about him. So he tried to check this theory out. He forced himself to look up to see if people *were* looking at him. And they weren't. He gradually found a way to get some more certainty, or probability, into his interactions with the world. He got back on his feet, and has recently enrolled to do a PhD in cognitive science and philosophy. I would suggest that Joe went from an overly radical form of Skepticism (nothing is true) to a healthier form of Skepticism (some hypotheses are more likely than others, based on the evidence), and this was key to his returning to health. We can all benefit from this sort of measured Skepticism toward our emotional beliefs about the world, so that when we find ourselves thinking, "that person hates me," we can ask ourselves, "Is that really the case? Are you sure? Where's the evidence?" According to CBT, what typically causes emotional disorders is overconfidence in our dogmatic interpretations of the world. A depressed person is *sure* things will go wrong. A socially anxious person is *sure* other people dislike him. We can learn to question our own rigid dogma, and open up to new ways of interpreting our experience.[5]

The helpful head of publicity at Landmark, Deb Beroset Miller, apologized for Joe's experience but said it was not representative, and that most participants find the course deeply rewarding (although the program's legal waiver form says that others with no history of mental illness also reported experiencing psychotic episodes following the course). Deb tells me that the leader of Joe's course, Alain Roth, who was also the subject of a critical French documentary,[6] no longer works at the organization, and that Landmark has "totally altered" its methods in the past five years. We can't directly blame Joe's psychotic episode on Landmark — he was already feeling depressed before the workshop, and probably shouldn't have participated. But perhaps Landmark should provide people with clearer warnings that the course is not appropriate for everyone: its website, for example, trumpets the miraculous benefits of the course, but doesn't say anything about the risks.

COULD SKEPTICISM BE THE FOUNDATION FOR A COMMUNITY?

In the ancient world, Skepticism was used as the foundation for small schools and communities, but what about the modern Skeptics — that ragtag army of unbelievers I met at The Amazing Meeting in Las Vegas? Could such a doubtful and diverse bunch ever truly be a community? Judging by my few days attending TAM in Las Vegas, and by the size of the global Skeptic movement, the answer would have to be yes. Modern Skepticism has proved you don't need to believe in God to create a community of belief. "I was brought up in a Mormon family," says Sariah, attending her first TAM. "I left that family. Maybe I've found a new family here." Yes, I ask her, but how deep are the connections and obligations in this community? Would you really trust any of these strangers with your children? She thinks for a bit. "I think I would. I've met some really nice people."

Part of the reason for Skepticism's success as a grassroots movement, perhaps, is that Skeptics, like the Catholic Church, know how to put on a good show. The Skeptic movement is full of magicians, illusionists, comedians, paranormal investigators. It's a fun scene to be in. And there's a lot of laughter to be had at other people's folly. But the main reason modern Skepticism is a thriving mass movement is that, unlike ancient Skepticism, it has positive values and beliefs: it believes in science. Michael Shermer, the founder of the *Skeptic* magazine, tells me: "Skepticism is really just science — it's a scientific way of thinking, beginning from doubt and looking for testable evidence, which we use to try and make the world better." And every positive has a negative: in Skeptics' minds, the noble forces of science are engaged in a "zero-sum war" with the irrational and destructive forces of religion.

The modern Skeptic movement, like Christianity, is given a lot of its vibrancy by a sense that it has mortal enemies out there, and needs to be well organized to defend its values. Steven Novella, host of The Skeptics' Guide to the Universe podcast, told the TAM audience that he had been demonized by Christian fundamentalists for his work in support of vaccination. He told the audience: "You have to understand the mindset of these folks. They're not rational. They see us as an evil cabal carrying out a secret plan to take over the world." And yet I wondered, after spending a few days among the Skeptics in the Nevada Desert, whether modern Skepticism itself retains traces of this Us versus Them mentality. One speaker, the psychologist Carol Tavris, told the audience: "There's so few of us and so many of them. So we need to tolerate the differences within the movement and focus on the real enemies to scientific thought." Skeptics can sometimes portray themselves as heroic saints battling the demons of irrationalism in their culture: one T-shirt on sale at the main desk shows Randi battling a demonic-looking woman, with the slogan "Round One: Debunk!" Randi tells the conference: "I can guarantee you'll return home from these few days in the desert even better prepared to face down the nonsense you encounter every day," as if TAM is some sort of desert shamanic training. In here is "a clear-thinking oasis" as Richard Dawkins puts it. Out there, just a few meters away, is a world full of flimflam, bunkum, woo woo, bullshit, and it has to be denounced as bullshit, over and over, like Luther spitting obscenities at the Catholic Church. The bullshit must be hunted out, and extirpated from the land, like St. Patrick expelling the snakes from Ireland. It's not enough to quietly suspend belief while tolerating others' irrationalities, as the ancient Skeptics did. If modern Skepticism is to be a genuine social movement, then it needs a mission, it needs campaigns and battles. Above all, it needs enemies. This is one paradox of modern Skepticism — it champions tolerance, yet sees itself engaged in a zero-sum war with religions. "There are more theocrats in Congress today than ever before," thunders Sean Faircloth, executive director of the Secular Coalition for America. "This is the time of maximum danger, and we need to spread the word!"

SKEPTICAL ABOUT SCIENCE?

This sense of a good-versus-evil war between "science" and "religion" can lead to some quite uncritical statements, like "I believe in science" or "science is good," both of which I heard at TAM, and to an almost cultic reverence for scientists like Richard Dawkins. More interesting Skeptics do not content themselves merely with ridiculing religious fundamentalism or New Age quackery (that's easily done) but also hold up our culture's faith in science to critical examination.[7] For example, we have arguably replaced our old, irrational faith in the power of soothsayers with an equally irrational confidence in the power of economists and social scientists to explain the world and predict the future. As the Skeptic Nassim Nicholas Taleb pointed out in *Black Swan: The Impact of the Highly Improbable*, this excessive confidence in the social sciences can cause just as much harm as religious fanaticism. The Credit Crunch wasn't caused by the Religious Right, it was caused by banks' faith in economic risk-modeling, and investors' faith in Alan Greenspan, and Alan Greenspan's faith in the market's perfect rationality. Another instance of our culture's excessive faith in science is the sometimes noxious influence of psychoanalysis. Our culture put a huge amount of faith in psychoanalysis, with many psychologists feeling a religious veneration for its founder, Sigmund Freud. But the Freudian dogma that all neurosis is caused by childhood sexual trauma (real or imagined) wasn't just wrong — it caused a great deal of damage, not least in several instances where analysts succeeded in implanting false memories of sexual abuse in their patients, as the Skeptic Elizabeth Loftus has very ably illustrated.[8] A more interesting Skepticism recognizes that it's not simply religions that give rise to irrationalism and fanaticism. It's our inherent human tendency to be overconfident in authority figures and systems of belief, and to attack anyone who criticizes those beliefs.

Sensible Skeptics would agree, I think, that the "scientific method" is not inherently "good" — it's a method which can be used for good or evil, depending on your values. The finest scientists in the world could invent you the atom bomb — you still have to decide whether to use it. That's why more and more governments and research institutes use bio-ethics committees — simply saying "science is good" is not enough. Some modern Skeptics also seem to me to be overly dogmatic in their absolute certainty that there's no God and the universe has no purpose. Quantum physics asks us to believe such strange things — that time can go backward, observation can alter matter, that there are multiple universes where every possibility happens — that it seems to me at least feasible that the universe is connected by some sort of conscious intelligence, as the Stoics interpreted God. But in other areas, modern Skepticism doesn't seem dogmatic and punchy enough. Why is the movement so silent on the issue of climate change? Why does it not attack all the examples of bad science and willful ignorance on this critical issue? Why do Skeptics spend so much energy attacking Deepak Chopra and James Van Praagh, and so little attacking Exxon, Chevron, and their Washington lobbyists? The answer, I think, is there's a clash between the movement's natural libertarianism and the need for global legislation to control and curtail fuel emissions.

From a long-term historical perspective, obviously the rise of Skepticism has greatly helped our culture. You only have to look at countries where witch doctors still sacrifice children in fertility rites to appreciate the triumph of Western rationalist science. New Agers may mourn the passing of the age of magic and animism, but I'm personally very grateful we no longer cower before knife-wielding druids. And I am sure that, if I lived in the United States and was surrounded by phony evangelists, fundamentalist senators, and fear-mongering shock-jockeys, I would be a card-carrying Skeptic. But I don't. I live in Britain, where our society is already deeply secular, and church attendance is in long-term decline. From the perspective of the UK, Dawkins and his ilk look like quaint historical reenactors fighting battles long since won. They don't seem to me to be fighting the critical battles of our time: climate change, for example, or the moral crisis in capitalism. And in their crusade against believers, Skeptics seem to willfully ignore any benefits we have gotten from religious traditions — including many of the therapeutic techniques now used by Western science, like cognitive therapy and meditation. Religions are a great storehouse of knowledge about the emotions and techniques to transform them. We can appreciate that, while still criticizing religions in their more extreme and destructive forms.

Now it's time for our final session, Politics, where we explore further the question of how philosophers should engage with society, and try to transform it. In the next lesson, we'll meet the Cynics, who have a rather radical solution to society's ills.

LATE-AFTERNOON SESSION

Politics

9. Diogenes and the Art of Anarchy

IN FRONT OF THE SOLEMN PILLARS of St. Paul's Cathedral, a multicolored mushroom patch of tents has sprouted. Businessmen hurrying to the London Stock Exchange ignore the signs covering the columns of Paternoster Square: "The beginning is nigh," "Say no to usury," "Kill the policeman in your head," "We are fantasy." There's a man in medieval armor and a Guy Fawkes mask clanking around the tents. Another is carrying a large plastic skull and a banner saying "Dance on the grave of capitalism." Several people are dressed as zombies (it is Halloween) and are practicing the jerking shuffle of the undead. There's a food tent, a "tranquillity center," a makeshift cinema, and a "tent city university" with a full schedule of daily workshops on everything from meditation to well-being economics. This, of course, is the Occupy London camp, or #occupylsx as it's known on Twitter, one of several anarchist occupations that appeared at the end of 2011 like an outbreak of boils on the face of global capitalism. Mainstream media commentators looked on in scorn, then in wonder, then in genuine confusion: "Who are they? What do they want? What are their demands?"

Perhaps the Occupiers weren't demanding anything, exactly. They were exhibiting. They were living and acting out an alternative vision of society on the streets of New York, London, Bristol, Berlin, Oakland, and elsewhere. The camps were an anarchist version of the Ideal Home Show. They exhibited a communal way of life that tries to abolish authoritarianism and enhance participation. "Come and see what real democracy looks like," one of the London banners said. Every few hours, the Occupiers held a general assembly on the steps of St. Paul's: someone took to the microphone to express a point of view, then the assembly broke into small groups to discuss the idea, then feed their opinions back. The Occupiers expressed their sentiments through a common language of hand signals — jazz hands expresses consent, a T gesture means you have a technical point, crossed wrists means you block the vote. The Occupiers were exhibiting an economic system based on sharing and gifts rather than property and capital. They were exhibiting a lifestyle based on imagination, satire, and play, rather than lives spent sitting at a desk watching the clock. And they tried to show how little one needs to be happy: a piece of pavement, a tent, a sleeping bag, and some friends. How's *that* for austerity measures?

Kalle's Story

The Occupy movement began on September 17, 2011, when a Vancouver-based anarchist collective named Adbusters called for a tent occupation of Wall Street, to emulate the occupation of Tahrir Square in Cairo earlier that year. Adbusters is an anticonsumerist magazine and protest movement dedicated to "culture jamming." Its founder and guiding spirit is Kalle Lasn, who at the age of seventy shows no signs of weariness in his efforts to overthrow capitalism. Kalle tells me: "We're at the beginning of a cultural revolution. Our present system is ecologically unsustainable and psychologically corrosive. It screws our planet, and it screws our mind. Corporations have taken over the media systems, which bombard us with consumerist messages. At least 75 percent of the population is caught in a consumer trance. They're completely brainwashed. One day, all of a sudden, people will wake up after the Dow Jones has gone down by seven thousand points, and say: 'What the hell is going on?' They'll see their life as they know it collapse around them. And they'll have to pick up the pieces and learn to live again."

Perhaps surprisingly, Kalle started his career in advertising. He was the child of Estonian immigrants who'd fled the Soviet Union. He grew up in a deported persons camp in Germany, then moved to Australia, then moved again to Japan, where he worked in the booming 1960s advertising industry. He says: "It was a very thriving time, business-wise. I got a taste of what the advertising industry is all about. I found it was an ethically neutral business, where people didn't really give a damn whether they were selling cigarettes, or alcohol, or Pepsi-Cola. For them it was all one big interesting game, and the social repercussions were somehow irrelevant." He then moved again, to Canada, where he got involved with the fledgling environmental movement. By 1990, Kalle was working with an environmentalist group campaigning against logging. The group wanted to buy TV airtime to run a campaign ad. "We were told we couldn't. The $6 billion forestry industry could, but we couldn't. Everything we've done since then has grown out of that outrage, from realizing that one side gets on TV and the other side doesn't. We want to have our say. Democracy doesn't really work unless everyone can have a say."

In the early 1990s, Kalle and his friends set up *Adbusters* in Vancouver. The magazine, which quickly built up a worldwide circulation of 120,000, runs journalism pieces by the likes of Matt Taibbi and Bill McKibben, alongside witty spoof ads designed by Kalle and other refugees from the advertising industry. One ad showed Joe Camel, the 1990s mascot for Camel cigarettes, in a hospital bed undergoing chemotherapy. Another showed a flaccid vodka bottle, with the caption: "Absolut Impotence." Another showed a male model peering down his Calvin Klein boxer shorts, with the slogan: "Obsession. For Men." Kalle says: "We're exposed to so many messages each day trying to get us to consume — hundreds, maybe thousands. What we're trying to do is get a few messages out there saying the opposite." The idea for the fake ad campaigns came, Kalle says, from the Situationist movement of the 1960s and 1970s, which likewise tried to deface the currency of industrial capitalism, using street art, posters, and countercultural graffiti. Kalle says: "One of the big things the Situationists talked about was *détournement* — it's a French word that means taking an existing situation, and in a deft, judo-like move, creating a feedback loop that destroys it. So you're a culture jammer and you're facing Nike, which is a massive corporation that has all kinds of power on its side. But because you're fleet of foot, and nimble, you grab them and throw them on the mat with a beautiful, aesthetic, intellectual tour de force that somehow outwits them."

In 1992, Adbusters launched Buy Nothing Day, a day in which participants voluntarily put themselves through a twenty-four-hour consumer fast. Kalle says: "Many people who decide to take the personal plunge suffer — it's as hard as giving up smoking for some people. It's hard to resist the urge to buy a coffee or a Mars bar. People go through a cold turkey experience. They sweat, and they realize the extent to which this impulse to buy is a bit of an addiction." The hope of the Adbusters movement is that people will kick the consumer habit and embrace a life of simplicity, freedom, and creative endeavor. Kalle says:

> The simplicity movement is made up of people who have been stung by consumer culture. Either they're stressed-out, or they've got some kind of mood disorder, or they lost their job — they're people who have really suffered because of the dog-eat-dog world of capitalism that we live in, and they've said: "You know, I don't need a car, I don't need a big house with a TV in every room, I don't need to max out on my credit card every Christmas. I'm just going to downshift, I'm going to live a simpler life, and I can get by on the money I have, and get a job that I really love instead of a job that pays a huge amount of money." These are people who radically changed their personal and working lives.

This sounds homely enough, but Kalle is aware that only a minority of people show any desire to give up consumerism, so he thinks the struggle against capitalist civilization may need to get violent. He has written: "America needs to be liberated from itself...We will wreck this world." He tells me: "God knows what will happen after the revolution. We'll have to build a new system from the bottom up, and I have no idea how the system will look." Does he worry that a revolution will lead to an even more authoritarian system in which, as in revolutionary France, Russia, and China, a handful of intellectuals enforce their philosophy onto the masses? He says:

Of course it's a danger. I've been a student of revolution all my life, and every revolution faces that danger. In the early stages it's full of idealism and truth and sincere authentic people. But as soon as they win, it turns into a monster, like in Russia. I believe we are at the beginning of a huge cultural revolution. I'm sure that, years down the road, when we've won, some of us will turn into monsters. That's just the way the human spirit works. But nonetheless I believe it's very important for us to win, and worry about how badly we behave later. Right now we need to pull the current monster down.

A DOG'S LIFE

The therapy of ancient philosophy often had a political dimension. Emotional disturbances come from our beliefs, but our beliefs may come from our society, from its economic and political structure and values. So philosophers had to decide how to engage with their society. The Stoic response was to quietly declare inner independence from society's toxic values. The Epicurean response was to leave society and set up a commune of friends. Both of these responses were apolitical — Stoics and Epicureans accepted that the philosopher was powerless to reform society, so they should focus on their own personal fulfilment. But there were other, more optimistic visions for how the philosopher could change society, and free not just themselves, but their whole society from the discontents of civilization. We're going to look at some of those responses in the late-afternoon session.

The first response we'll look at is Cynicism. The Cynics suggested we should abandon civilization, and their radical and extreme lifestyle is being reerected on our streets. One of the first Cynics, and certainly the most famous, is Diogenes the Cynic, who you can see in the front of Raphael's *School of Athens*, sprawled out on the marble steps like he owns the place, his ragged blue cloak tossed back to reveal his sinewy torso. Diogenes was a native of Sinope, a city on the coast of the Black Sea. His father was a banker, and either he or Diogenes was accused of "defacing the currency" of Sinope, which led to Diogenes being thrown out of the city. He arrived in Athens as an exile, under a cloud of scandal, but he embraced his notoriety, became a radical philosopher, and declared it his mission in life to "deface the currency" of civilized conventions. Diogenes decided that humans' emotional discontents arose from the false values of civilization. To cure ourselves, it is not enough to stay within civilization while practicing inner freedom from its values, as the Stoics did. Civilization must be abandoned, and the false values of civilization have to be actively defaced. Like the Occupiers, Diogenes acted out his philosophy of freedom on the streets, dressing in rags, feeding on leftovers, and living in a barrel in the center of the Athenian marketplace, to show the bemused Athenians how simple and happy the natural life could be. These animal antics earned him the name Diogenes *Kynikos*, or Diogenes the Dog-Like, which is where the word "cynic" comes from. Originally, then, "cynic" meant someone who has abandoned the false values of civilization to follow a natural life of poverty, asceticism, and moral freedom. Diogenes said: "Instead of useless toils men should choose such as nature recommends, whereby they might have lived happily, yet such is their madness that they choose to be miserable."[1]

Why do we choose to be miserable? Because we want to be accepted by our civilization. Living in a dense metropolis forces us to be polite, which comes from the Greek *polis*, meaning city-state; and urbane, from the Latin *urbs*, meaning city. If we want to get on in the city, if we want to make something of ourselves, we have to consider how our behavior is affecting the millions of people around us. We have to behave ourselves and acquire metropolitan manners, because otherwise we won't be accepted into civilized society. We need to win the approval of the strangers we live among, and avoid their censure. It's our inherent sense of shame and our desire for public approval that enables civilization to exist. We internalize the gaze of others, and this internal spectator becomes all-powerful over us. But Diogenes insisted that our sense of shame has become so overrefined by civilization that we've become anxious, neurotic, alienated beings, who are terrified of making a bad impression on others. We spend all our energy trying to look good to strangers, putting forward a carefully tended mask of civility, while hiding anything from the public's view that might seem uncouth, rude, or primitive. This terror of making a bad impression is the cause of many of our civilized discontents. Diogenes abandoned this value system, and instead decided to "live according to nature." If a behavior is natural, why should we be ashamed of it? Why should we hide it from public view? The Cynic breaks down the wall between public and private selves, and between public and private morality. Diogenes ate and slept in public, defecated in public, he even masturbated in public. Why shouldn't we masturbate in public? Either it's a vice, and we shouldn't do it in public *or* private, or it's not a vice, and we shouldn't be ashamed of doing it in full view of the public. We happily fart in private. So why are we so ashamed to fart in public? It's a neurotic suppression of behavior that is perfectly natural. A disciple of Diogenes's called Crates heard about one young man, Metrodus, who farted while giving an important speech. Metrodus was so horrified by his faux pas that he shut himself up at home, determined to kill himself. Crates came round to see him, and let loose a joyous self-affirming fart. "From that time forward Metrodus was his pupil, and became proficient in philosophy."

The Cynic way of life involves a sort of voluntary desensitization against public ridicule and disapproval. We're far too worried about what others think of us, and are terrified of their disapproval. As a result, we end up anxious, miserable, and trapped in inauthentic lives. So we need to declare our independence, by refusing to hide our natural behavior, and training ourselves not to care if others laugh at us or ridicule us. We need to attack our inner censor, kill the policeman in our heads. Civilized values have misdirected our natural sense of shame, so we have to reprogram ourselves, so that we feel shame about acts that are *truly* shameful, while feeling no shame about acts that are natural. Cynicism involves a revolution in personal morality — Cynics move from a false morality based on appearances to a genuine morality based on adherence to a personal moral code. Cynics don't want to look good to strangers. They want to *be* good, according to their own personal code.

SHAME-ATTACKING

As extreme as it sounds, this Cynic technique of retraining and redirecting our sense of shame is used today in modern psychotherapy, where it's called "shame-attacking." Once again, the person who redeployed this ancient technique was Albert Ellis, the pioneer of cognitive therapy, although he seems to have taken it from behavioral therapy rather than Cynic philosophy. When he was a teenager, Ellis was terrified of being rejected or laughed at by girls. So, when he was eighteen, he decided to free himself from this crippling sense of shame. He went to the Brooklyn botanical gardens, and set himself a task: he would sit next to a girl on a bench and start a conversation with her. He would do this with a hundred different girls, until he overcame his embarrassment and anxiety. He remembered: "Out of the one hundred conversations, I made one date, and she didn't turn up. But I overcame my fear of talking to girls, and eventually became one of the best picker-uppers in New York."[2] (In fact, he eventually wrote a book called *The Art of Erotic Seduction*.) In the 1950s, when Ellis devised Rational Emotive Behavioral Therapy, he drew on this experience, insisting that it's not enough to challenge our beliefs in the therapy room — we also need to get out and practice in the street, in real-life situations. Each time we challenge our fears successfully, we lessen their hold over us. So, if we're terrified of being looked at or laughed at (as people with social anxiety are) then we should practice intentionally drawing ridicule onto ourselves, to desensitize ourselves to the experience. Ellis set his patients "homework" — they would walk down Madison Avenue with a banana on a leash, or ask passersby directions to the North Pole, or sing loudly in supermarkets. Naturally, people would look at them strangely, but so what? A bit of ridicule wouldn't kill them — and that's the whole point. They turned what they most feared into a personal triumph. By changing their attitude, an external humiliation became an internal victory. Many people have since found the technique useful for overcoming social anxiety, which affects as much as 10 percent of the population. The comedian Will Ferrell, for example, says he was painfully shy as a child but managed to conquer it by intentionally inviting ridicule. "I always just forced myself to do crazy things in public," Ferrell told *People* magazine. "In college, I would push an overhead projector across campus with my pants just low enough to show my butt. Then my friend would incite the crowd to be like, 'Look at that idiot!' That's how I got over being shy."[3]

Dave McKenna, a young man in Lancashire, tells me he also used shame-attacking to overcome his crippling social anxiety. He says:

> I hated being the center of attention, and used to feel really self-conscious. My social anxiety was so bad, I didn't have any mates, or girlfriend, or job. It was my dream to be a professional footballer, but I'd get terrible stage fright every time I played in front of a crowd. Then I heard about this "shame-attacking" technique from a social anxiety support website, and thought I'd try it out. I came up with a three-month plan. I planned to come to this shopping center in Bootle, and do shadow-boxing, to get used to people staring at me. I kept a journal, like a little folder, where I planned it all out — you need a structured plan, so you can review the progress you are making as you go along. I planned it for weeks, but then I'd come down here with my boxing gloves, and I'd just be too scared, too self-conscious. I'd feel sick with fear, and would turn around and go back home.

And then finally, one day, he took the leap:

> I got out the boxing gloves, put them on, and started doing shadow-boxing! The first time I did it, it was terribly uncomfortable. But after about a week it started to get a bit easier. So I ramped it up a bit, and tried it in fancy dress — I dressed up as a scarecrow. That was when I noticed a real difference. I was walking to the shopping center, dressed as a scarecrow, and I noticed I didn't feel anxious or cripplingly self-conscious. Just a few weeks before, I'd been so self-conscious I could barely leave the house. Now I was able to walk down the street dressed as a scarecrow, and it didn't bother me.

STATUS ATTACKING

But Cynicism was not simply a personal therapy. It was more radical than that. It is also a critique of civilization, of its social, moral, and economic values. Diogenes was a tramp — he lived in a barrel in the middle of the Athenian marketplace; his only possession was a rough cloak; he fed off rubbish and scraps thrown to him by the amused Athenian public. Such a life is the complete opposite of the "American Dream." It's most civilized people's worst nightmare. Adam Smith, the great philosopher of capitalism, wrote in his *Theory of Moral Sentiments* that, for most people, to be seen by others as a beggar or tramp is a fate "worse than death." We're terrified of being seen as failures by others. And so, to seek the approval of strangers, we devote our whole lives to trying to look as rich, glamorous, and successful as possible. In the words of the economist Tim Jackson: "We spend money we don't have on things we don't need to make impressions that don't last on people we don't care about."[4] Smith himself admitted that, if we ever do "make it" and become rich and successful, we often discover that we're not actually any happier than when we began. We might even be *less* happy, more anxious, more bad-tempered, and stressed. We realize we've been chasing an illusion, attempting to please an imaginary crowd of phantom spectators. And yet, Smith decides, it's *good* that we've been chasing this false dream, because all our neurotic production and consumption helps the economy to grow (or, as he puts it: "It is well that nature imposes on us in this manner. It is this deception which rouses and keeps in motion the continual industry of mankind."). Smith's contemporary, Bernard Mandeville, pointed out that if we were all ascetics like Diogenes, the capitalist economy would collapse.[5] Capitalism needs us to be vain, deluded, insecure, and miserable.

Diogenes refused to buy into that rat race. Instead, he embraced a life of poverty, flaunted it even, to show that it's only our beliefs that make such a life seem terrifying. He insisted that the life of a vagabond is *happier*, less complicated, less anxious than civilized life. You have nothing to fear because you have nothing to lose. It's more independent, as there's no need to "play the game" and suck up to the rich and powerful. When Alexander the Great visited Diogenes in his barrel, and asked him what he could grant the philosopher, Diogenes replied "only that you move out of my sun." The Cynic life is more free and more honest: civilized people have to lie and dissemble, while for the Cynic, the sweetest activity is free speech. Cynics had no need to keep up polite appearances, and they took delight in heckling and insulting passersby. And the Cynic life is more moral, because it rejects the false external goods of status and luxury and embraces the inner riches of the Socratic life. Epictetus, who like many Stoics was a great admirer of the Cynic way of life, wrote, in words that could be the motto of the Occupy movement: "How is it possible for a man who has nothing, naked, without home or hearth, in squalor, without a slave, without a city, to live a tranquil life? Look, God has sent you one to show that it is indeed possible. 'Look at me, I have no house or city, property or slave: I sleep on the ground, I have no wife or children, no miserable palace, but only earth and sky and one poor cloak. Yet what do I lack? Am I not free of pain and fear?' "[6]

The Cynics were the first anarcho-primitivists in Western culture.[7] They were the first to suggest that civilization was incurably sick, and that we should return to a state of nature. We should abandon the *polis* and become cosmopolitans — citizens of the universe, children of nature. Cosmopolitans don't need the protection of the state, because they're so tough and resilient. As Charles Dickens put it much later: "The men who learn endurance are they who call the whole world brother."[8] Conversions to the Cynic life could be sudden — it was known as the "short path to virtue." People would suddenly look at their complicated and stressful lives and think "What the hell am I doing?" We hear of Monimus, a banker, who suddenly woke up from his trance. Rather like the hero of Chuck Palahniuk's novel *Fight Club*, Monimus faked insanity to get fired from his job, and happily went to live in the streets with his fellow Cynics.

And yet despite rejecting civilization, Cynics never actually *left* it. Instead, they practiced a sort of street theater, a daily performance of their rejection of civilized conventions. Diogenes was as famous for his pranks as for his teachings — walking through the streets with a lamp "looking for an honest man," asking a statue for money "to practice being rejected," pissing on passersby, disrupting the lectures of Plato by pulling out a chicken. His exhibitionist antics made him a much-loved figure in Athens, even a tourist attraction — they built a statue to him after he died. In some ways, the Cynic wasn't really *that* independent, because he required an audience. He may have freed himself from the need for public approval, but not from the need for public attention (the Stoics, who were less attention-seeking, perhaps avoid this danger of conspicuous anti-consumption). And as a political response to civilization, Cynicism was surely inadequate. The Cynics had no program for the disestablishment of the state. In fact, they continued to live off it and enjoy the protection of its laws.

THE EVOLUTION OF CYNICISM

After Diogenes's death, Cynicism split into two streams: literary Cynicism and practical Cynicism. In both Athens and Rome, some followers of Diogenes chose not to embrace his radically antisocial lifestyle, but they still carried on his project of trying to deface the currency of social conventions through satire. Satire is, after all, a way of tearing off the mask of civilization to expose the grinning goat beneath. Cynic satirists like Menippus and Lucian wrote biting satires of contemporary hypocrisy, and the tradition was carried on in the modern age by writers like Jonathan Swift, who called his eighteenth-century satire of English society *A Tale of a Tub* in homage to Diogenes's barrel. This type of Cynicism continues today, in satirical magazines like *Private Eye*, which holds its lamp up to modern politics in an effort to find an honest man (it is entirely appropriate, in this respect, that one of the largest American private detective companies is called Diogenes). Cynics of this sort perform an important social function, by exposing the corruption that lies beneath civilized appearances. Think of Enron, which managed to convince the world it was the perfect corporation, until its lies were exposed by a hedge fund named Kynikos Associates (the firm's Greek founder Jim Chanos, says the name was inspired by Diogenes's example).[9] Kynikos Associates "defaced the currency" of Enron's corporate spin. We need that sort of Cynicism more and more.

Cynicism as a way of life also survived for many centuries, to the extent that Lucian complains in the second century AD that "the streets crawl with these vermin." Some academics think Cynicism was an influence on early Christianity, perhaps on Jesus himself. There's more than a whiff of Cynicism in the life and writings of St. Paul, who says: "We have become, and are now, as the refuse of the world and the offscourings of all things..."[10] (or "the all-singing, all-dancing crap of the world," as a later Cynic, Tyler Durden, put it in *Fight Club*). You can see the influence of Cynic *askesis* on the Christian asceticism of the desert fathers, who unlike Diogenes actually *left* the city, and on later anticapitalists like St. Francis of Assisi, who abandoned his wealth and stripped off to become a naked mendicant. In the Enlightenment, Jean-Jacques Rousseau was labeled a mad "descendant of Diogenes's dog"[11] as he lambasted his age in very Cynic terms (he also liked to expose himself to passersby in Paris, which is quite Cynical). Civilization, he declared, had made us miserable slaves to public opinion. Civilized man "lives outside of himself and can only live in the opinions of others."[12] To free himself from this alienation, Rousseau abandoned Paris to go and live in the countryside, but this Cynic experiment didn't work very well: he ended up stewing in neurotic isolation, and wrote his *Confessions*, a long and paranoid justification of himself to the public. Like Diogenes, the more Rousseau declared his independence from public opinion, the more he seemed to crave attention.

In the nineteenth century, Henry David Thoreau declared his independence from American society and went to live by Walden Pond for two years. He did so in conscious imitation of "the ancient philosophers," and in scorn of modern academic philosophy. He wrote: "There are nowadays professors of philosophy, but not philosophers...To be a philosopher is not merely to have subtle thoughts, nor even to found a school, but so to love wisdom as to live according to its dictates, a life of simplicity, independence, magnanimity, and trust."[13] Thoreau successfully proved how little one had to work and spend to support oneself. Yet his rejection of civilization didn't take him very far into the wild — he only got as far as the garden of his friend Ralph Waldo Emerson.

THE REVIVAL OF CYNICISM

For a while, the anarcho-primitivist critique of capitalism was eclipsed by Marxism–Leninism, but Cynicism returned as the Soviet Union lost credibility. You can see Cynicism's influence on Situationist philosophy,[14] and the protesters of Paris 1968, who aimed not to replace the capitalist state with a communist state, but rather to do away with the state altogether through a revolutionary campaign of poster art and ironic graffiti. You can also see the influence of Cynicism in the Yippies (or "Youth International Party") of the 1960s and 1970s, who were notorious for their "Groucho Marxist" stunts, like causing chaos at the New York Stock Exchange by throwing wads of fake money onto the trading floor.[15] You can see the Cynic response, too, in the anticapitalists of the 1990s, like Reclaim the Streets, who tried to disrupt the dream of capitalism with pranks, raves, carnivals, and street theater.[16] The artist Banksy, perhaps, is a modern descendant of Diogenes, using street art to deface the values of consumer capitalism. Banksy quotes Diogenes in one of his works, and he also literally defaced the currency, printing ten-pound notes with Princess Diana's face on them. This sort of anticapitalist agitation seemed to peak at the 1999 Seattle protests against the World Trade Organization, only for the "antiglobalization movement" to subside somewhat in the Noughties. But it has come back strongly in the last few years, spurred on by the obvious dysfunctionality of our present financial and political system. More and more people have started to think that the present system is rigged: private banks keep their profits, while expecting taxpayers to pay for their losses. Government budgets are slashed and currencies inflated to protect private banks from bankruptcy. And every government in the world seems to be hoping that climate change will simply go away. Faced with such a system, going to live in a tent doesn't seem such a ridiculous option.

CLIMATE CAMP

In 2009, as the world's governments tried and failed to broker a climate change agreement, I visited Climate Camp, which a group of anarcho-primitivists had erected in south London. Climate Camp was maybe a 150 meter-diameter circle filled with tents, with a metal fence around it, in the middle of Blackheath common. You had to enter through a steel gate, over which hung a sign saying "Capitalism is crisis." Crusties sat on straw bales beneath the sign, perusing the new entrants like monkeys outside a Hindu temple. The crusties were on "gate watch" to make sure the police didn't enter. The Camp for Climate Action handbook, which I picked up as I entered, told me: "Whatever you have to offer, from vegan cakes to tripods, do come to the defense center and be a part of making our vision of a community free from authoritarianism a reality." I entered a welcome tent on the left, where a middle-aged lady gave us a brief induction. She told the new recruits about the various ways we could join in: we could be on food duty, washing-up duty, well-being duty ("going round, checking on the welfare of the camp"), dismantling duty (the tents, not the state, sadly), and so on.

"Any questions?"

"What are you trying to achieve?" I asked, like the cynical journalist I am. "Well, it's not 'you.' Hopefully it's 'we,' " she replied. "We're here in London, the center of the global financial system, because we're opposed to the system. We think it sucks. We don't want to reform it, because as soon as we start to debate that, we get into arguments, and it hurts my head." She banged her head to illustrate this. "But we agree that we would rather the present system…" collapsed? "…went away." She was a veteran of direct action. She'd helped set up — and dismantle — the Kingsnorth camp, protesting against E.ON's plans for a new coal-fired power station. "My personal favorite is superglue. I like gluing myself to things," she confided, as if confessing a fetish. "I've always wondered about that," said a well-spoken lady on her right. "How do you come unstuck?" "Turn that video camera off and I'll tell you," said the woman. A young man videoing the induction dutifully turned his camera off. "You use soap and water."

Climate Camp didn't have any obvious impact on governments' failed attempt to agree on a climate agreement. But it looked like a fun experiment in living. However, it's one thing to run a "community free from authoritarianism" in the relative seclusion of Blackheath common on the outskirts of London. Imagine trying to run an anarchist community with no borders or police, where everyone has a say and the citizenship is constantly changing, right in the heart of London, amid all the noise, traffic, pollution, tourists, drunks, thugs, and the ringing of the cathedral bells…

THE LIMITS OF ANARCHISM

Two years later, at Occupy London, I witnessed an angry debate take place at one of the general assemblies. The evening before, a protester had been turned in to the police for assaulting another protester. The camp had attracted a lot of tramps, some of them with mental, behavioral, or substance-abuse problems, and keeping order was proving difficult. The Occupiers debated whether to grant the Tranquillity Center (a group charged with maintaining the well-being of the camp's members) executive powers to eject anyone from the camp who threatened the physical or mental well-being of any other member of the community. During the debate, one of the members of the Tranquillity Center spoke out against the motion: "Don't give us these powers," he said. "We don't want them. It should be the collective responsibility of the community." Despite his concerns, the motion passed, through a mass showing of jazz hands. "I'm a gay ethnic minority," said one protester. "We need to feel safe." "I block the motion!" shouted one skinhead. "You can't, we've been through the process," said the facilitator. "Yes, I can! I can do what I want. There's no police. So I block it." "It's already passed," snapped the weary facilitator. "Let's move on." And so, with one vote, the Occupy commune quietly passed from anarchist to...not quite so anarchist, and I had a fleeting vision of the future, once the Occupiers had taken control of England, and we have learned to fear a bang on the door in the middle of the night, and the shout: "Open up! It's the Tranquillity Center!"

At the camp's Tent City University, I found myself caught up in a two-hour workshop on "acknowledging your emotions." "I want you to pair up, and share your feelings," we were told. It reminded me rather of the Landmark Forum. The BBC documentary maker Adam Curtis has blamed the "human potential movement" of the 1970s (out of which Landmark grew) for killing off the Sixties revolution, because it turned angry Sixties protesters into the mellow self-help freaks of the 1970s.[17] Yet, at that Occupy workshop, I realized the two strands have come together: both the revolutionary anarchism of 1968 and the human potential movement of the 1970s. The Occupiers take classes in meditation, in well-being economics, in "body work" and improvisation. The personal is tied to the political.

But perhaps the Occupy movement is so Utopian that the political takes second place to more unfocused emoting. "My name's Venus, I've started a global movement of love," one Occupier shared with me, before collapsing into tears: she'd been at the camp for two and a half weeks and like many of the protesters was suffering from advanced sleep deprivation.

Revolutions have always been deeply emotional affairs. Plato, who we'll meet in the next chapter, first used the word "privatization" in *The Republic*, to describe how, in liberal capitalist democracies, our feelings have been "privatized" — we never feel collective emotions anymore, except when watching Susan Boyle sing "I Dreamed a Dream" on *Britain's Got Talent*.[18] But after the revolution, he suggested, we would all think and feel as one. And he was right, sort of: during revolutions, people get brief and intoxicating flashes of that tribal emotional experience — a whole people, thinking and feeling as one. As Wordsworth put it, reflecting on his youthful trip to revolutionary France:

> Oh! pleasant exercise of hope and joy!
> For mighty were the auxiliars which then stood
> Upon our side, we who were strong in love!
> Bliss was it in that dawn to be alive,
> But to be young was very heaven![19]

Revolutions are in part a reversion from bureaucratic and technocratic politics to a more primitive emotional feeling of communion. But then, of course, you come down from the high, and go home. Or you might actually gain power...and then you have to work out new bureaucracies, new institutions, new technologies of control when the oxytocin has run away, and the distrust and loathing come back.

LEAVE IT ALL BEHIND

Maybe we don't need to dismantle industrial capitalism — it seems to be doing a pretty good job at bringing itself down. We simply need to pop up our tents, brew some tea, and prepare ourselves for the inevitable collapse. One person who is better prepared than most is Neil Ansell, who lived in a cottage in the Welsh hills for five years, during which time he hardly saw other people. He says: "I just felt like spending some time on my own." Neil decided to go and live in the hills after spending several years living in a Simon Community in London, which is a commune run for homeless people according to strict anarchist principles. Both volunteers and the homeless exist on the same income of £7 a week, everyone eats together, and all sleep together on the floor. "It was set up by a Catholic anarchist, and attracted a strange mixture of people," Neil says. "You had hardcore anarchists next to former monks. Most people spent a few months there — I stayed there for three years, and ended up running the place, with between fifty to a hundred homeless people living there at any one time." He says, contrary to the Romantic notion, the life of a tramp is not carefree. "Most homeless people are deeply unhappy with life. They struggle with the brutal reality of it, and escape it through substance abuse. One year, over twenty people I knew died of heroin. It's not a safe life — I knew one guy who was killed for a £5 debt."

Neil then went travelling, visiting fifty countries in five years. He hitchhiked, slept rough, picked up work as an agricultural laborer. He ended up back in London, living in a squat in Highgate with twenty to thirty other squatters crammed into fifteen bedrooms. "It was bedlam. You have no control over who moves in, so you get people with drug problems, alcohol problems, antisocial problems." While there, Neil heard from a woman he'd helped in his Simon Community years. She'd recently married a lord, who had a hill cottage on his estate in Wales, which she offered to Neil to live in. "I felt I needed to stay still, to learn what it's like to be in one place. I hadn't spent a single day in isolation in the last decade, and I wanted to see if I could." Neil wasn't exactly abandoning civilization, because he'd "always lived on the edge of it." But he certainly led a simple life in his Welsh retreat. He had occasional visitors but spent most days alone. Was it lonely? He says:

> Choosing solitude is the opposite of loneliness. I was never bored, because there was always so much to do. It took a couple of years to get everything up and running, but I became pretty much self-sufficient,

growing my own vegetables, foraging for berries and mushrooms, making my own elderflower wine. When I wasn't active, I wasn't really thinking. It was almost like a meditative state. The internal chatter fades away, and I became absorbed in the environment around me. I kept a journal while there, and as the years go on, I disappeared from it and it became basically a nature diary.

Toward the end of his time in the hills, Neil fell seriously ill with a thyroid infection. He was barely capable of sustaining himself. "It made me reflect on the level of confidence I had in my powers of self-sufficiency. I realized it was conditional on things like health and not having dependants." After five years, Neil left the cottage, met a girl, got married, and had two kids. Having children brought him back into civilization, and the family moved to Brighton. He admits: "It's very difficult to bring up a family in the hills — it's very bleak in winter, very physically hard." Neil got a job working at the *Big Issue* office, and then became an undercover reporter, Cynically exposing corruption. He says: "The job is all about nerves, you have to be able to keep your bottle. I can do that. Living in the wild made me centered, it gave me an inner core of peace, the strength to take risks." His daughters are now fourteen and nine, and Neil's devoted to them. "This is the longest time I've ever spent in a town. I now live for two other people, and that changes the way you think."

The Cynic response is perhaps too extreme to be practical. Most of us want to have families, and we need the protection of the state for children, for the sick, for the elderly, for minorities. Anarchy isn't a practical option, although the Cynics do teach us not to take the comforts of our civilization for granted, and to train ourselves for a possible collapse. Our next teacher, Plato, had a different political solution to the problems of his day. He wondered if the state was necessarily beyond repair. Could it not perhaps be reformed and redeemed, if it was taken over by philosophers?

10. Plato and the Art of Justice

ALEXANDER IS A THIRTY-FOUR-YEAR-OLD PLATONIST, living in Dallas, Texas. He admits: "Dallas is not really the most philosophical city in the world." As a young man, Alexander searched far and wide to try to find something more to believe in than capitalism. He decided the spiritual approach that made most sense to him was Islam, and in particular Sufism. He heard about a school in Yemen offering Arabic classes so, in his mid-twenties, he quit his job and travelled to Tarim, in the Hadhramaut Valley in Yemen, and enrolled at the Dar al-Mustafa religious school. The school taught Arabic and Islamic philosophy in a monastic environment. The five hundred students, including many foreign students, slept in dormitories together, ate together, prayed five times a day together, and studied Islamic philosophy together. "It becomes a routine, part of your life, so that if you miss a prayer, it doesn't feel right," Alexander says. Tarim is the religious center of Yemen, but it's still quite a bit smaller and poorer than Dallas. Yet Alexander loved the place:

> The roads aren't paved, the houses are all built of mud-brick, the buildings are all close together. It's very simple, which gives it a spiritual atmosphere. It's not like an American city, like Las Vegas, where each building competes with the others to attract attention and be unique. The whole environment was spiritual — even the people in Tarim who aren't part of the religious community understand that

the people there had high ideals and were trying to build a closer relationship to God. They're trying to capture a spiritual experience, to create moments of ecstasy where they come closer to God.

Alexander lived in the community for almost two years. But he became somewhat disillusioned with Islam.

I came across other Muslim traditions and sects in Tarim, and each one claimed to be the true Islam. As I studied the sources, it seemed to me that none had a true claim. I lost faith, or interest, in Islam as a historical force, but became more interested in Islamic philosophy. It made a lot of reference to "the ancients," meaning the ancient Greeks, so when I came back to the United States, I started to read the Neo-Platonists, who inspired a lot of Islamic philosophy. I read Proclus, Plotinus, and especially Damascius. And through that, I came to read Plato himself, which I found far superior. The Neo-Platonists don't capture the brilliance of Plato's irony, his playfulness. They're fundamentalist in their interpretation of him — they take everything he says as a direct fact.

For the past five years, Alexander has made the study of Plato the cornerstone of his spiritual practice. He says: "Most Western spirituality has its foundation in Plato. The mystic traditions of Christianity, Judaism, and Islam are deeply indebted to Plato. For me, Platonism is a way of seeing things. It's a desire, a longing to see truth, not just as a fact, but as something that is essentially good, beautiful, and orderly. Plato believed that all the good, beauty, and order you see in the universe is the manifestation of eternal Good. Individuals become more real as they become transparent to that Good. So, day to day, I try to maintain that vision of participating in the Good. Everything I do, I try to do with reverence." He now works as an operating room nurse in Dallas. "I don't see that simply as a way to earn money, but as an attempt to make the world better."

He admits to feeling a bit out of place in modern America. He says: "The fundamental idea in Plato is how the part relates to the Whole, to the

Absolute. In the United States, everyone tries to be so unique, so they're scared of giving up the self for something collective. In Plato's ideal city, all the buildings, all the art, all the citizens, would be joined and harmonized through their relationship to the Whole. The American city by contrast is a mess of different styles. It lacks any common beauty." Think, for example, of the Strip in Las Vegas, where a giant Roman palace sits next to a replica of the Eiffel Tower, next to a medieval castle, next to an Egyptian pyramid. There's no sense of order, no sense of the whole. Everything is privatized — even the streets are named after the casinos. There's no sense of the civic good, of the good of society as a whole. In fact, the Strip isn't even part of Las Vegas, it's a tiny tax island called Paradise. And everything is permitted in Paradise. "Plato wrote that, in a democracy, all your desires and pleasures are given an equal voice," says Alexander. "It's an anarchy of desire. There's no sense of a hierarchy of goods. Plato suggests we should build a society that places our highest aspirations at its center, rather than our lowest appetites." Our highest aspiration, according to Plato, is — or should be — a longing for God. A community built around that aspiration would be a theocracy, says Alexander, "not in the sense of simply following the word of *The Republic*, but in the sense that each soul would do their best to come closer to the Divine and to live in the constant presence of the Divine."

Does Alexander really think Platonic philosophy could ever be used as the foundation for a community, or even a whole state? "It would be very hard. Plato wanted to create philosophical communities, but he knew how difficult it was to pull off. You'd have to get people away from the idea that wealth and power is desirable. You could try and form an institution like the Christian Church, but it would have to pander to the lowest common denominator, which is not very philosophical. You see, again and again, how holy men set up institutions, and then they get bogged down." Platonism, after all, is quite an elitist philosophy. "You can't just jump into Plato. The idea of the elite is that the truth is only open to those who take the time to prepare their minds to see the Whole, and to let go of their previous concepts. Most people are not intellectually and emotionally available to put all their thoughts on the table." Instead of striving to establish a Platonic commune in the Texas desert, Alexander has kept his ambitions small, setting up a meet-up group called The Platonists of North Texas.[1] He says: "A few people show up. The focus is on the spiritual aspects of Platonism, and the demand that we transcend our thoughts and try to comprehend the Whole. That's difficult for some people who are trained in academic philosophy and want to master intellectual concepts. And others worry that Plato will demand they give up their luxuries, which is true to some extent, but it's not exactly a monastic austerity."

PLATO, THE LAST SHAMAN

In primitive human societies, the religious and the political exist side by side. In tribal societies, the chief is in charge of terrestrial affairs, while the shaman or witch doctor is in charge of spiritual affairs. The shaman was (and in a handful of cultures, still is) a strange, otherworldly figure. As a teenager, he or she would have fallen into a sort of nervous sickness, which drove them from their society, and which only abated when they were initiated into their shamanic profession. This initiation involved dying to the world, and being reborn in the world of the spirits. The shaman then returns to their worldly community, in it but not quite of it, and acts as an ambassador between the tribe and the spirit world, to which they travel by working themselves into an ecstatic trance and then flying up a ladder into the sky (that's how it's described in Siberian shamanism, anyway, and the ladder image is found in many other cultures, like Jacob's ladder in Genesis). The shaman has clearly defined social and political functions — they predict the future, they cure sicknesses, they secure the spirits' blessings for war, hunting, and agriculture, they protect the tribe from evil spirits and the wrath of the gods, and they act as spirit-guide to the afterlife when members of the tribe pass away. They are both the priest and the doctor for their tribe.[2]

This millennia-old relationship between the religious and the political was ruptured by the birth of philosophy, a mere 2,500 years ago. As we've seen, Greek rational philosophers in the sixth and fifth centuries BC started to challenge the shamanic account of the natural world, and to provide more convincing rational accounts of phenomena like, say, lunar eclipses, thunder, or epilepsy. Philosophers challenged the idea that there was a spirit realm which gave humans their laws and customs. If that was the case, why did every culture have its own idea of the good? Perhaps, some daring philosophers suggested, laws weren't handed down by the gods. Perhaps humans invented them. Perhaps there's no absolute right or wrong, merely what seems right or wrong to humans at particular times. Perhaps "man is the measure of all things," as the Greek philosopher Protagoras put it at the end of the fifth century BC.[3]

This was a direct challenge to the authority of priests. It meant there was no point in trying to discover the will of the gods, and even less point in making sacrifices, kneeling to the priests, or any of that mumbo jumbo. Instead, in a secular democracy, what mattered was the will of the people. They were the true arbiters of right and wrong. So if you really wanted to study something useful, you should study public relations, learn to understand the moods and whims of the public, and how to manipulate them with rhetoric and oratory. By the end of the fifth century BC, Athens was full of philosophers or sophists (which can be translated as "pedlars of wisdom") who claimed to be able to teach young people the art of living, by which they really meant the arts of rhetoric and public relations. In a democracy, they insisted, an initiate in the dark arts of public relations could become truly powerful. They could pretty much do whatever they wanted. This was far more relevant than trying to become closer to God. Who believed in God anyway? And so, the witch doctor was gradually replaced by the spin doctor.[4]

A young disciple of Socrates, called Plato, watched this secular, liberal revolution with horror. As a young man, Plato had encountered the mystical philosophy of Pythagoras, and it had made a deep impression on him. Like Pythagoras, he believed that the study of geometry, logic, and music revealed the eternal truths behind the apparent flux of material reality, which human reason could discover if it was sufficiently enlightened and disciplined. From his other great teacher, Socrates, he took the technique of dialectic, and the method of restlessly searching, through dialogue, for better and more comprehensive definitions of moral terms like freedom, beauty, and justice. Plato suggested that, just as there exists a pure realm of mathematical truths, in which 2 + 2 always equals 4, so there must exist a pure realm of moral values — Truth, Beauty, Justice — which we can approach through dialectic. Sophists had tried to deny the existence of these moral absolutes, suggesting that "truth," "beauty," and "justice" were simply words, conventions, resting on nothing more substantial than public opinion. So the search for the good degenerated into the effort to win the public's favor in an *X-Factor*–style popularity contest. But surely, Plato insisted, good music is not simply "whatever the public votes for"? Surely some music is genuinely better than others, some art is genuinely better than others, some lives are genuinely better than others? If so, then the work of the philosopher is not to discover public opinion, as the Sophist and the spin doctor try to do. It is to try to discover reality.

THE ASCENT OF THE SOUL

This is not some dry academic pursuit. Discovering reality was, for Plato, a journey on which the whole of the personality must go. Plato put forward a sophisticated account of human psychology, which anticipated many modern theories of the psyche. He suggested, first of all, that we don't have one self, but several. Our psyches are made up of different competing systems, each with their own agenda. He suggested a tripartite structure — there is a rational, reflective system; a spirited or emotive system; and a basic system of physical appetites. One can compare this to the triune brain structure put forward in the 1960s by the neuroscientist Paul D. MacLean, who suggests humans have a reptilian instinctive system, a mammalian emotive system, and a neo-mammalian system of higher reasoning.[5] Plato was also the first Western thinker to suggest we have an unconscious, which is free to express its unlawful desires (such as the desire to sleep with a parent) when we're asleep.[6] Plato believed that different political systems affect our psyches in different ways. Members of a liberal capitalist society typically possess what Plato called the "democratic personality," in which there is no order or hierarchy to the different parts of the psyche. One moment, the emotive system is in charge, the next our rational system is in charge, the next we're in the grip of our physical appetites. In such a society, we're not one person but many — and our consumer society encourages us to gratify all the multiple sides of us. Our personalities are like a society in civil war, as Plato put it, or a ship without a captain, where every crew member is shouting out different directions.[7] This view of the psyche as a riot of competing impulses and systems is now very popular in neuroscience — indeed, David Eagleman wrote an entire book, called *Incognito*, putting forth the idea that our selves are like a parliament where different political parties compete for control (I'm not sure Eagleman is aware Plato said this first — if he is, he doesn't mention it).

But what Plato insisted, and what neuroscientists and cognitive psychologists are beginning to accept, is that we can train our rational or "neo-mammalian" system to override the other systems, to try to make more rational, intelligent, and long-term decisions. At its simplest, this might be resisting the impulse to smoke or eat another portion of pudding. Plato, like the Stoics, suggested that each time we practice using our conscious reason to override our impulses, we strengthen its rule. If we practice this our whole lives, we can gradually bring the competing systems of our psyche into harmony, like notes in a chord (he took this idea from Pythagoras). Then, instead of being pulled this way and that by each competing impulse like a puppet, we become "master of our selves."[8] We become a unified self, a whole person, rather than a babel of different selves. Becoming a whole person involves a sort of shamanic training. It involves physical as much as mental training, because the pull of our physical impulses must be tempered and modulated. The body must be broken like an unruly horse, as Plato often puts it. Physical desires cloud our reasoning and prevent it from ascending to truth. Only when we have disciplined the body and purged our reason of its influence can our minds rise unhindered to the Divine. Just as the shaman dies to the world and then flies up into the spirit realm, so the philosopher's reason, freed from the prison of the body, flies up to the pure realm of truth.

Plato, who had initially wanted to be a playwright, gave Western culture some very beautiful descriptions of this ascent of the soul. The philosopher, he suggested, grows wings, and flies up through the world of appearances to an ecstatic union with the Absolute. Philosophy is really a form of love-madness (philosophy literally means "love of the truth"), in which the soul remembers its spiritual home, and longs to see it again. Lovesick, the soul wanders the earth desperate to see the face of its lover, Sophia (or Truth). We fall for this girl or that boy, because they're beautiful and they remind us somewhat of the Divine. But then we realize they are just a particular manifestation of something higher and more universal. So the philosopher gradually ascends from the particular to the Whole, until at last they gaze upon the face of Absolute Beauty, and are consumed in ecstasy.[9] Or, in another famous myth, the philosopher "wakes up" and realizes that the phenomenal world is really a cave of illusions, and what they took to be reality is nothing more than a shadow puppet show projected onto the wall of the cave. The philosopher manages to free him- or herself from this illusion, to emerge from the cave blinking into the light. And then, like Neo in *The Matrix*, the philosopher decides to go back into the cave, to try to wake up their fellow humans and make them realize they are watching a show.[10] But what if the humans don't want to be woken up? What if they get annoyed with the philosopher for blocking their view? What if they angrily tell the philosopher to sit down or, even worse, start laughing at them?

Society's Rejection of the Philosopher

This was the problem that Plato faced. The shaman had a clearly defined social and political role. He or she was a respected figure, whose authority was fixed in collective myths and rituals practiced for millennia. But the philosopher, as a cultural figure, had only been around for a century or so (Pythagoras was the first to use the term in the sixth century BC), and was still an object of deep suspicion. Plato tried to create new myths to cement the new role of the philosopher-shaman. But Athenian democratic society showed an irritating reluctance to accept the authority of the philosopher and to bow before his superior wisdom. In fact, the philosopher was often a figure of ridicule rather than veneration. Socrates, for example, was mocked in Aristophanes's comedy *The Clouds* for, literally, having his head in the clouds. Rather like today, philosophers were teased for being pale, unworldly, stammering creatures, who babbled nonsense and were completely unfit for political affairs.[11] Worse still, some actually saw philosophers as a corrupting influence. In the popular mind, no distinction was made between genuine philosopher-shamans like Plato and Socrates, and philosopher-Sophists who deconstructed conventional morality without necessarily putting anything in its place. This confusion led to Socrates — "the best and wisest man I ever knew" as Plato described him[12] — being sentenced to death for impiety at the end of the fifth century BC.

The death of Socrates was a traumatic event for Plato, and indeed for Western culture as a whole. Where before the shaman and the chief had existed side by side in a symbiotic relationship, now the philosopher-shaman stood apart from his society, despising it and wanting nothing to do with it. Socrates had wandered the streets of Athens, engaging his fellow citizens in philosophical dialogues and urging them to take care of their souls. But after his death, Plato seemed to have lost faith in democracy and in his fellow citizens. Philosophy, he wrote, "is impossible among the common people."[13] Philosophers, recognizing the corruption of the democratic state, should "live quietly and keep to themselves...they see the rest of the world full of wrongdoing, and are content to keep themselves unspotted from wickedness and wrong in this life, and finally leave it with cheerful composure and good hope." Philosophy becomes an individual journey to spiritual fulfillment, and a private declaration of independence from the corrupt values of modern society. It becomes personal mysticism, or self-help.

DREAMING OF UTOPIA

And yet Plato couldn't help but wonder: What if philosophers were in charge? What if they *forced* the public to listen to them and to follow their orders? This was the conceit of *The Republic*, Plato's most famous dialogue, and probably the most famous work in Western philosophy. It declared that "there will be no end to the troubles of states, or indeed...of humanity itself, till philosophers become kings in this world, or till those we now call kings and rulers really and truly become philosophers." Plato then imagines a perfect society where philosophers rule. *The Republic* draws an analogy between the individual and the state. It suggests there are three main classes in any society, which correlate to the three centers of the psyche — the intellectuals, representing the reasoning system; the soldiers, representing the spirited or emotive system; and the merchants, representing the system of physical appetites. As in the psyche, each of these classes has their ruling motivation: the intellectuals want truth, the soldiers want glory, and the businessmen want money. Just as justice for the individual involves reason controlling and ordering the other systems of the psyche, so justice for the state involves the intellectuals, or philosopher-kings, controlling and ordering the other classes in society. Each class should respect their own function, or "mind their own business" as Plato puts it, which means only the philosopher-kings will practice philosophy. Everyone else will obey orders and ask no questions.

The philosopher-guardians of Plato's imaginary republic are, from birth, subjected to an extremely austere and rigorous education. Plato's overriding aim is the spiritual unity of society. He wants to break down his guardians' sense of the individual ego, their sense of "me" and "mine," so that they identify completely with the Whole. The future guardians are taken away from their parents at around five, and are never told who their biological parents are, so that they have no private attachment to particular adults. They're brought up in state-run boarding schools, in which every aspect of their lives is controlled by the director of education, which Plato says is the most important position in the republic. The director controls what the students eat, how they exercise, what they read, what music they listen to. Every aspect of their childhood must be controlled by the state, because everything they encounter leaves an impression on their wax-like psyches. Particularly close attention must be paid to the stories they read and the music they listen to — Plato was worried by the toxic influence of modern music and theater on Athenian youth, and by the restless innovation of Athenian culture. He wrote: "the music and literature of a country cannot be altered without major political and social changes." Therefore, the state must carefully control and regulate the arts, in order to guide the people's passions toward Truth and Beauty. There was, in fact, no need for innovation in the arts or any other aspect of the republic, as long as the philosopher-kings remained in close communion with the Divine Forms of reality. As they grew up, the young guardians should be introduced to philosophy, and initiated into the deep mysteries of the Absolute. And when it became time for them to breed, the state should subtly marry off the best male guardians to the best female guardians, so that the genetic purity of the class was enhanced. Any specimens that appeared mentally or physically disabled should be killed off.

But why should the philosopher-guardians, once initiated into the mysteries of the Absolute, care about life back on earth? After all, the true philosopher, in Plato's view, cares nothing about earthly matters, nothing about the self, or the family, or the state, or even life itself. They care only about the Absolute, the Divine, the Cosmic Whole. So how can they be persuaded to float back down to earth to worry themselves about things like transport policy or the city's plumbing system? Plato thought it might be necessary to resort to a white lie. He thought that all members of the republic should be told as children that they had sprung from the very soil of the republic, so they were all brothers and sisters, and the republic was, in a sense, their mother. This "noble lie," he hoped, would be enough to persuade his philosophers to reluctantly engage with political administration, though really they just want to contemplate the Absolute all day long.

It's hard to know quite how seriously to take *The Republic*. Throughout this chapter I have written "Plato says," but actually, Plato doesn't say anything himself in any of his dialogues. Rather, he creates a sort of puppet theater, in which various characters voice various opinions. Socrates, his chief puppet, does not offer one coherent philosophy throughout Plato's books, but changes position in different dialogues. And it's hard to tell when Plato is in earnest and when in jest. Sometimes he clearly seems to be joking, like when Socrates claims to have proven that the philosopher is precisely 729 times happier than the tyrant. There's quite a lot of self-conscious artifice, even game-playing, in Plato's philosophy. Typically, Socrates will unfurl some incredible vision of the afterlife, complete with flying philosophers and palaces of pure light. And then he will say something like "but this is just a pretty story" or "maybe some such thing is true."[14] Perhaps this is to prevent us from being too fundamentalist in our relation to his work. We have to ascend to the truth ourselves rather than take Plato's word for it. Partly, also, Plato is protecting himself politically, so that if anyone accused him of plotting a revolution he could say "but the whole thing was just a silly story." But this playfulness also shows what a modern author Plato is: he is self-consciously creating religious myths for his society, while also pointing out the myths' fictionality.

Some modern academics *have* taken Plato's *Republic* seriously, and criticized what they see as a template for totalitarianism.[15] As in twentieth-century totalitarian states, private life is eliminated in the republic. The state's reeducation of its citizens is total, reaching into every aspect of their life. As in modern totalitarianism, we meet the unfortunate metaphor of the state as doctor, "purging" the body politic of moral sicknesses and, if necessary, cutting out any cancerous elements. Perhaps the comparison between the individual and the state is just an analogy, just a metaphor. But metaphors are dangerous things. They can escape out into the world and cause damage. And the dangerous thing about that particular metaphor is that in one important way, a just society is *not* like a just individual. An individual or religious commune may choose to put themselves through harsh ascetic training in order to attain spiritual wisdom. That's their choice. But a large multicultural society is unlikely to make that choice as one, because people have different views about the good life, which means a handful of intellectuals will subject the population to the most austere control and discipline against their will, "for their own good." From that perspective, *The Republic* presents a frightening first glimpse of that very modern figure, the intellectual revolutionary, who is deaf to all appeals for pity as he shapes his perfect society.

THE SCHOOL OF ECONOMIC SCIENCE

We may decide Plato's Utopian scheme is impractical or dangerous for an entire state. But perhaps there could be Platonic communes on a smaller scale, in which consenting adults join together to try to work toward the

Absolute? That was the vision behind the School for Economic Science (SES), founded in the UK in 1937 by a barrister called Leon MacLaren, and still going strong today. The school has a plush headquarters off Bond Street in London, a large country estate in Oxfordshire called Waterperry House, eighteen other regional centers around the UK, and affiliated schools in fifteen countries around the world. SES estimates it has around twenty thousand members globally, including the actor Hugh Jackman. MacLaren set up the school after having an epiphanic moment by a lake in Wimbledon Park, when he realized "that there was such a thing as truth, and there was such a thing as justice, and that they could be found, and being found, could be taught." He wanted to set up a school "in the manner of the ancients," particularly with Socrates in mind (although Socrates didn't actually set up a school). Evening classes would bring enquiring minds together to study the natural laws underlying man, society, and the cosmos — the laws MacLaren believed were revealed in Plato, the Bible, and Shakespeare. In the 1950s, MacLaren met and was deeply inspired by an Indian guru, Sri Shantanand Saraswati, and henceforth the school's curriculum combined Platonic and Neoplatonic mysticism with Eastern Vedic philosophy. Meditation classes were taught alongside Socratic group dialogues. But the dialogues were not exactly open-ended, as Plato's early Socratic dialogues are. It was never questioned that the truth was out there, or that an eternal spirit realm *did* exist. It was an article of faith that Shantanand Saraswati was in close contact with the Divine Realm — indeed, he was considered the closest thing to God on earth, and therefore worthy of absolute reverence, trust, and obedience. And MacLaren was considered the next rung down on God's ladder, likewise worthy of complete reverence and obedience. In total submission, the students would discover total freedom. In the abnegation of their egos, they would discover their true selves. The relationship with a living Indian guru was key for the development of the school, because really the members, like Plato himself, were trying to invent a religion. To some extent, they could rely on the authority of ancient texts, and SES members are still working on translations of Plato and the Renaissance Neoplatonist Marsilio Ficino. But the words of long-dead philosophers were not nearly as inspiring as the words of a living guru, who could actually give them directions as they groped their way in the dark.

The school was in existence for around fifty years before it attracted much attention. It was only in the 1980s that the British press started to wonder what went on at this strange organization. Some academic philosophers complained, for example, that the school's prominent ads for philosophy classes, still seen in newspapers and on the Tube, were really false advertising, considering the course did not offer an introduction to philosophy in general, only to one particular religious philosophy. In 1984, two *Evening Standard* journalists wrote an exposé called "Secret Cult," criticizing what the authors saw as the school's cultlike insider mentality, whereby school members only really fraternized with each other, and ostracized any members who left. The members' unquestioning obedience to the leader was also seen by the reporters as cultic. So too was the school's practice of "philosophical service," whereby members had to give the school many hours of hard, unpaid menial labor each week. Also seen as dangerous was the general attitude of "school first, everything else second" — even when "everything else" included your children. The school's attitude to women, who were seen as irrational, overemotional, and in need of the rational guidance of men, struck outsiders as backward. And the school was even accused of trying to infiltrate British politics — one of SES's leading members, Roger Pincham, was also chairman of the Liberal Party from 1979 to 1982.

Ian Mason, the school's principal, tells me the school has been misunderstood: "The idea is not to break down the ego for the sake of it, but rather to put you in touch with yourself, to help you distinguish what's real or not, and to nourish and strengthen the mind. But perhaps there was too unquestioning an attitude to the leader in earlier years. People took things that MacLaren said and applied them without intelligence." To be fair to the school, if Plato set up his Academy today, or Epicurus set up his Garden, they would probably be accused of being cults. Philosophy schools, it seems to me, can be structured in two ways. They can offer a variety of different philosophies to be considered and reflected upon, without any real commitment being demanded from the pupils. This liberal model is basically what places like the School of Life and the Idler Academy offer. Or you could have a philosophy school closer to the ancients' conception, in which pupils are taught one particular philosophy, one ethical way of life, which they commit to in an effort to completely transform their personalities. The closest thing we have to that today is the School of Economic Science, so it's interesting to see how it fared, and what mistakes it made.

UNWILLING PLATONIC GUARDIANS

The school set up two children's schools in 1975, for the children of SES members. MacLaren was inspired by the example of *The Republic* and Plato's last work, the *Laws*. Both of these books are educational treatises as much as works of political philosophy. Plato seemed to think that, if philosophers can't rule society, the next best thing they can do is set up schools to train the next generation of leaders. The exalted figure of the philosopher-shaman evolves into the more mundane figure of the schoolteacher. MacLaren set up two children's schools in central London: St. James School for Girls and St. Vedast School for Boys, both of them run by SES parents and staff. From the age of five to eighteen, the pupils were taught the school's philosophy. They were given classes in meditation, Greek philosophy, Eastern philosophy, Sanskrit, Vedic dancing, Vedic maths, Shakespeare, Renaissance art, and other subjects.

From the beginning, there was huge expectation put on the children's shoulders. They were expected to be the future spiritual elite, a generation of perfectly trained philosopher-guardians who would save Western civilization from itself. But some of the children didn't want to be philosopher-guardians. They resented being made to wear ridiculous uniforms, and being denied the normal lives they saw other children enjoying in London. They felt cut off from their society. Some of the teachers were good (the actress Emily Watson's mother was a respected teacher at the girls' school) but other teachers, who had themselves submitted with absolute obedience to the school's hierarchy, reacted very badly to any hints of teenage insubordination. They were not professional teachers, many were new to the subjects they taught and perhaps felt insecure. Perhaps, like Plato's philosophers, they had their eyes so fixed upon the Divine that they had no pity for the imperfect beings here on earth. Whatever the reason, some teachers subjected the pupils to a regime of terror. Pupils were ridiculed, caned, punched in the face and stomach, thrown across classrooms, hit with cricket balls and gym ropes. And if the pupils complained to their parents, they often received no sympathy. The parents were members of the same deeply hierarchical organization. These abuses came to light in a 2006 independent report,[16] only after former pupils shared their horror stories on the internet. The teachers involved were given a "formal warning," and no longer work at St. James, although they're still part of the School of Economic Science.[17]

St. James School is apparently run a lot better now by professional teachers, attracting the children of well-to-do parents in Brook Green. Today, only around 10 percent of the children have parents involved with SES, so there's inevitably been some dilution of the schools' spiritual philosophy, and a gradual shift closer to the mainstream of society. But there are still many lives that were damaged by that decade of incompetence and abuse. And some past practices of the school have still not received enough attention, such as the occasional practice of marrying off female graduates of St. James when they were over eighteen to older SES men, and even to teachers at the schools. Principal Ian Mason, for example, who taught an extracurricular course in law at St. James School, has married not one but two former St. James pupils (the first marriage was suggested by MacLaren, and didn't work out, the second has fared better; Mason points out he didn't teach either of them, and they were both adults in their twenties when they married him). The present leader of the SES, Donald Lambie, also married a former pupil of the school. There were even two balls arranged for eighteen-year-old female pupils and older male SES members, which led to some marriages. Mason says: "The balls were a response to requests from young women for opportunities to meet some eligible young men in the SES and were pretty innocent occasions. I should emphasize that there was no coercion involved." One can understand that the school wanted to encourage in-group marriage to preserve its countercultural values: many religious groups practice that. Nevertheless, as Mason admits, "It's a bit weird."

I personally don't think SES is a "secret cult." It has lost its charismatic and authoritarian leader. Its membership is declining. Ian Mason, who was helpful and open to me in my research, accepts that his two teenage daughters "show no interest in meditation, and complain about only meeting other SES families." SES seems to me to be an interesting experiment, an interesting attempt to turn Eastern and Western ancient philosophy into a genuine community and way of life. But aspects of the school's history also show how such communities can become dogmatic in their devotion to a charismatic leader, and how careful one must be in imposing one's philosophy onto one's children.

In the next lesson, we'll meet Plutarch, a schoolteacher who consciously set out to create great leaders from his pupils, so that they could go out and transform their societies as philosopher-heroes. Let's see if his ideas are more practical for our own time.

11. Plutarch and the Art of Heroism

LOUIS FERRANTE GREW UP IN QUEENS, in a neighborhood that had street gangs covering "every area and section." He remembers: "It was normal to be in a street gang, whether it be an Irish gang, an Italian gang, black, Spanish, or Asian." He was a small, stocky kid, who didn't like studying, but he was good at fighting: "Everyone at that age is lost and confused, looking for a group to fit into. I identified with the street gangs, because it was an outlet for testosterone. We all thought we were pretty tough guys." At thirteen, he joined a gang called the Hill Boys, which hung out on Queensboro Hill. He says: "We graduated from fists to baseball bats to knives to guns." He quickly began his career in organized crime. "Initially we were just hanging out, trying to make a dime with things like breaking open mailboxes to get credit cards. But a few of us graduated into harder crime, like hijacking and armed robbery." He started to move in mobster circles, and to get their attention: "My first big heist was a hijacking of a truck with about 100,000 dollars of tools and toolboxes inside of it. That got the wise guys' attention."

Louis eventually started to work for John Gotti, the head of the Gambino family in New York. He says: "I shylocked money for John, but my main profession was hijacking. I had a crew working under me. We did a lot of business. So, for example, a guy might owe the mob 150,000 dollars, and he'd say, 'Don't break my legs, I work for a major trucking company, they have a safe with 300,000 dollars in it, take it all.' Then the mobster would call me, and I'd take care of it." Louis enjoyed the life: "We used to walk into restaurants and be given the best tables. It gave me a sense of ecstasy — to achieve status at such a young age. I felt on top of the world." It was a culture of flashiness defined by Gotti: "Some of the other dons were more secretive, but he would always flash his money. He liked his nice cars, nice clothes. When I was eighteen, I pulled up in front of him and his crew in a brand-new black Mercedes. They just said, 'Nice car.' "

In 1993, at the age of twenty-two, Louis was arrested and charged with a string of armed robberies and credit card fraud. He was sentenced to twelve and a half years in jail, and was sent to a maximum-security prison at Lewisburg, Pennsylvania. "The place was in the middle of a civil war between the Aryan Nation and the Black Muslims. My first day there, there was a double homicide. Welcome to the prison system." Yet even in Lewisburg, mobsters received special treatment: extra cigarettes, wine, comfier mattresses, their own stoves to cook on. But the glamour of the life was beginning to fade for Louis. "I was gradually thinking more and more about the things I'd done. What gave me the right to put a gun to a man's head?" He was also beginning to feel distaste for the other mobsters in the jail. "We were raised by the mob code, told you only kill someone if they do something horrible against the family, because that was like treason. So if someone disappeared, you never asked questions. Now, in prison, I came across a lot of mobsters charged with murder. And nine out of ten times, it was about money. Maybe as little as seven thousand bucks. And I thought, my God, these people are animals, killing over money. I thought no one should die even for a billion dollars. I didn't even want to be near them." Before, when Louis was in the presence of John Gotti, it was like being in the presence of the pope. Now, in jail with him, he saw him as just a man. "It was like seeing Caesar without his cloak. And Gotti was always complaining. I thought, 'Is this guy kidding me? He has the nerve to complain?' I realized, 'I'm guilty, I'm wrong for what I did.' And that's something most mobsters never understood. If they ever said they were sorry, it was just to get a lighter sentence. It was their parents' fault, or the judge's, or the FBI's. The greatest thing I ever did was to realize the Feds were just doing their jobs."

He was once thrown into "the hole" — a solitary-confinement cell where his food was passed through a slot in the door. "The guard there called me an animal. And I thought, 'I really am like an animal. I can't walk the streets, I'm getting my food pushed through a slot in the door.'" When he got out of solitary, he started to read. "Before, I'd never read a book in my life. I cheated my way through school, scammed it." But now he started to read biographies: "I read Martin Gilbert's biography of Churchill, and I loved it. I fell in love with reading biographies, reading about people who had achieved amazing things in their life, against the odds, people who had surmounted all obstacles. And they're human beings. Churchill was just a man, like me. You have to realize, all circumstances might be against you, but the same God that created you, created Churchill, Newton, Einstein." He was inspired by Nelson Mandela's *Long Walk to Freedom*: "I was serving eight and a half years [his sentence had been shortened], and Mandela was inside twenty-something years, just to liberate his country. He could serve triple what I was serving, because he had a goal. His story helped teach me the uselessness of violence as a means to achieve your goal. It was a real lesson for me, as someone who always tended to use their fists to achieve their ends." He particularly loved Plutarch's *Parallel Lives*: "I loved his stories about figures like Cicero, who stood up for what he believed, and gave his life for it." He enjoyed the book so much he stole it from the library and put it in his locker. "I was lying on my bunk, thinking about it, and I thought, 'How could I do what I just did?' I felt like a lowlife. It hit me like a ton of bricks. The next day, I returned it, and that was the last time I committed a crime." Louis is now out of prison, a published author, and a campaigner for literacy. He says: "Reading really turned my life around. It gave me a moral compass, a desire to live a good life."

You Are Who You Imitate

Louis may not have realized it, but he was using a technique known as the *exemplum*, or moral example, that was an important part of the therapeutic toolkit of ancient philosophy. The theory behind the technique is both simple and very profound: it's based on the observation that we're social animals, and a lot of our moral behavior comes from observing and emulating others. The social psychologist Albert Bandura has called this "modeling." He writes: "Most human behavior is learned observationally through modeling: from observing others one forms an idea of how new behaviors are performed, and on later occasions this coded information serves as a guide for action." Bandura illustrated this with his famous "Bobo doll" experiments in the early 1960s: a child was left to play in a room full of toys, and then watched as an adult, playing in another corner of the room with a Bobo doll, started to attack the doll, punching it, hitting it with a hammer, and so on. The adult then left, leaving the child alone to play with the toys in the room. Those children who saw the adult hitting the Bobo doll aggressively were much more likely also to attack the doll. And those who saw an adult of the same sex as them being aggressive toward the doll were particularly likely to ape this behavior themselves.

The experiment has since been replicated and copied many times; for example, by showing adults violent videos and seeing how it affects their subsequent behavior.[1] It shows that we're intensely social creatures, whose moral decisions are deeply informed by the behavior of those around us. That's why many emotional and behavioral problems, from obesity to loneliness, have been shown in recent studies to be socially contagious. We're more likely to be lonely when we have lonely friends, more likely to smoke when our friends smoke, more likely to overeat when our friends overeat, and so on. We are who we know. But even more than that, we are who we imitate. All of us use other people as patterns to copy, or as standards to measure ourselves against. Louis, for example, naturally imitated the dominant male figures in his environment, who happened to be gangsters — and it cost him dearly. But this process does not have to be unconscious and automatic. We can learn to be more conscious of the role models we choose and the patterns we emulate. The ancients, aware of how much of our behavior comes from modeling and emulation, used the *exemplum* to try to steer people in good directions. They wrote lives of philosophical sages or military heroes, so we would not merely hear their words, but see their lives, all the better to imitate them. Appropriately enough, the most famous practitioner of this technique was Plutarch, the Greek philosopher, priest, and historian of the first century AD, whose *Parallel Lives* Louis stole from the prison library, before having a change of heart and putting it back.

EUROPE'S SCHOOLMASTER

Plutarch was born in roughly 46 AD, into a wealthy family in Chaeronea, a small town in the Greek region of Boeotia. At twenty, he studied philosophy for three years at the Academy in Athens, before travelling through Sparta, Corinth, Egypt, and Rome, where he gave public talks on Platonic philosophy. He returned to Chaeronea, and was eventually appointed priest of the Delphic Oracle. He set up his own version of the Academy, where students included his nephew, Sextus, who became Marcus Aurelius's tutor in philosophy. One scholar has commented that Plutarch was "for centuries, Europe's schoolmaster," which is well put, because his genius was as an educator. He thought deeply about how to instill and cultivate character in young people, and for many centuries his method was at the heart of Western education.

Plutarch argued against the Stoic doctrine that we should try to entirely eradicate any passion within us. Instead, he followed Plato in arguing that eradicating our passions "is neither possible nor expedient." Instead, we should strive "to keep them within due bounds, reduce them into good order, and so direct them to a good end; and thus to generate moral virtue, which consists...in the well-ordering of our passions."[2] In education, it is our job to guide the passions of young people "to a good end" by instilling in them good habits. "Character," he wrote, "is habit long-continued."[3] We're all of us a combination of reason, passions, and habits — but, thankfully, most of us are free to change our habits using our reason. This is particularly true for young people, "for youth is impressionable and plastic, and while such minds are still tender, lessons are infused deep into them."[4]

The most important part of education consists in the guidance and shaping of children's passion for emulation, which means the ambition to equal or excel another. As Albert Bandura's Bobo doll experiments showed, children watch, imitate, and constantly absorb lessons from their environment. They set themselves models, or standards, and then measure themselves up against that standard and compete with it. This is a natural animal passion, which the Stoics would seek to remove, but which Plutarch says we must rather guide to good ends. The chief object of children's emulation is their parents — particularly, for sons, their fathers, and for that reason fathers should, Plutarch said, "make themselves a manifest example to their children, above all by not misbehaving and doing as they ought to do. Thereby children, by looking at their fathers' lives as in a mirror, may be deterred from disgraceful words and deeds." Unfortunately, it sometimes happens that the father sets a terrible example to his son, creating perhaps a pattern of adultery, drinking, violence, lawbreaking, or simply not being there for his family. Today, a third of American children live apart from their biological fathers, and one quarter grow up in single-mother homes. This places a huge economic and emotional burden on single mothers and their children. For the children, it means they are statistically more likely to have emotional and behavioral problems, to run away from home, and to end up in prison. They are denied the emotional and financial support of a father — and they're also denied a pattern to imitate.[5]

Parallel Lives

While we can't choose our parents or the people we grow up among, we can choose our own role models. We can bring to mind great figures either from our life or from literature, and then try to live up to the standard they set. For that purpose, Plutarch completed the great work of his life, *Lives of Grecian and Roman Noblemen* (commonly known as *Parallel Lives*), in which he sketched the lives of forty-six of the great military and political heroes of Greece and Rome, always pairing a Greek hero off against a Roman hero, to measure them against each other, and to inspire the reader likewise to measure themselves against the heroes of old. The book presents vivid portraits of Alexander the Great, Cicero, Brutus, Pericles, Pompey, and others, and contains some of the great setpieces of historical writing:

the assassination of Julius Caesar, the romance of Antony and Cleopatra, the suicide of Cato. His *Lives* inspired Shakespeare's Roman plays, and are written with an artist's sense for the grand scene, and a journalist's eye for the revealing detail. But his chief aim was ethical. He wanted to create examples of both virtue and vice for young people to emulate. He wrote: "Our intellectual vision must be applied to such objects as, by their very charm, invite it onward to its own proper good. Such objects are to be found in virtuous deeds; these implant in those who search them out a great and zealous eagerness which leads to imitation."[6]

Plutarch saw the power of emulation in his biographical subjects. Alexander the Great, for example, was obsessed with emulating and competing with Achilles. He put Achilles's motto above his tent — "Ever to be the best and far above all others" — and paid homage to Achilles's tomb at Troy. Julius Caesar, in turn, was obsessed with emulating the life of Alexander. As a young man, Caesar read a life of Alexander, then burst into tears. When his friends asked what was wrong, he replied: "Do you think I have not just cause to weep, when I consider that Alexander at my age had conquered so many nations, and I have all this time done nothing that is memorable." Machiavelli, who was profoundly influenced by Plutarch, thought that this sort of conscious emulation of historical figures was a key part of the education of a ruler. He wrote:

> To exercise the intellect the prince should read histories, and study
> there the actions of illustrious men, to see how they have borne them-
> selves in war, to examine the causes of their victories and defeat, so
> as to avoid the latter and imitate the former; and above all do as an
> illustrious man did, who took as an exemplar one who had been
> praised and famous before him, and whose achievements and deeds
> he always kept in his mind, as it is said Alexander the Great imitated
> Achilles, Caesar Alexander, Scipio Cyrus.[7]

Plutarch, aware of the power of this youthful desire to emulate and exceed the feats of the past, tries to steer it in good directions. So, in his portraits, he directs our approving gaze to those heroes who exhibit the classic

Socratic virtue of self-control. He admires Alexander the Great for his self-control in sexual matters. Alexander, we are told, never laid a hand on the captured women in the family of Darius, King of Persia, even though Darius's wife was "far the most comely of all royal women." This may have been because Alexander was gay, but Plutarch insists Alexander restrained himself because he "considered self-mastery a more kingly thing than the conquest of his enemies." The Roman general, Mark Antony, by contrast, brings disgrace on himself and on Rome through his inability to control his passion for the Egyptian queen, Cleopatra. When Cleopatra flees the Battle of Actium, Antony can't help but follow her, like a slave: "Antony made it clear to all the world that he was swayed neither by the sentiments of a commander nor of a brave man, nor even by his own, but...was dragged along by the woman as if he had become one body with her and must go where she did."

Plutarch also admires those subjects who are capable of controlling their temper. If you're in politics, he suggests, people are going to attack you, so you'd better not bear grudges, because then your statecraft will be swung by personal prejudice rather than the interests of the state: one thinks of Gordon Brown and Tony Blair, and how their personal animosity ended up harming the governance of the state. Nick Clegg, the British deputy prime minister, seems to have been shocked by his fall from media darling to public punchbag.[8] Well, that's politics. Lycurgus, the great Spartan statesman, so incensed wealthy Spartans with his reforms that he was set upon by a mob, and one young man succeeded in blinding him permanently in one eye. Rather than taking his revenge, Lycurgus took the boy into his house and became his tutor. The boy "thus became a devoted follower of Lycurgus, and used to tell his intimates and friends that the man was not harsh nor self-willed, as he had supposed, but the mildest and gentlest of them all."

Perhaps the most important passion the ruler must learn to control is the passion for fame and popularity. Plutarch is on slightly dangerous ground here, in that the entire project of the *Lives* is designed to spur young men to feats of courage, emulation, and derring-do. And yet the passion for fame and distinction, if it's not reined in, can be very damaging to the state. Alcibiades was a heroic general with a genius for warfare, but his overwhelming passion for glory led him to "inflame the desire" of the Athenian public for reckless military adventures. Pericles, by contrast, had no such need for fame or popularity, and so was better able to check the public's mood swings, rather than being swung by them like a weather-vane. This, in fact, is one of the key roles of the ruler — just as he or she must control their own passions, so they must be able to control and steer the turbulent passions of the public using rhetoric, like a captain steering a vessel through a storm. One thinks of Churchill, and how he steered the British public between excessive complacency and excessive despair before and during the Second World War, guided by what his biographer, Martin Gilbert, calls the "twin pillars" of his oratory: realism and vision.[9]

In all of this, the ruler needs philosophy. They need to be educated in philosophy by an experienced teacher from an early age, as many of Plutarch's heroes were — Alcibiades by Socrates, Pericles by Anaxagoras, Alexander by Aristotle. Philosophy gives rulers the "equipment," as Plutarch puts it, that they need to rule: a knowledge of rhetoric, of history, of statecraft, and above all a knowledge of how to rule themselves and live a good life. A good ruler needs a good character. They also, however, need a bit of luck. On this theme Plutarch attempts to distinguish what a person achieves through their own character, and what simply happens to them through good or bad fortune. The Stoic, we remember, is virtuous no matter whether lucky or unlucky. But the Plutarchian hero, out in the rough world of geopolitics, needs to be more than simply virtuous. They also need to be lucky, and to be able to judge the moment correctly in order to act decisively at the right time. Sometimes, in politics, that might mean doing things that are not, in fact, virtuous — like marriages of convenience, bribery, or even murder (there is a realpolitik side to Plutarch, which would appeal to Machiavelli). But Plutarch seems to have a confidence that the ideals of philosophy are not at odds with the world of geopolitics. Indeed, he suggests that Alexander the Great might actually have been the greatest philosopher ever, because his armies spread Hellenistic philosophy across half the known world, albeit at the end of their swords.[10] Plutarch's political solution for his society, then, is for philosophers to train an elite of military and political heroes, who will reshape their society through the sheer force of their personalities. You don't need a revolution, he suggests. You just need the right person in the right place at the right time.

THE CULT OF THE HERO

For centuries, Plutarch's cult of the hero was hugely influential in Western civilization. The early Christians condemned it, of course, as a manifestation of pagan pride and vanity. But even as they condemned it, they drew on Plutarch's psychology to create their own role models, in the lives of the saints, which they spread through their culture in stories, woodcarvings, tapestries, and stained-glass windows. Medieval culture was filled with artistic and literary portrayals of heroic knights, as clerics tried to civilize young rulers through chivalric romances. The Renaissance was obsessed with the heroes of the classical world, and tried to re-create the classical ideal of the hero in their own age. Giorgio Vasari, for example, wrote his *Lives of the Painters* to inspire Italian artists to feats of emulation, and designed the Uffizi in Florence as a walk-through education in classical role models. The Romantic era also saw a revival of the hero-cult, in the writings of Emerson, Carlyle, and Nietzsche, and in the figures of Byron and Napoleon. Carlyle, in particular, thought that the cult of hero-worship could somehow replace Christianity and act as the glue to keep modern society together. But the cult of the hero faded from modern culture after the Second World War. Today, we see military adventurers like Napoleon as war criminals, and Carlyle's idea of worshipping heroes seems Fascist. So, is Plutarch's conception of the hero completely irrelevant to modern life and modern politics?

To find out, I went to meet Rory Stewart, one of the few people in modern politics who seems to engage consciously with Plutarch's ideals. At thirty-eight, Rory has already lived what the *New York Times* called "one of the most remarkable lives on record." While studying at Oxford, he served as part-time tutor to Prince William and Prince Harry. He then worked for the Foreign Office in East Timor and Montenegro before, at the age of twenty-five, setting off for a six-thousand-kilometer walk across

Asia, including a final leg across Taliban-ruled Afghanistan. At twenty-eight, he became deputy-governor of two provinces in occupied Iraq. He wrote two bestselling books about his experiences, the movie rights to which have been bought by Brad Pitt. He then went back to Afghanistan to set up an arts school, before returning to the UK in 2009, to become an MP. I emailed him asking if I could interview him about Plutarch — he must be the only MP who would agree to such a strange request.

We meet in Rory's office in Westminster one rainy morning in July 2011, and I begin by asking him when had he first became enraptured by tales of classical military heroes. "It must have started very young," he says. His father, a senior officer in MI6, "tried to teach me ancient Greek when I was five, and spent a lot of time laying out ancient battlefields on the nursery floor with plastic soldiers." When he was six, Rory named his toy horse after the horse of Alexander the Great. He has written of Alexander that he was "haunted by competition with dead lives," and this seems true of the young Rory as well. He says: "I was always very interested in how old people were when they achieved things. I always found myself flipping back to the beginning of books to remind myself when people were born, and if I discovered that, for example, John Stuart Mill had already written two books by the time he was eleven, and I was eleven, I'd be very worried. So there was a competitiveness with people who were dead." This emulation of classical and modern "heroes" (he was particularly inspired by Lawrence of Arabia) spurred him on to great deeds, to audacious feats like his trek across Afghanistan, or his youthful deputy-governorship of two Iraqi provinces. Yet he became increasingly conscious there was something anachronistic, even ridiculous, about the Plutarchian hero in the modern world:

> The great person of the classical sort requires an audience that thinks they're great. In the absence of that, they're simply absurd. All of the classical heroes tread a very, very narrow line between greatness and absurdity. The classical hero by his very nature is a fantasist, boastful, liable to have a somewhat exaggerated opinion of himself.

They're trying to be godlike, and believe they really do have magical powers.

He thinks the last time that such a character was not seen as ridiculous — or even as pathologically sick — was the generation of T. E. Lawrence, Churchill, Shackleton, and Scott, in other words, the "heroic" last generation of the British Empire. The Empire gave this generation a playground to act out a grander Plutarchian conception of themselves.[11] Rory says:

> There's no doubt that from the late eighteenth century onwards, British India becomes a place where young people can get away from the Industrial Revolution and live out these fantasies of being knights in shining armor. But, typically, such figures come back to Britain and find it very hard to adjust. The Victorians can get excited by such figures, can write about them or paint portraits of them. But they are always treated with a certain distrust and contempt by the Establishment when they come home.

After the Second World War and the collapse of the British Empire, there's simply no stage for that grand conception of self. Stewart is fascinated by the careers of Michael Foot and Enoch Powell, two postwar politicians who both had a "grand classical conception of themselves," and who took themselves "very seriously indeed." But both men, Rory tells me, "ended up looking ludicrous in the modern world." In a world without empire, we no longer revere military values or military heroes, and we're suspicious of "people who self-consciously set out to be heroes" as Caesar or Alexander did. We prefer, Stewart notes, our heroes to be accidental. The old Plutarchian ideal of the hero still lives on, but "in a very simplified form, largely pushed out of everyday life and onto the big screen." Thus, contemporary American men may still find it thrilling when Maximus, the hero of *Gladiator*, declares: "What we do in this life echoes in eternity." But such figures only really exist in fiction, expanded to ever more ridiculous proportions on our cinema screens. "You might conceivably compare yourself to a classical hero," says Stewart ruefully, "but how could you possibly compete with an intergalactic superhero like the Green Lantern?"

Stewart is no doubt aware that some of the modern criticisms of the self-aggrandizing classical hero have been directed at him, and that some people wonder if he will manage to fit in to the more prosaic world of Westminster politics. When I ask him how he is finding it back home, there is a long, long pause. But he insists he has finally "liberated" himself from the allure of the Plutarchian hero-cult. He says that partly he "got it out of my system" when he walked across Afghanistan. But also his experience as a deputy provincial governor in Iraq changed him. "I had this incredible power, an eye-watering budget, military units under my command... and I achieved nothing. That sort of power is very empty. You issue commands, but you're so detached that nothing happens, or if it happens it's not because of you." By contrast, he says one of the most satisfying experiences of his life was setting up an arts school in Afghanistan. "It was a very small project, it only took up two or three blocks in Kabul, but I was on the ground, I could affect things, I could develop relationships, I could see things happening. It was all much more concrete. And yet clearly setting up an arts school does not fit with the classical template of the hero." Perhaps he has simply outgrown the hero-cult. He says: "It's no accident that Alexander died at thirty-three, that Shelley and Byron both died in their mid-thirties. That incredibly Romantic conception of the self is sort of a delayed adolescence. And it can't be maintained indefinitely in the reality of the world."

Today, the great military heroes of the past look, to modern eyes, to be little more than war criminals. Historians of the twentieth century convinced us that there was no such thing as "great figures of history," only the vainglorious puppets of economic forces and luck. More recently, situational psychologists like Philip Zimbardo convinced us that there was no such thing as "good character" or "bad character," because our behavior depends on the situation we're in. Zimbardo illustrated this with a famous experiment in 1971, called the Stanford Prison Experiment.[12] He took twenty-four normal, healthy male volunteers, and made twelve of them "guards" and twelve of them "inmates," put them in uniforms, then placed them in a simulated prison in the basement of Stanford University's Jordan Hall. He and his colleagues tried to make the experience as realistic as possible, to see how the volunteers would react to the situation. The experiment was meant to run for two weeks, but had to be stopped after a few days, because the guards became so sadistic some of the inmates had emotional breakdowns. They got lost in the situation, even right in the middle of Stanford campus. The experiment seemed to undermine the Plutarchian idea of "character," and to suggest who we are depends on the situation in which we find ourselves.

Yet it's interesting to note that Zimbardo seems recently to have moved closer to Plutarch's idea that our characters can be strengthened by reading about and emulating the lives of great figures. In 2010, Zimbardo launched a new venture called the Heroic Imagination Project, which tries to instill heroic habits of behavior in young people, partly by soaking their imagination in stories of everyday heroes who stood up for justice.[13] Perhaps we can say that some historical figures are genuinely heroic, that Nelson Mandela is heroic, or Ernest Shackleton, or Aung San Suu Kyi. There's a value in reading the lives of such figures because, even if we can never become as brave as Shackleton, as defiant as Churchill, as stoic as Mandela, we can still raise our aspirations to become a little closer to such heroes.[14] In the absence of such aspiration, we become obsessed with the trivial, with people who are famous merely for being famous (look, for example, at that modern Plutarch, Piers Morgan, whose show *Life Stories* featured such heroic figures as Katie Price and Peter Andre). We are what we watch. Humans are inescapably social creatures, and we can't help but imitate and emulate the people around us. But this process doesn't have to be entirely unconscious and involuntary. We can, to some extent, consciously choose the models we emulate, to try to bring out the best and highest in us, rather than the lowest or the worst.

Our penultimate lesson is with Aristotle, and it takes us back to Socrates's conception of street philosophy, and the optimistic idea that philosophy is not just for the hero, or for a Platonic elite, but should be taught to every citizen. Let's see if this is really a practical option today.

12. Aristotle and the Art of Flourishing

AS I APPROACHED THE COMPLETION OF THIS BOOK, I decided I needed to get up from my desk and stretch my legs. I set off one May morning to walk the Camino de Santiago, the old medieval pilgrimage route that weaves (in its most popular route, the Camino Francés) for 780 kilometers across northern Spain to Santiago de Compostela. The pilgrimage had once been an expression of the unity of Christendom: travellers from all over Europe found a common identity as pilgrims, and a common goal in Santiago. In the modern age, the Camino has been revived by the European Union as a symbol of Europe's cultural, economic, and fiscal unity — although as I walked through Spain, the Eurozone seemed to be collapsing. Today, few pilgrims really think that walking the Camino will give them an express pass through purgatory, as their medieval counterparts believed. But for some, walking the Camino is still a serious act of religious devotion. I met one intense young Englishman called Arthur, a recent convert to Catholicism, whose eyes burned with terrifying ardor. He described himself as a professional pilgrim. One day he'd walked eighty kilometers before collapsing and sleeping in a field. I asked him what he'd do when he reached Santiago. "I want to do another pilgrimage," he said. "A *proper* one this time."

Quite a few pilgrims had been inspired by Paulo Coelho's book *The Pilgrimage.* They believed, in a vague New Age way, that the universe would show them signs when they were on the right path. "I almost missed my flight here," one pilgrim told me. "But when I changed flights, my backpack was the very first to appear on the luggage carousel. That's when I *knew* I had made the right choice to come here." Others had less spiritual reasons for following the Way. Jenny, a white witch from Wales who made a living selling sex toys for Ann Summers, was doing the walk with her boyfriend for fun. They kept on leaving the Camino to slip into the bushes for a quickie. Others wanted a month to walk and reflect on their lives, like Anna, a German lady who was trying to decide whether to stay in her marriage (she decided not to), or Alberto, a roly-poly Ecuadorian, who'd been sent on the Camino by his mother to find a wife. I wasn't looking for redemption or a wife, but as it happens I fell in love with a Texan economist called Claudia, who was also unsure why she was on a pilgrimage, and we walked the Camino together. Despite the pilgrims' various nationalities, ages, professions, and beliefs, for one month we were united in a common way of life. Every morning, the pilgrims woke up at six, had breakfast, put on our backpacks, and walked west. We ate together, walked together, shared stories, tolerated each other's snores. We may have lost medieval Christendom's sense of common values or the common heavenly goal of life. But for one month, we shared a common geographic goal, handily pointed out by the yellow arrows painted on the sides of trees and houses.

I began the pilgrimage very much a Stoic, and spent the first few days striding silently along listening to my iPod, seeing how many kilometers I could walk in a day. That didn't last long. My feet gave out, I felt lonely and cut off, and wondered why I was putting myself through this solitary ordeal. By the end of the pilgrimage, I'd changed my philosophy, because I had been helped so much by my fellow pilgrims (and perhaps because I'd fallen in love). To go on a pilgrimage is to make yourself vulnerable, to put yourself at the mercy of others. You learn to accept the gift of others' help, and to accept your own dependency.[1] I realized the ideal of self-sufficiency one often encounters in ancient Greek philosophy is not sufficient for a good life. We are not, and should not try to be, invincible Stoic supermen, safe in our lonely fortresses of solitude. We need each other. We need to admit this need, and embrace it. In modern liberal society, we have struggled for centuries to wall off the individual from the interference of church, state, and community. We have won our individual freedom and privacy, but at the cost of terrible loneliness. We place a great emphasis on the free, private, autonomous individual. If we hurt, we hurt in private. The pilgrimage broke down this liberal isolation through sheer necessity. It was all too obvious who was in pain and who needed help: often it was the younger pilgrims, the ones you'd think would be physically hardy, but who ended up needing help from pilgrims in their sixties. We had to care for each other, share paracetamol, swap tips on how to deal with tendonitis, tend to each other's injuries and, above all, listen to each other's stories and encourage each other on.

ARISTOTLE AND THE GOOD LIFE

I took Aristotle with me on the walk. Or rather, I took his *Nichomachean Ethics*, the book he wrote for his son, Nichomachus. I'd always thought of Aristotle as a boring encyclopedist, a systematizer, an enemy of street philosophy. Yet on the walk, I belatedly realized how wrong this view was, and how much Aristotle has to offer. He was born in 384 BC in Stageira, on the northern coast of Greece, the son of the personal physician to King Amyntas of Macedon. At eighteen, he was sent to Athens to study under Plato at the Academy. Aristotle would become Plato's most famous pupil, and his greatest critic. He studied at the Academy for twenty years, but left Athens after Plato died, and then travelled through Greece and Asia Minor, before being invited by Philip II of Macedon to be tutor to Philip's son, Alexander the Great. Aristotle encouraged Alexander's military adventures, advising him to be "a leader to the Greeks and a despot to the barbarians"[2] (this racism was one of Aristotle's least attractive features: he argued that some people were naturally slaves, and also seemed to think philosophy was beyond the powers of women and children). He eventually left Macedonia and returned to Athens, where he set up his own school, the Lyceum, so called because it was built in a grove sacred to Apollo the Wolf-God. Aristotle taught there for the next twelve years, but fled Athens again after Alexander's death. He died in 322 BC.

In Raphael's *School of Athens*, Plato and Aristotle stand in the center of the school, Plato pointing up to the heavens, Aristotle down to the ground. This has been interpreted as a reference to the different mentalities of the two great philosophers: Plato is not interested in the terrestrial or the particular, but in the abstract and divine. Aristotle, by contrast, was much more of a scientist, fascinated by how things function here on earth. According to professor Armand Leroi of Imperial College, Aristotle was the greatest biologist ever.[3] He was never happier than when pottering around Greek islands with a net, finding octopi or cuttlefish to examine and dissect. Aristotle was an astonishing polymath, writing definitive works on everything from biology to logic to literary criticism. Plato is by far the better writer, but no one, except perhaps Shakespeare, has ever had so broad and comprehensive an intellect as Aristotle. He created a philosophy that encompassed the entire universe, from biology to psychology to literature to ethics to politics to astrophysics. And, for several centuries, through the Catholic Church, this philosophy was the foundation of medieval Christendom. Only Karl Marx's philosophy had such a broad scope and historical impact — and Marxism, although also a "total philosophy," is far more narrow in the topics it encompasses.

Aristotle's two most famous works — the *Nichomachean Ethics* and the *Politics* — offer us a unified vision of human psychology, ethics, and politics. Aristotle rests his ethics on a biological theory of human nature: he suggests our psyche has both a rational and an irrational component, and that it's also essentially social, political, and spiritual. The good life is one which fulfills this nature and guides it to happiness and fulfillment. His vision is teleological — everything is designed for a purpose, and it achieves the good when it fulfills the purpose for which it is designed. Humans achieve the good life when they fulfill the design of their nature. Unlike the Stoics, Aristotle didn't think humans should use their rationality to completely conquer their irrational mind and free themselves from passions. He was closer to his teacher Plato — he thought we should use our reason to steer our emotions into good habits. But unlike Plato, he didn't think we could discover virtue in some absolute, eternal, and unchanging form. Rather, we have to use our discrimination to try to discern what is the right thing to do in ever-shifting circumstances.

Like Plutarch's hero, we need to know how to do the right thing at the right time. Aristotle introduced the idea that there are certain cardinal virtues — courage, temperance, good humor, friendliness, patience, and others — which exist in a "golden mean" between excesses. Courage, for example, is the golden mean between the excesses of rashness and cowardice. Good humor is the golden mean between the excesses of oversolemnity and buffoonery. Knowing how to hit the right mark between these excesses takes practice. The only way we can acquire the virtues is by practicing them in real-life situations, until they become automatic. He compares ethics to playing the lyre: just as a lyre player gets better with practice, so we as human beings can improve our characters through practice, until eventually, after long training, we perfect our habits and automatically do the right thing at the right time. If someone harms us, we feel appropriate indignation and respond with appropriate force. If we're in political office, we act with an appropriate balance of prudence and daring. If we're at a dinner party, we make jokes of appropriate levity. We become a virtuoso in living well. And we achieve happiness as a sort of free bonus to our ethical fulfillment. True happiness, Aristotle insists, is not simply pleasant feelings or the absence of pain, as the Epicureans believed. No, true happiness is *eudaimonia*: the joy that comes from fulfilling what is highest and best in our nature. "Happiness," he wrote, "is an activity of the soul in accordance with virtue." And we might even find that highest happiness in the sacrifice of our life for a "higher cause" like our country or God. Epicureans would think that was barmy.

The Politics of Flourishing

The good life for Aristotle has an inescapably social and political dimension. The Stoic doesn't need other people to follow the good life. They can do it on their own, in exile, in a prison cell, anywhere. But for Aristotle, many of the virtues are social, such as good humor, friendliness, and patience. That means we can only achieve the good life together. We're naturally social and political creatures, which is why we feel fulfilled when we're working on a common project, uniting with others in friendship. Friendship is a key virtue for Aristotle — he devoted a whole book of the

Nichomachean Ethics to it. The Epicureans also emphasized the importance of friendship, but theirs is a friendship disconnected from political life. It's a private friendship. For Aristotle, friendship in its highest form has a political or civic dimension. We love our friends not just because we like each other or are useful to each other, but because we share the same values and ideals for our society, and come together to advance those ideals.

The good society, then, is one which enables its members to reach human fulfillment. Humans are happy when the highest drives of their natures are fulfilled — the drive to know, to master skills and virtues, to connect with other people and work on common projects. Aristotle's vision of human nature was tested out, in the 1970s, by two psychologists called Edward Deci and Richard Ryan. They found that humans are not the profit-motivated creatures that liberal economics believed. In fact, a series of experiments run by Deci and Ryan suggested humans will actually work harder at projects for less money, or even no money, if they find these projects to be meaningful, challenging, socially engaging, and fun. That's why humans are prepared to spend so much time and effort on projects like blogs or Wikipedia, which don't necessarily make a profit. We're not killing time, we're making meaning. As Aristotle predicted, we're seeking ways to fulfill the higher drives of our nature for meaning, mastery, engagement, transcendence, and fun.[4] A good society creates opportunities for its citizens to fulfill these drives. Aristotle thought the best constitution for the pursuit of the good life is democracy, because democratic societies enable people to join together and set up clubs, associations, networks, communities of friends, which can practice philosophy and reason their way to the common good. And the solutions they come up with will be better than in a tyranny where only a handful of minds are engaged. In a democratic society, *everyone* is thinking, everyone is engaged.

Beyond Self-Help, to Group-Help

Aristotle offers us a very optimistic vision of philosophy's role in society. It takes us beyond self-help, and into group-help. We can't help ourselves on our own, we need to connect with other people and work on common projects. But his political vision asks a lot of us. It asks that we *all* become philosopher-citizens, so that we can reason our way to the common good. At the moment, that doesn't happen. Only a handful of people — a Platonic elite — runs our society. Aristotle's vision asks that we take education a lot more seriously, that we allocate more time and resources to it, because this is the foundation of a good society. And it asks us that we trust in government to play a more paternalist and intrusive role, actively instilling good moral habits in the citizens' psyches, particularly when they're children. Unless we can access the right education, Aristotle suggests, the good life is impossible to achieve. Is this a practical vision? If we look back to the early Renaissance, then Aristotelian philosophy was, for a while, the official philosophy of the whole of Christendom, thanks to the Dominican priest Thomas Aquinas, who synthesized Aristotle's philosophy with the Christian faith and persuaded the Vatican to endorse it. Of course, only an intellectual elite really studied philosophy, but Thomist Aristotelianism still provided a foundation for European culture, a sense of common values, and a bridge between science and culture, reason and faith, man and the cosmos. This foundation helped pave the way for the sublime visions of Chaucer, Dante, Raphael. But, unfortunately, because Aristotelianism became the official philosophy of the Catholic Church, it calcified into religious dogma. If you disagreed with Aristotle, you were a heretic, and would be burnt. And in some important ways, the dogma turned out to be wrong.

The Rise of Relativism

In particular, Aristotle's theories of astrophysics turned out to be wrong, notably his theory that the sun revolved around the earth. He lacked the empirical method developed by Galileo, Bacon, Kepler, and others during the Scientific Revolution of the sixteenth and seventeenth centuries, and his scientific theories, although advanced for his day, were naturally quite out of date by the seventeenth century. When the natural philosophers of the Scientific Revolution successfully challenged Aristotle's astrophysics, it opened up the way for further challenges to Christian Aristotelianism's ethics and politics, and for the great explosion of competing ethical philosophies that took place during the Enlightenment. The decline in the intellectual authority of the Church meant that, from the eighteenth century to the present day, the West no longer has any common philosophy of the good life or the common good. Instead, the Enlightenment gave rise to a bewildering array of competing ethical theories — Utilitarian, Kantian, Burkean, Lockean, the moral sentiment theories of David Hume and Adam Smith, the socialist theories of Marx and Lenin.

Modern philosophy successfully undermined the moral authority of the Catholic Church, but failed to provide a replacement for Christianity, in the form of ethical systems for ordinary people, grounded in symbols, stories, rituals, festivals, or genuine forms of community. What relevance did Kant have to the struggles and concerns of ordinary men and women? What hope or consolation could he offer them? The only Enlightenment philosophy that attempted to create a total philosophical system to rival Christian Aristotelianism was Marxism. (Marx was planning a series of lectures on Aristotle before he abandoned academia to become a journalist, and he referred to Aristotle as "the great investigator.") Marxism, like Aristotelianism, created a philosophical framework for the flourishing of human beings, which connected the intellectual to the people, and the social sciences to the humanities. But alas, the brutal reality of twentieth-century Marxist societies was a long way from the dreams of its intellectual supporters. In fact, so murderous were the Soviet and Maoist regimes that, in the second half of the twentieth century, Western policy-makers came to accept that governments should not be in the business of telling their citizens how to find happiness and fulfillment. After all, how could you prove that your version of the good life was better than anyone else's, and therefore what right had you to impose it on others? Perhaps it was a "metaphysical chimera," as Sir Isaiah Berlin put it, to imagine there was one single answer to the Socratic question "How should I live?" — and therefore any attempt to impose a single answer onto the masses would necessarily lead to coercion and the concentration camp.

In place of the totalitarian systems of Maoism and Marxism–Leninism, modern liberal societies embraced a much more limited conception of the state: it should be a nightwatchman, as the philosopher Robert Nozick put it, which protects its citizens' physical and economic security, while leaving them to decide for themselves how to be happy.[5] In Berlin's famous definition, the state should defend citizens' "negative liberty" — i.e., their freedom from interference by others — while leaving them to pursue their own "positive liberty," their own personal conception of the good life.[6] The state should resist the temptation to meddle in its citizens' private lives, it should never try to heal their souls or guide them toward a particular conception of human fulfillment. That was a recipe for tyranny.

In accordance with this limited conception of the state's role, politics increasingly became a technocratic affair carried out by a small group of bureaucratic experts, mainly with a view to increasing a nation's GDP. Meanwhile, the pluralism of the postwar period slowly turned into the postmodernism and moral relativism of the 1960s and 1970s, in which it seemed to some that no one had the right to tell anyone else how to live, and all moral agendas were really covert attempts to impose your own interests on others. Postmodernists insisted that there's no such thing as an essential and unchanging human nature, so any attempts to ground a view of morality in human nature is really a disguised form of power and domination. Morality, and truth itself, is not grounded in human nature, but rather is an artificial construct, a convenient fiction. The aim of philosophy should be not to promote a particular model of the good life, but rather to expose all models of the good life as self-interested fictions.[7] The good life is whatever works for you. If you're into aromatherapy, that's your thing. If you're into sadomasochism, that's your thing. Everyone should be free to pursue their own thing, as long as they tolerate other people's thing. Whatever works for you. Whatever turns you on.

THE RETURN OF ARISTOTLE

This sort of postmodern moral relativism reached a high water mark in the 1980s. At that point, a handful of thinkers started to revive Aristotle's belief that some ways of living are simply better than others, and that it is the proper role, even the duty, of government to encourage the flourishing of its citizens by educating them in the art of living. Governments should not merely defend the negative liberty of their citizens, but also support the positive liberty of human flourishing and spiritual fulfillment. Liberalism, it was argued, had left us lonely and atomized, rattling like loose change in the pockets of the corporate state, adrift in mega-cities with no common values, not even knowing the names of the strangers we live among.

At first, only a few voices put forward this rather provocative and negative view of liberalism, such as Alasdair MacIntyre and Allan Bloom, both of whom published influential books in the 1980s suggesting that moral relativism had left the West in a deep moral crisis, and that we needed to return to a classical idea of the virtues and of human flourishing.[8] The Neo-Aristotelian cause was taken up in the 1990s by the likes of Martha Nussbaum and Michael Sandel, both of whom tried to find a balance between liberal democracy and virtue ethics,[9] and in the first decade of the new millennium Neo-Aristotelianism had become a new consensus, unifying Anglo-Saxon thinkers across the political spectrum, such as David Brooks, James Q. Wilson, Jeffrey Sachs, Jon Cruddas, David Willetts, and Richard Reeves, the last of whom announced: "In political and policy circles the Aristotelian idea of a good life informs contemporary concerns."[10] As the *Daily Telegraph* put it, with some justification, "Our leaders are all Aristotelians now."[11] Both Nicholas Sarkozy of France and David Cameron of the UK announced, in the early years of this decade, that they would make well-being the end, or goal, of public policy. The European Union looks likely to follow suit. Partly, governments will simply measure their citizens' happiness, in the Epicurean sense of positive feelings. But the Office of National Statistics says it is also taking a "eudaimonic approach," by asking citizens how worthwhile or meaningful they think their life is. As one cabinet minister put it: "Aristotle didn't get everything right, but he got most things right."[12] So, some centuries after the decline of Christian Aristotelianism, it appears Europe will once more have a common Aristotelian goal of human flourishing.

The Psychology of Flourishing

What has given intellectuals and policy-makers this new confidence that, firstly, there is such a thing as the good life, and secondly, that governments can, and should, actively intervene in the lives of their citizens to promote it? One source of confidence is the proven success of cognitive therapy in helping people overcome emotional disorders. There's no point in governments trying to promote the good life if our personalities, habits, and happiness levels are fixed. What CBT has successfully proven is that we can change our personalities and personal habits. We can become happier by learning basic cognitive and behavioral techniques. CBT has quite limited aims — it has the negative aim of removing the symptoms of sicknesses, rather than a positive aim of encouraging human flourishing. However, a younger colleague of Aaron Beck at the University of Pennsylvania, Martin Seligman, started to wonder if the techniques of CBT could be taught to *everyone*, not just for the negative aim of removing sickness, but for the positive aim of encouraging human flourishing.

In 1998, Seligman used his presidency of the American Psychological Association to launch Positive Psychology, which aimed to move psychology beyond its negative focus on sickness and pathology, and instead get it to study and promote the positive goal of human flourishing. At the core of Positive Psychology were the basic techniques taken by Aaron Beck and Albert Ellis from Stoicism — changing your emotions by changing your habitual beliefs. But Seligman added the Aristotelian idea that there existed certain universal virtues, or "character strengths," which were recognized in all human cultures.[13] Seligman insisted that science could quantify the extent to which a person possessed these strengths using basic questionnaires. And then it could help people to enhance these character strengths. So Positive Psychology wasn't simply teaching happiness or positive emotion. Rather, as Seligman told me in an interview:[14] "I'm interested in the meaningful or virtuous life, what the Greeks called *eudaimonia*."[15]

This, then, was the new Renaissance promised by Positive Psychology — ancient philosophy tested by modern empirical science, to create "a vision of the good life that is empirically sound while being understandable and attractive," as Seligman has said.[16] Positive Psychologists, armed with their clipboards and questionnaires, could finally tell us what *really* makes us happier, stronger, and more resilient. From the start, Positive Psychology was a wonderful marketing proposition — who doesn't believe in science? who doesn't want to be happier? — and Seligman proved a genius at attracting funding, both from private charities like the Templeton Foundation, and from schools, education boards, and government departments. Positive Psychology has been taken up and taught to employees by corporations like the shoe company Zappos,[17] and governments have also started to finance the dissemination of Positive Psychology to their citizens. The British government, for example, paid Seligman and his colleagues at Penn to design a three-year pilot program to teach "emotional resilience" to secondary school children. In 2009, Seligman really hit the jackpot, when the Pentagon wrote a check for $125 million for Seligman and his colleagues to teach resilience to every American soldier — as we saw in chapter 2. These are the first steps in what Seligman called a new "politics of well-being," where governments would use their finances to teach the science of human flourishing to their citizens — like the Medicis used their wealth to spread Platonic philosophy across Renaissance Florence (to use Seligman's analogy).[18] The politics of well-being shows no signs of slowing: at the end of 2011, as Europe teetered on the brink of financial collapse, the president of the European Council, Herman Van Rompuy, sent a book on Positive Psychology to two hundred world leaders, accompanied by a letter calling on them to make well-being their main policy focus in 2012. "Positive thinking," he wrote, "is no longer something for drifters, dreamers, and the perpetually naive. Positive Psychology concerns itself in a scientific way with the quality of life. It is time to make this knowledge available to the man and woman on the street."[19]

BEYOND PLURALISM?

It seems that Western societies are moving beyond pluralism and moral relativism back to a political vision close to medieval Christendom, in which all of Europe was joined together under common values and the common goal of human flourishing. But instead of priests and clerics, politicians are turning to psychologists and neuroscientists to guide us to happiness. The fact that Seligman is a scientist, and that Positive Psychology puts itself forward as an objective and morally neutral science, allows governments to roll out a specific vision of the good life to their citizens, while also claiming they are not being morally paternalist. Positive Psychology is a science, Seligman insists, not a moral philosophy. It "does not tell people what to do," it "is not a moral theory. It does not tell us what is right and wrong, good or evil, fair or unfair."[20] It describes the good life, without prescribing it, he says. And Seligman insists that it does not put forward one model of the good life. He suggests there are five different versions of happiness, which he calls PERMA: Positive emotion, or feeling good in an Epicurean sense; Engagement, or feeling absorbed in an activity; Relationships; Meaning, or feeling like you're serving a worthwhile higher cause; and Achievement.[21] He says these five versions of flourishing can be scientifically measured, and that a good life will probably involve some combination of these different types of happiness, but it's not for the humble social scientist to tell us definitively which is best. So Positive Psychology is not really telling anyone how to live. It's simply measuring what interventions lead to these various types of flourishing.

But, in fact, if you look at how Positive Psychology is taught to children and to soldiers, it is very prescriptive, coercive, and didactic. Take the Comprehensive Soldier Fitness course, which every American soldier must take. There's a lot to welcome in the course — it teaches soldiers the Stoic idea that we can become more resilient by understanding how our beliefs and interpretations lead to our emotions. But it also tries to teach "optimistic thinking," a particular thinking style which involves not blaming yourself for mistakes, while taking the credit for successes.[22] This was never part of CBT, and it's certainly not part of Stoicism. It's actually quite a dangerous idea — it trains us to take responsibility when things go well, and to shirk responsibility when things go badly. Equally misleading is Seligman's claim that questionnaires can quantify how meaningful our lives are, and to what extent we possess "character strengths." Every

American soldier now has to take a barrage of computerized question-naires that Seligman designed, called the Global Assessment Tool. Sol-diers answer a few simplistic questions on a seven-point scale, and then the program gives them a numerical score for their mental fitness, their emotional fitness, even their "spiritual fitness." If they score too low in this last domain, a box pops up on the computer screen with the message:

> Spiritual fitness is an area of possible difficulty for you. You may lack a sense of meaning and purpose in your life. At times, it is hard for you to make sense of what is happening to you and others around you. You may not feel connected to something larger than yourself. You may question your beliefs, principles, and values. Nevertheless, who you are and what you do matters. There are things to do to pro-vide more meaning and purpose in your life. Change is possible, and the relevant self-development training modules are available.[23]

This strikes me as a weird sort of automated spirituality — the medieval priest replaced by a spiritually enlightened computer. And notice that ques-tioning "your beliefs, principles, and values" becomes a sign of weakness or even sickness — we've come a long way from what Socrates and the Stoics had in mind, and closer to the Catholic idea that any deviance from the official path to happiness is sickness or even heresy. I'm not surprised some soldiers have found it offensive and intrusive. Likewise, when Posi-tive Psychology is taught in schools, it is certainly prescriptive and simplis-tic. Wellington College, for example, which made Positive Psychology part of its curriculum, put forward a "ten-point well-being program," which headmaster Anthony Seldon said, "encapsulates what every single child and adult *needs* to follow if they are to make the most of life" [my italics].[24] The school's well-being teacher, Ian Morris, says he has been struck by the lack of skepticism from the "the students." But is that really something to celebrate? Shouldn't lessons in the good life train students to be skeptical?

I have no problem with schools or the army teaching moral values to young people, but I do when values are taught as "scientific facts" which cannot be disputed. And the empiricism backing up the science of flourishing is often very weak and blunt, considering the boldness of the intervention into people's characters. Do Positive Psychologists really think a quick computerized questionnaire can accurately quantify how "spiritually fit" a person is, or to what extent they possess *eudaimonia*? You can ask someone how meaningful or virtuous they *think* their life is, but who's to say they're right? You could ask them to what extent they feel they're serving a "higher cause," but that won't tell you if the cause they're serving is actually a *good* cause. A questionnaire can only tell you how a person sees themselves: it can't tell you how they actually behave in real life. Seligman himself, desperate to avoid the charge of moral paternalism and to preserve his scientific credentials, has insisted that a person could score highly in Positive Psychology's tests for flourishing, and still be an immoral person. He gives the example of Osama bin Laden, who he says would probably have scored high in tests of PERMA. But surely if Osama bin Laden fits your model of the good life, then there's something terribly wrong with the model.[25]

This is the danger of trying to turn ancient philosophy into a science. There is this pernicious idea that you can "prove" the validity of a certain model of the good life, so there's no longer any need for people to debate it or consent to it. Such claims become dangerous when overhasty policy-makers decide that, because the research "proves" it, the science should be instantly transmitted to the masses, and installed in their personalities via automated programs and prewritten scripts. It marks the triumph of instrumental technocracy, and of the scientific expert, at the cost of practical reasoning, personal freedom, and choice. Seligman and his political backers are so keen to build an "objective science," and to avoid the charge of moral paternalism, that they have built a model of the good life that leaves out moral judgment, ethical debate, and free choice — all of which, I would suggest, are fairly crucial aspects of human flourishing.

THE UNEASY MARRIAGE OF PHILOSOPHY AND PSYCHOLOGY

I am not suggesting that Positive Psychology has been a complete waste of time. I welcome much of its work, particularly in spreading the ideas and

techniques of ancient philosophy, and testing out these ideas with empirical science. That is a really valuable project. Without empirical research,
moral philosophy is a brain in a vat, cut off from real-world situations. But
a purely scientific model of the good life without moral reasoning is like
a chicken without a head. We should resist the idea we can arrive at some
proven scientific equation for the good life that excludes the need for ethical debate and public reasoning. In the words of Aristotle: "It is the sign
of an educated person to look for precision in a subject only so far as the
subject allows." If we become too eager to spread one vision of flourishing to the whole of society, to automate it, install it, and indoctrinate the
masses in it, we will end up with an official version of the good life that is
simplistic, reductive, intrusive, and ultimately damaging.

What I've tried to show in this book is that Greek philosophy offers
us not one model of the good life, but several. All of them rely on the
same core Socratic beliefs — we can know ourselves, we can change ourselves, we can make ourselves happier through rational philosophy. But
they take these Socratic beliefs in quite different directions, with respect to
our relationship to society and to God. These philosophies involve different value judgments that the individual must make for themselves. Science
can "prove" that the core Socratic beliefs are, on the whole, true. So in
that sense, Socratic ethics do seem to "fit" our nature, and perhaps governments could teach the basic Socratic techniques of CBT to children and
adolescents in schools. But science can never *prove* what model of the good
life is true, because we can never be sure whether there's a God, whether
there's an afterlife, whether there's a transcendent meaning to human existence. Nor can science "prove" what emotional reactions to the world are
healthy and appropriate. How long is it appropriate to grieve after your
partner has died? That's not a question science can objectively answer. It's
a moral, cultural, and philosophical question — and a personal one.

So if governments want to teach "the good life" in schools, universities, or adult learning centers (and I think they should) then I suggest they
teach the various different ethical approaches, and highlight the differences
and arguments between those approaches, rather than pouring them all
into the same punchbowl and stirring them until they lose their edges, their

differences, their arguments with each other. We need to empower people to consider the multiple approaches to the good life, and then to experiment, innovate, and decide for themselves. Otherwise the education process is far too passive: the expert spoonfeeds the art of happiness, and the masses kneel and swallow it. And I'm not so arrogant as to think the models of the good life presented in this book are anything close to exhaustive. All the schools we've met share some basic Socratic assumptions and values. In particular, they all share Socrates's idea that the good life is rational, self-controlled, and self-sufficient. That might be some of the answer to the question of the good life. But it's not *necessarily* all of the answer.

MEETING JEAN VANIER

On the first evening that I walked the Camino, I stayed in the church hall at Roncesvalles, in the damp Pyrenees Mountains, together with some two hundred other pilgrims. I remember sitting on my bed, hiding in a book, somewhat shocked at my forced collectivization with so many strangers. I was used to having my own space. That evening, I went to the only place serving dinner, and was told to sit at a table with some other pilgrims. So I sat at a table with a young Irishman called Ciaran. We got into a conversation, and I told him a little about this book. Ciaran told me that, as it happened, he was going to work with a philosopher after he completed the pilgrimage — a man by the name of Jean Vanier, who had set up a community in France where volunteers lived with the mentally handicapped. Vanier had originally studied Aristotle at university, before leaving academia to set up a community called L'Arche (or "The Ark"). He and a friend had started the community in 1964, with two mentally handicapped people. Slowly, the community had grown, and today there are 150 L'Arche communities in thirty-five countries around the world. I was intrigued, and after finishing the Camino, I got in contact with Ciaran, and travelled to Trosly-Breuil in France, where Ciaran was spending a year living in a house with five volunteers and six mentally handicapped "core members." Having seen the conditions in some state-run mental asylums, I was impressed — the severely handicapped core members were treated as human beings, worthy of respect, care, and love, and had clearly formed warm relationships with the volunteers who lived with them for years at a time.

Jean Vanier still lives in the same small cottage in Trosly, though he seems too big for it, like a kindly polar bear living in a shed. He's eighty-three now, and an internationally respected figure, but he lives simply, without any sort of veneration or hullabaloo, and I could sense that, unlike other "gurus" I had met and interviewed, he was not vain and had no insecure need for publicity. I must have struck him as a strange sort of person, turning up on his doorstep to talk about Aristotle, but he was generous with his time. I asked Jean if Greek philosophy could form the basis of a genuine spirituality or way of life for our society. He replied: "Aristotle understood our deep human desire for happiness and fulfillment, and the importance of friendship. However, he was obviously an elitist. He defined humans as 'rational, free Greek men,' which is far too narrow. By that definition, a barbarian is not a person. Women and children are not really persons. The mentally handicapped are not persons." Vanier pointed out that Greek philosophy — not just Aristotle, but almost *all* Greek philosophy — tends to strive toward an ideal of perfect rationality and complete self-sufficiency. Even Aristotle, who emphasizes the social virtues of friendship and political participation, still puts forward the ideal of the "great-souled man," a sort of superman, who doesn't really need anyone else. And the Stoics certainly put forward a model of the sage as an invulnerable fortress of rationality. Now, there's something valuable in that ideal: as adults, we need to learn to stand on our own feet, to achieve autonomy, to recognize that we don't necessarily need the things we think we need. Yet we can become *too* independent, can strive for too much autonomy and invulnerability, ending up lonely and cut off. Loneliness, Vanier has written, is the great sickness of our time — and it partly comes from our shame at admitting that we're all flawed, imperfect, wounded creatures.[26]

Aristotle would have considered the mentally handicapped residents of L'Arche subhuman. Yet Vanier says the volunteers at L'Arche learn from the core members about their common humanity: "They teach us that we're all weak, we're all handicapped. We're all fragile. And that's okay. That's part of being human. We learn to accept our own weakness and fragility, which is extremely difficult in today's society, which puts such a great emphasis on being competent, and efficacious, and strong, and self-sufficient." Vanier's philosophy is, in fact, close to Thomas Aquinas's version of Aristotle, combining Aristotle's emphasis on reason with a more Christian sense of humility and compassion for our common limitations. Where Greek philosophy can overemphasize the superhuman isolation of the sage, Vanier's philosophy is based on meeting, on relationships, on genuine friendship and love. He says: "A good society is one in which you enable people to meet, not to tell each other what to do, not to prove we are better than each other, but to reflect on our common humanity, to create friendship, to celebrate life by eating together, living together, dancing together. There's not much dancing in Greek philosophy."

This is a much smaller vision than some Neo-Aristotelians would like to create. It doesn't attempt to create a government-sanctioned model of the good life to be spread to the entire Western world. Rather, Vanier suggests, it's about "small groups coming together and meeting. That's what we're doing here — living in small groups with disabled people, showing that they're people too." He says: "I believe in the village. There's a danger of our society becoming too big, too technical, so that people become closed off and passive, and relationships are not fostered." Instead, he and the other L'Arche members are trying to create "a new way of living, based on the idea of meeting. One person meets another. And meeting another person is revealing not just that I have qualities, but also that I have weaknesses, difficulties, that I need your help."

We live in exciting times for philosophy, when old beliefs and structures are collapsing, and individuals and governments are searching for a common vision of the good life that they can bring to society. There is a new confidence that governments can make us happier and wiser, that we can construct what the journalist Simon Jenkins calls, rather ominously, a "state infrastructure of joy." But there's a risk we may end up with a politics of well-being that is mechanistic, instrumentalized, and reductive, that replaces human relationships with automated box-ticking, and that grants too much authority to "well-being experts" at the cost of the citizen's autonomy. We're in danger of committing the same mistake made by the followers of Karl Marx, who turned his living philosophy of the good life into a lifeless, technocratic, and coercive state system.

My hope is that we can find a better balance between the ancient idea of the good life, and a modern, pluralist, and liberal politics. It would recognize that well-being is not a simple concept that can be objectively defined, pinned down, and measured by empirical science, and the world would be a much more boring place if it was. We should explore the plurality of philosophical approaches to well-being. We should treat citizens as rational adults who deserve to be brought into the conversation as equals. Empiricism balanced with practical reasoning. Science balanced with the humanities. Not one version of the good life, but several. Not a mass enforced march to an official well-being target, but groups of friends helping each other in their search for the good. That's what I would like to see.

Graduation: Socrates and the Art of Departure

THOMAS DALEY JOINED THE US MARINE CORPS in 1978, when he was seventeen, and retired in 2008, having completed tours in Beirut, Grenada, Panama, in the two Iraq wars, and in Afghanistan. He had been injured and evacuated five times while fighting for his country. Probably his most challenging situation was in November 2004 in the Second Battle of Fallujah in Iraq, where some of the most intense urban fighting involving American forces occurred since the battle for Hue in 1968, during the Vietnam War. Over the course of 2004, Iraqi and foreign insurgents had built up strong positions within the "city of mosques," positioning snipers and improvised explosive devices (IEDs) around the city in preparation for a showdown with the Marines. The Pentagon believed the city had become the stronghold of around five thousand Al Qaeda forces, led by Abu Musab al-Zarqawi, the leader of Al Qaeda in Iraq.

On November 8th, the Marines began an assault on the city, codenamed Operation Phantom Fury. The US Army moved in first in Bradley Fighting Vehicles, then Marines followed on foot supported by artillery and heavy weapons. They entered in the north of the city, and worked their way south house by house. Tom says: "I would describe Fallujah as like driving in a car, and then the car hits a patch of ice and starts to spin out of control. So you turn the wheels into the skid. It's instinctual. It was a very dangerous environment. In such situations, it's very obvious you are mortal. I would honestly tell myself, in some of those hairy situations, that everybody dies sometimes, and that sometimes, for the good of the whole, you have to put yourself at risk, or send others into risky situations."

Tom came across ancient philosophy when he was twenty-seven, and took a graduate degree in Humanities. Through that, Tom encountered Marcus Aurelius, and read his *Meditations*. He says: "I liked the fact he was a soldier. I liked the fact he was writing for himself. It wasn't an outreach program. He was trying to work out how to conduct his own life. I think people should show how to live by example, not by forcing other people to believe what you believe." Tom took Aurelius, Epictetus, and Seneca with him during recent tours in Iraq and Central Asia, and read them whenever he had a spare moment to himself. He says philosophical ideas and techniques often gave him strength to cope with dangerous situations:

> I feel a strong sense of duty, it's one of the key reasons I'm into Stoicism. People who have served, who have been in conflict, they know what it's like. They don't want to go into conflict, and they don't want to have been there. They know it's not like the movies, that there's no glory in it. They're just doing a job. Sometimes you're in situations you don't like, but you have a job to do. Most soldiers love to complain. I try not to complain about what I'm asked to do.

Tom retired from the Marines in 2008, and returned home to his wife and his newly purchased home — six and a half acres near Dallas, Texas. He says: "I want to come back, settle, and live a peaceful life. I've been doing some work with the online Stoic community, which I'd like to see expand." But Tom's plans didn't work out like that. He tells me, at the end of our interview, that he had discovered the day before that he had a brain tumor. He said: "The doctors confirmed it yesterday. I haven't told my wife yet. I'm going to tell her after Christmas [the interview took place on December 22]. I don't want to spoil her Christmas. She might not like me keeping it from her, but that's just how it is. Then the doctors want to operate on me as soon as possible, so that will be the first week of January."

I am somewhat stunned, and say how sorry I am to hear it. I ask him how he feels about it. He says: "Well, it's not what you want to hear. That's why I was thinking about the house: Will my wife be provided for, if something happened to me? In fact, the mortgage is insured, so if something happens, my wife would get to keep the house." I ask how serious the tumor is. He says:

It's difficult to get a straight answer from the doctors. I've done several tours in Iraq and Afghanistan. There have been several situations I've been in where it's been likely I would be hit. And I have been injured five times in my career. But I still never believed I would die in those situations. With this situation, it's different. For one thing, it's not immediate. I also know I'm likely to be injured. I've already suffered the loss of some language skills. I've also had some memory issues. A friend of mine passed away in 2007, it was almost exactly the same thing. He had surgery on a tumor in December, and by August he had gone. So I may have around six months left.

I ask him, tentatively, what his attitude is to the prospect of dying. He says:

A part of me thinks "This is your fate," like Socrates facing his death. Another part of me thinks the doctors are here for a reason, that they could help me. Marcus Aurelius says something like, you could have a day left, or ten years left, but everyone has to go sometime. That's not being courageous, it's just accepting the inevitable. Statistically, it doesn't look good — if everyone in history has died, then it's pretty likely it will happen to me too. I would prefer it not be tomorrow, but it's not something I have control over.

Does he believe in an afterlife? "I think so, but there might not be. Again, Marcus Aurelius says, as I remember it, 'If there is a God, be comforted. If we're just atoms, then you won't feel anything anyway.' If there is a God, I am sure he will understand the way I think, and why I think like I do." Would he say the news has changed how he thinks?

I guess people should think constantly about the life they lead. Am I the kind of person I'd like to be? Have I misled anyone? There are things I have no control over — the past, or the future. I get caught up in life like everyone else. I don't always think first, but I try to review myself and my actions. I am a work in progress. Whether I get to complete that work in progress is not up to me. But I will try now in a more expedited fashion. I would like to have time to write my own version of the *Meditations*, with advice on how to live, for my son to read.

So, as a Stoic, should he fight his situation, or accept it? "The two aren't mutually exclusive. It's like going into battle. I accept that I might die, but it doesn't mean that I won't go down without a fight. If it's not my time, then I'll have fought through it. If it's my time, then I'll go without crying."

Tom went into surgery on January 4, two weeks after our interview. After initially making a good recovery, his condition worsened, and he went into a coma. He died on the morning of January 26, 2010.

Is There Such a Thing as a Good Death?

Can dying be a spiritual exercise? The ancient Greeks believed so. In fact, for them, dying was *the* spiritual exercise, the one for which all other exercises were preparatory. To philosophize, as Socrates put it, "is to practise dying."[1] Seneca believed "It takes a whole life to learn how to die."[2] Marcus Aurelius agreed: "Even dying is part of the business of life, and there too no more is required than to see the moment's work well done."[3] For ancient philosophers the moment we face death was the ultimate test of the strength of our philosophical practice. Have we really transformed ourselves and attained unshakeable tranquillity, or were we just talking? How well do we die? We hear, in Plato's *Phaedo*, that in his last hours Socrates was every inch the philosopher. The dramatic scene is laid out by Plato with consummate skill: Socrates's friends surround him, sobbing; his wife, Xanthippe, is wailing so uncontrollably that she has to be led from the room; the executioner waits to one side, holding a cup of hemlock.

And there, amid this emotional turmoil, is Socrates: "...his mien and his language were so noble and so fearless in the hour of death that to me he appeared blessed."

There is something deeply theatrical about Socrates's death — Plato, after all, initially wanted to be a tragic playwright. There is nothing tragic about his death, however. In some ways, the *Phaedo* is an anti-tragedy. All the elements of a tragedy are there — the injustice, the murder, the weeping friends and family, the hero dying before his time. And yet in this case, the hero is obstinately insisting that nothing bad is happening to him and everyone should stop crying. That is the message of the *Phaedo*: death is not an evil. Socrates tries to convince his friends that death is not an evil by "proving" to them that the soul is immortal, and then describing the fate of the soul after death. The *Phaedo* was meant to be sort of a map for the soul, to prepare it for its journey, and some Greeks and Romans read it before they died, just as some Buddhists have the *Tibetan Book of the Dead* read to them on their deathbeds as a preparation for the soul's journey.

Socrates tells us that after death, the *psyche* leaves the prison of the body, and journeys up into the heavens "to converse with pure souls." Then it comes to a place of judgment, where souls that are still attached to material things are reincarnated, after forgetting their past lives, while those who have purified themselves with philosophy "live henceforth altogether without the body, in mansions fairer far than these, which may not be described." But where the *Tibetan Book of the Dead* exhibits a brazenly confident knowledge of the exact stages of the soul's journey, Socrates says rather less certainly: "I do not mean to affirm that the description which I have given is exactly true — a man of sense ought hardly to say that. But I do say that, in as much as the soul is shown to be immortal, he may venture to think not improperly or unworthily, that something of the kind is true." Death, then, is not an evil according to Socrates, because the soul is (probably) immortal and will finally attain union with God after leaving the body. Death is, in fact, the end of the philosopher's long searching after truth, the moment when his or her quest for God finally reaches a climax.

Therefore, says Socrates, "Will he not depart with joy? Surely he will, my friend, if he is a true philosopher."

THE GOOD EPICUREAN DEATH

But what if you don't believe in the afterlife, or aren't sure what happens to the soul after death? Is there still such a thing as a "good death"? Epicureans didn't think the soul survived after death, but they still insisted that death was not an evil, and that the wise man or woman could "die well." Death cannot harm us because harm exists in unpleasant sensations, they argued, and once we are dead we don't experience anything, therefore death does not harm us, and is not an evil. A "good death" for Epicureans is one where we take our leave of life calmly and in good cheer, surrounded by our friends and fondly reminiscing about all the good times we have shared, without any unnecessary anxieties about the afterlife, safe in the knowledge that death is "more peaceful than the deepest sleep," as Lucretius puts it.

An example of such a death might be the passing of David Hume, the eighteenth-century philosopher and atheist. In his sixties, after a long and distinguished career as an essayist, historian, and philosopher, Hume fell ill with a disorder of the bowels that was probably cancer. His friend, the philosopher Adam Smith, tells us that Hume initially fought the disease. But the symptoms returned, and "from that moment he gave up all thoughts of recovery, but submitted with the utmost cheerfulness, and the most perfect complacency and resignation" to his death. When Smith visited him shortly before his death, Hume remarked cheerfully: "I have done every thing of consequence which I ever meant to do; and I could at no time expect to leave my relations and friends in a better situation than that in which I am now likely to leave them. I therefore have all reason to die contented." In his last days, we read that Hume was "quite free from anxiety, impatience, or low spirits and passes his time very well with the assistance of amusing books." He died "in such a happy composure of mind, that nothing could exceed it."[4] But what if we haven't "done every thing of consequence" which we "ever meant to do"? In that case, surely death is an evil? We might agree that, lacking proof of an afterlife, death is certainly what Albert Ellis would call a "pain in the ass," particularly if it cuts us down in our youth, before we have enjoyed what's normally considered a long life. Then again, what's a long life? I'm now thirty-six, which means if I existed during any other time or place, I would be lucky to have made it this far.

BETTER AND WORSE DEATHS

Even if we disagree with the Greek philosophers, and insist that death is an evil, we can still agree that there are "better" and "worse" deaths. Few of us can choose what we die of, but some of us can choose, to some extent, the manner of our departure, and having the ability to control the process, even to a limited extent, seems to give the dying some peace and satisfaction in their final weeks and days. The contemporary British thinker Charles Leadbetter lost both his parents in the autumn of 2009. But he says (in a speech he gave in 2010), that they had "utterly different deaths": his father's death was a "bad death," while his mother's death was a "good death." His father died

> in a dreadful ward, Ward 3 of Airedale General Hospital. The room in which he died had stained ceiling tiles, masses of equipment every-where, nothing that relieved the standardization and monotony. It wasn't in any sense clean. When my mother visited my father, she would clamber over the equipment to give him a kiss, and just for a moment, this dreadful ward was brought to life with intimacy. Yet the image of her clambering over the equipment to give him a kiss summed up what was wrong with the situation: all that clutter was in the way, it should be cleared, to make room for intimacy.

Charles's mother fell ill a few days after his father died, and she was taken to Bradford Royal Infirmary.

> Out of a determined rationality, she decided she wanted to die. But she was in a very good hospital, and the staff there wanted to keep

her alive as a matter of passion. When they brought her all the drugs to keep her alive, she asked them, "Can't you just give me one big pill [to let me die]?" And they said, "No, we can't do that"…Then she realized, if she stopped taking her drugs, she would die. So finally they moved her to a nursing home, where she died, just after they'd given her her cornflakes at 9:30 in the morning. The signatures of my mother's death are a sense of coming together, of achievement, of looking a situation squarely in the face and deciding what she wanted to do. There's no doubt she was in charge of it. She was in a system in which she had little control, but she had navigated her way through it to find the death that suited her. In the end, this was a death in which she was the main protagonist. The main protagonists in my father's death were nurses and doctors. They were the heroes, heroines, and villains. The main protagonist in my mother's death was my mother.

Leadbetter concludes: "There's way too much bad death in our present system. Fifty percent of complaints in the NHS are to do with the way people die. There's not enough good deaths, where the script can be written by the person dying…What we need is a way for people to write their own scripts."[5] Perhaps so — although it depends if we have decided to die or not, doesn't it? If we have decided to do everything we possibly can to battle our illness, for the sake perhaps of our family, then inevitably we grant a lot of control over our lives to doctors.

Choosing a Death

The idea of writing the script of one's death, of "navigating one's way" through dying, is very Stoic. The Stoics were the pioneers of dying as the ultimate lifestyle choice. Seneca wrote: "Just as I choose a ship to sail in or a house to live in, so I choose a death for my passage through life."[6] Just as we saw Socrates, in the *Phaedo*, masterfully stage-managing his own death, defining it, using it as an opportunity to express his values, so the Stoics tried to "choose the script" of their own deaths. They tried to turn their own deaths into Stoic assertions of their dignity and autonomy in the face of the uncontrollable. We read in Diogenes Laertius, for example, of the last moments of Zeno of Citium, the founder of Stoicism, who, as an old man, tripped and broke his toe upon leaving the Stoic school. He beat on the ground and cried out: "I come of my own accord, why then call me?" And then he killed himself, either by holding his breath, or by starving himself. His successor, Cleanthes, likewise starved himself to death, when he fell ill in his advanced years, and decided that he had lived long enough. Other Stoics chose to die rather than allowing themselves to be captured or killed by tyrants: Cato the Younger stabbed himself in the stomach rather than let himself be captured by the tyrant Julius Caesar. Seneca slit his wrists rather than be murdered by the troops of Nero. Their suicides were, for them, an expression of defiant freedom and self-determination in the face of tyranny. These Stoics tried to write their own scripts for their deaths, and there was certainly something theatrical or even histrionic in their deaths, as if they are consciously playing the role of Socrates, as laid down in Plato's masterful prose.

And yet their actual deaths were sometimes not as well rehearsed and smoothly produced as Plato's fiction. Seneca's death, for example, initially followed the Socratic model: Seneca calmly accepted the news he must die, and scolded his weeping relatives for letting their emotions get the better of them. But then the scene rather fell apart. Seneca slit his wrists, but the blood flowed out too slowly to kill him. So he slit the veins in his knees and legs, but that still didn't kill him. So he took a poison, but it moved too slowly through his blood. Finally, to end what the historian Tacitus described as the "tedious process of dying," he was carried into a hot bath, where he rather pathetically "anointed" his servants with water, before eventually suffocating in the steam.[7] The lesson in the poignant, slightly farcical manner of Seneca's death is that there's always a tension between our attempts to control our death and make it a "good death" (i.e., an expression of our autonomy and dignity), and the fact that, ultimately, this is Death. It defies our ability to manage it.

Is Suicide a Sin?

The ancient Stoics, it must be said, seemed fairly blasé about suicide, apparently believing it's fine to take our lives whenever we find them intolerable or even uncomfortable. Seneca writes: "If you like, live; if you don't like, you can go back where you came from." But do we have the right to take our own life? If so, under what circumstances? Isn't choosing to die a rejection of the circumstances that God has given us to live in, and therefore a Stoic sin? This was certainly Socrates's position in the *Phaedo*. He says that humans are the "possessions of God," and therefore our lives are not our own to take: "a man should wait, and not take his own life until God summons him, as he is now summoning me." Socrates didn't see his own death as suicide: he has been ordered to drink hemlock by the city of Athens, so he drinks it. It's an execution. But of course, in some ways Socrates is choosing to die, by choosing not to flee Athens, as his friends urged him to do. He is obeying God's summons to death, he suggests. The Stoics also defended suicide in instances where God has apparently "summoned" us to die. We should wait, as Marcus Aurelius puts it, "like a soldier waiting for the signal to retire from life's battlefield."[8] But how do we know when God has summoned us? A manic-depressive might believe God summons them six times a day. If even a broken toe can be taken as a summons from God, who of us would make it to adulthood?

The Stoic defense of suicide, such as it was, had a profound impact on Roman law, which asserted that choosing the manner of one's departure from life is a person's right, and to deprive someone of that right is worse than killing him. This legal acceptance of suicide continued in the early centuries of Christianity. After all, the Bible contained no clear condemnation of suicide. Although most of the seven suicides in the Bible happen to "bad men" (the worst being Judas Iscariot), not all are bad: Samson, for example, is still considered a hero of Judaism and Christianity despite the fact that he took his own life. It was only when Christianity became the official religion of the Roman Empire that attempts were made to legislate against suicide. The Christian prohibition of suicide began with St. Augustine in the fourth century AD, who returned to Socrates's original point that we are the possession of God, therefore our lives are not ours to take. In the sixth century, the Catholic Church had begun to legislate against suicide, forbidding priests from giving mass to the self-killed, or from burying them in holy ground.

By the twelfth century, medieval theologians frequently revisited the issue of suicide and explained why it was a sin. As they did so, they were engaging in a fight with the Stoics. Indeed, the word "suicide," from the Latin neologism *suicidium*, was first coined in a twelfth-century religious tract written against Seneca's position on self-killing.[9] We see these tensions between Stoic and Christian attitudes to suicide reemerge during the Renaissance, when Seneca enjoyed a return to great popularity. The most famous dramatic speech in English literature, from Shakespeare's *Hamlet*, is really a discussion of whether the Stoics or the Christians are right on the issue of the "right to die":

> To be, or not to be: that is the question:
> Whether 'tis nobler in the mind to suffer
> The slings and arrows of outrageous fortune,
> Or to take arms against a sea of troubles,
> And by opposing end them?

By the eighteenth century, as Christianity declined as a cultural force in Europe, and people's belief in the supernatural began to weaken, philosophers and writers dared to voice their support for people's right to kill themselves, should life become unbearable. David Hume, for example, attempted in an essay called "On Suicide," written in 1755, to "restore men to their native liberty by...showing that [suicide] may be free from every imputation of guilt, or blame, according to the sentiments of the ancient philosophers." Hume argues that "such is our natural horror of death... no man ever threw away life while it was worth keeping." But Hume did not dare to publish his defense of suicide in his lifetime — his essay was published posthumously in 1783. The debate carries on in our time: as I write this, a commission in Britain has just recommended the government legalize assisted suicide. The argument is still split between the Stoic and Epicurean defense of the right to choose death, and the Christian and Platonic insistence on the sacredness of life. Perhaps the Stoics are winning, as the baby boomers embrace their idea of dying as the ultimate lifestyle choice.

AND THEN?

What awaits us after death? Does our soul fly up to palaces of pure light, to be judged and assigned a new body? Or does our consciousness fizzle out and our body decompose back into the atomic stew? Or does something else happen — something completely different from what we have imagined? Modern philosophers have tended to assume that death is the end. I know of few Western philosophers today who seriously defend a belief in life after death. William James, the philosopher and psychologist (and brother of the novelist Henry James), did try to do so, and spent a lot of time investigating spiritual mediums and near-death experiences when he was president of the Society for Psychical Research. Academics typically view this aspect of his research as a cranky hobby, not to be confused with his more serious academic output. But the reason I think William James is such a wonderful thinker is that he was open to the variety of human experience. He did not rule out any experience as unworthy of attention or investigation, and insisted that philosophy and psychology should consider all the available data — objective and subjective. And people have some pretty weird experiences. They have out-of-body experiences, near-death experiences, precognition and telepathic connection experiences, mystic visions, flashes of inspiration, prophetic dreams, memories of past lives (such experiences might be imaginary, but they seem significant to the people who experience them). Even sober academics have such experiences, though they rarely admit it in public conferences.[10]

At the beginning of this book, I said I'd managed to overcome the emotional disorders that affected me in my teens and early twenties thanks to practicing cognitive therapy and ancient philosophy. This is true, but it's not all of the truth. In fact, what initially helped me to see through my problems was what you might call a vision, or a near-death experience. In 2001, I travelled to Norway, where some of my family come from, to go skiing in the mountains of the Peer Gynt region. On the first morning of my visit, I flew through a fence on the side of a black slope and fell about thirty feet, breaking my left leg and three vertebrae, and knocking myself unconscious. When I came to, I saw a bright white light, and felt filled with ecstasy. Up until that moment, I had, for several years, suffered from post-traumatic stress disorder. I was terrified that I had permanently damaged myself and would be psychologically wounded for the rest of my life. Yet that moment, lying on the side of the mountain in a pool of my own blood, I felt sure there is something in all of us that cannot be damaged, something immeasurable and invulnerable that is always within us. I had forgotten this, and as a result I went begging for other people's approval and other external validations of my worth. I realized, in that moment, there was no need to worry or beg. Others' approval or disapproval couldn't add to or take away from that treasure within. I just had to trust in it, and stop grasping anxiously at externals.

For the next few weeks and months, I felt wonderful. I was in hospital, patched up and incredibly weak, but psychically I felt restored, strong, and full of love (even when I wasn't on morphine). And, in those few weeks after the fall, I somehow knew that the experience I'd had was described in ancient philosophy, particularly in Socrates and the Stoics, who spoke of trusting in the soul within rather than grasping at externals. To quote Montaigne: "We are all of us richer than we think we are; but we are taught to borrow and to beg... [and yet] we need little doctrine to live at our ease; and Socrates teaches us, that this is in us, and the way to find it, and how to use it." After a few months, however, the experience faded from my memory. I got caught up in life again, and I found some of the old fears, anxieties, and depressive thoughts coming back. I decided that the original epiphany wasn't enough, that I needed a more systematic way to encode those insights into new automatic habits. So I did the CBT course, and discovered how much CBT owes to ancient philosophy. That's how I came to study ancient philosophy, and how I came to write this book: it's all thanks to my inability to ski in a straight line down a mountain.

I don't know what happened to me that day. I really don't. I can think of secular interpretations: perhaps the accident finally gave me an opportunity to be cared for by others, which I had denied myself by not really talking about my depression with my friends and family. Perhaps the shock of the accident jolted my brain and kick-started its natural regenerative powers. I can also think of spiritual explanations: God helped me, or my guardian *daemon*, or some local mountain-spirit. I really have no idea. But for a moment, I felt sure that there is something in us that can never die, something that is pure awareness and love. I wish I could feel it again.

Extracurricular Appendices

Appendix 1.
Is Socrates Overoptimistic about Human Reason?

IN THIS FIRST APPENDIX, I want to go back to chapter 1, and deal further with the challenge that Socrates and his descendants were overoptimistic in their assessment of human rationality. The ancient Greek philosophers suggested we can know ourselves, we can change ourselves, and can become wiser and happier through the daily practice of philosophy. This is the hope at the heart of philosophy, the humanities, and also of cognitive therapy. But is it true?

The idea has certainly come in for something of a battering in the last twenty years. Psychologists like Daniel Kahneman, John Bargh, and Dan Ariely have argued that, while humans do possess the capacity for consciousness, self-reflection, and rational choice, it's very limited and weak. These psychologists suggest that humans possess two thinking systems: a conscious, reflective, "slow" system, and an intuitive, emotional, "fast" system. We use the "conscious-reflective system" for some higher-level tasks, like maths, planning for the future, negotiations, and emotional self-control. But we use the automatic-emotive system a lot more, because it's faster, and it uses less energy. Kahneman, Bargh, Ariely, and others have shown how much of our thinking is automatic, and how often, when we think we're making conscious and rational decisions, we're actually following automatic cues or biases. We don't know what we're doing, or why we're doing it. Our conscious system thinks it's in charge, but it's not. It's less the "steersman" of our soul, and more a helpless passenger.

So far, I completely agree. And so would the ancient Greeks. They certainly didn't think humans were born perfectly rational and autonomous creatures. Plato insisted that we have rational and irrational systems in our mind, and that the irrational system is usually in charge. So did Aristotle, who suggested the irrational part of our psyche "fights and resists" the reasoning part, so that when our reason wants to move one way, our irrational mind moves us the other. Epictetus thought most human actions were entirely automatic. He told his students: "we are random and headlong...some impression strikes me, and straightaway I act on it." Socrates himself, although arguably more optimistic than any of his descendants, still insisted that most humans sleepwalk their way through life, never stopping to ask themselves why they're doing what they're doing. The Greeks were very pessimistic about human nature in its raw form. But they expressed a cautious optimism that humans could be trained to become more rational, more conscious, and more philosophical in their responses.

As I've said earlier, this involves a two-fold process working with both systems of the mind. Firstly, you bring your automatic beliefs and responses into consciousness, using techniques like Socratic self-questioning and the journal. And then you turn your new conscious insights into automatic habits of thinking and behaving, using techniques like memorization, repetition, role models, and some of the other exercises we've explored. So philosophy works with both the conscious-reflective system *and* the automatic-emotive system. It makes the automatic conscious, and the conscious automatic. And it also uses culture — most Greek philosophers suggested we should build philosophical communities or even philosophical societies to turn ideas into collective social habits of behavior.

Is this a completely far-fetched project? I don't think so. It's the basis of Cognitive Behavioral Therapy (CBT), which had a huge influence on later cognitive psychologists like Kahneman, Bargh, and Ariely. In fact, Beck helped to create the idea of the automatic mind these later psychologists rely on, through his research into unconscious self-talk in the 1970s. CBT has proven, I would suggest, that people *can* learn to become conscious of their automatic beliefs, and they can learn to challenge these automatic beliefs rationally, and then to create new automatic beliefs and habits. Through this process, they can learn to think and react differently to the world, and thereby overcome emotional disorders like depression and social anxiety. I've had firsthand experience of that. I put this cautious case for optimism to Kahneman, Bargh, and Ariely in interviews (or in the case of Kahneman, at a public talk he gave in London). They seemed to agree with me. Kahneman said: "In the case of CBT, yes, clearly people can be trained and 'System 1' [as he calls the automatic-emotive system] can be modified. In fact, we're continuously learning and adapting. CBT is a way of teaching emotional responses to change. That can be trained. What's unlikely to change is our capacity to assess the story we construct. You're not going to change how System 1 constructs stories."[1] Of course, there's a difference between the experiments that behavioral economists construct, and the real-life emotional crises with which CBT engages. Kahneman, Bargh, and Ariely typically look at decisions made in laboratories, where subjects are asked mathematical questions or posed hypothetical situations, and in those instances it appears people make the same cognitive mistakes over and over. But those mistakes don't really cost them anything in terms of their personal flourishing — unlike the cognitive biases that lead to serious disorders like depression, anxiety, rage, or alcoholism. If your cognitive biases give you a terrible temper, which in turn damages your relationships, then those biases are really costing you in terms of your personal flourishing. Likewise, if you habitually misinterpret your loved one's behavior to fit a jealous "narrative," and consistently alienate your partner as a result, that cognitive bias is costing you, and you have a very strong motive to deal with it.

In other words, I think humans *do* have the capacity to correct their habitual cognitive fallacies, if those fallacies are shown to be both wrong and damaging to their personal flourishing. But it's very hard, and takes a lot of energy, effort, and humility (no one likes to admit their story is wrong). So people only do it when it's really necessary, when it's obvious their present automatic course in life is harming them. In those instances, we *can* change our course. The broader point is that emotions are crucial to the practice of philosophy. We'll only really work to change ourselves if we have a *motive*, an emotional push to change ourselves, and this emotional push will probably come from some sort of crisis in our life and our relationships, and from our emotions telling us that something is deeply wrong with our present life-trajectory.

Appendix 2. The Socratic Tradition and Non-Western Philosophical Traditions

IN THIS BOOK I have put forward what I would call a "soft universalism," which claims that the cognitive theory of the emotions which Socrates and his descendants put forward fits with the biological facts of human nature, regardless of our particular culture. However, I have also been at pains to show that the tradition goes off in several different directions when it comes to a theory of the good life, and that it's dangerous to argue that any comprehensive theory of the good life is objectively true and should be imposed on a whole society.

Nonetheless, some readers might take issue with the limited universalism, essentialism, and ahistoricism of my claims. Am I really suggesting that the Socratic tradition fits, always has fit, and always will fit with human nature? Isn't that to impose Western, individualist, rationalist ethics onto the infinite variety of human experience? I would make three points in response. Firstly, my theory is not entirely ahistorical or universal: I don't think a Socratic approach to the emotions is appropriate in primitive, animist cultures. Socrates represents a key moment in the very recent emergence of a post-animist worldview in Western culture. He marks the shift from understanding one's passions as experiences caused by spirit beings, as animist cultures do, to understanding one's emotions as the product of one's own beliefs, which are under one's own control. This moment is the birth of the "self" and of individual responsibility. In an animist culture, emotional disorders are externalized and attributed to spirits, and the cure is also externalized, and carried out by a shaman. In a post-animist culture, emotional disorders are attributed to one's own beliefs, and the cure is carried out by yourself, or perhaps by yourself in partnership with a psychotherapist. Both these paths may work just as well, and it wouldn't necessarily be appropriate to try to import a post-animist worldview into an animist culture. So in that sense, the Socratic tradition is not universal and ahistorical, but rather emerges at a particular stage in human evolution (and it's quite a recent moment, only two thousand five hundred years ago).

Secondly, the Socratic tradition is itself historical and has taken many different forms at different times. Athenian Stoicism was different from middle period Roman Stoicism and the Stoicism of late antiquity, and each subsequent age has shaped its own version of that philosophy — the same is true for other philosophies in the Socratic tradition. All those versions might follow the first three steps of the Socratic tradition (humans can know themselves, change themselves, and create new habits of thinking, feeling, and acting) but they will take the fourth step in many different directions, according to individuals' personalities and the particular pressures of their time.

Thirdly, I would argue that the cognitive theory of the emotions on which the Socratic project rests does not only appear in Western philosophy, so I don't think it's an entirely Western construct. It's apparent in other philosophical traditions, particularly in Buddhism. We meet it on the first page of the *Dhammapada*, where the Buddha says: "'He abused me, he beat me, he defeated me, he robbed me,' — in those who harbor such thoughts hatred will never cease. 'He abused me, he beat me, he defeated me, he robbed me' — in those who do not harbor such thoughts hatred will cease." Buddhism also seems to share the Stoic ideal of the sage, who has turned themselves into a fortress against the passions: the Buddha speaks of the sage "making his thought firm like a fortress," while Marcus Aurelius talks of retreating to the "inner citadel" of the mind. Both traditions suggest we should free ourselves from attachment and aversion to external things, including to life itself, so that we preserve a calm benevolence in all circumstances. Both traditions also emphasize the idea of mindfulness, of guarding your mind so you're not swept away by automatic emotional responses (this is also a theme in Judaism, Christianity, and Islam). But Buddhism, to its credit, developed a whole arsenal of mindfulness techniques involving the breath which the Greeks seemed unaware of, despite the fact that their word for the soul, *pneuma*, is also the word for breath. Many modern Stoics use meditation in their practice, and we've also seen Greek and Buddhist therapeutic techniques combined in mindfulness CBT.[1] The Epicurean (and Stoic) technique of focusing on the moment, and of "not dragging up sufferings that are over," has obvious counterparts with Buddhism, particularly with Zen Buddhism, while the Skeptic technique of trying to go beyond all mental constructions also has some resonance with Eastern philosophy — indeed, Pyrrho came up with his Skeptic philosophy after travelling to India with Alexander the Great.

But there are also important differences between the Buddhist and Socratic traditions. Compassion does not play a major role in the Socratic tradition, while of course the cultivation of compassion is a key part of the Buddhist tradition. And Buddhism was originally a monastic philosophy, which encouraged its followers to leave society and set up their own religious communes — this is different from Stoicism, whose followers were actively political, but similar to the Pythagoreans, with whom Buddhists share a belief in reincarnation. Finally, what Buddhism managed to do, which Greek philosophies never did, is combine esoteric teachings with myths, rituals, and festivals for the masses, which is why, perhaps, Buddhism remains a mass religion and a living tradition today.

We can also draw parallels between Heraclitus's and the Stoics' concept of the *Logos*, and Taoism's concept of the *Tao*. Both Heraclitus and Lao Tzu, who may have been contemporaries, spoke of a divine law of nature which unites opposites. Both suggested that the sage transcends dualities to bring themselves into harmony with the ebb and flow of nature. And both suggested the sage should withdraw from politics and live in quiet obscurity. Lao Tzu's great rival in Chinese thought, Confucius, could perhaps be compared to Aristotle: both Aristotle and Confucius emphasize the idea that the habitual practice of the virtues can perfect our natures, and both express optimism that politics and philosophy can be brought together to enhance the welfare of the masses. Indeed, the Chinese government's rediscovery of Confucius and the "politics of well-being" can be compared to Western policy-makers' rediscovery of Aristotle.

The "religions of the Book" — Christianity, Judaism, and Islam — all contain figures who attempted to bring together their own traditions with the Socratic tradition, such as Philo of Alexandria in Judaism; Al-Kindi, Avicenna, and Averroes in Islam; and Clement of Alexandria and Thomas Aquinas in Christianity. All these religions also contained figures who condemned the Socratic tradition for its optimism in human reason and its confidence in the possibility of happiness here on earth. Jesus, who declared he was the *Logos* made flesh, was in some ways a philosopher as much as a prophet. We could compare his great message that the "kingdom of heaven is within" to Socrates's injunction to look within and know thyself. Jesus's parable of the houses built on rock and sand also reminds me of Marcus Aurelius's injunction to "be like the cliff against which the waves break, but which stands firm."[2] Medieval Christians celebrated the Stoics, and saw Seneca as almost a saint, and the Stoic concept of the City of God had an influence on Christianity, and on St. Augustine in particular.

But there are big differences as well: Jesus appeared to believe the end of the world was rapidly approaching, and that humanity was heading for a final apocalyptic battle between Good and Evil. He also believed in demons, and in a supremely evil being called Satan sent to test humanity. This is all quite far from the cheerful rationality of Greek philosophy. And Jesus's followers, from St. Paul on, showed a hostility to learning, culminating in orgies of anti-intellectualism like the sacking of the library of Alexandria and the murder of Hypatia, one of the great philosophers of the ancient world (to be fair, the Romans, including Marcus Aurelius, committed their fair share of Christian massacres). Although Christianity, like Stoicism, opened its doors to the entire brotherhood of man, it still retained the aggressive tribalism of the Old Testament: if you don't accept that Jesus Christ is the only Son of God, and the exclusive doorway to heaven, then you're going to hell for ever. I've never believed that. But I recognize that, in terms of creating spiritual communities bound together by collective practices, myths, rituals, and festivals, and in terms of encouraging charitable activities, Christianity leaves Greek philosophy far behind.

In conclusion, then, I would suggest that the cognitive theory of the emotions fits with our biological nature. For that reason, the Socratic tradition, which contains many interesting ideas and techniques for self-transformation and social transformation based on this theory, is likely to be of interest and use to many cultures. Nonetheless, there are valid criticisms of the Socratic tradition, such as its overemphasis on the self-sufficient rational individual and its lack of compassion and charity — criticisms I myself have made in this book. Indeed, there is a whole tradition in Western philosophy which is diametrically opposed to the Socratic tradition, which we shall examine in the final appendix.

Appendix 3. Socrates and Dionysus

FINALLY, I WANT TO CONSIDER a philosophical tradition that is hostile to and critical of the Socratic tradition. I call it the "Dionysiac tradition," and would include in it Romantic thinkers like William Blake, Friedrich Nietzsche, J. G. Hamann, D. H. Lawrence, Carl Jung, and Henry Miller.[1]

The virtues of the Socratic tradition are self-control, rationality, self-consciousness, and measure. The Socratic tradition typically puts forward a hierarchy of the psyche, in which the conscious, reasoning parts of the psyche are highest, and the intuitive, emotional, and appetitive parts of the *psyche* are considered lowest. Following this hierarchy, Socrates and his disciples suggest that the highest possible existence is the cerebral existence of the philosopher, as compared to the more physical or intuitive life of, say, the artist, the soldier, or the lover. The Dionysiac tradition celebrates a very different way of life. Where Socrates preaches self-control, Dionysus urges us to lose ourselves in sex, music, dancing, and ecstasy. Where Socrates preaches rationality and measure, Dionysus urges us to exceed all measure and constraint. One of his names was *ho lysios* — he who grants release.[2] He releases us from all prudence, caution, and temperance. Where Socrates preaches a conscious and scientific knowledge of the self, the followers of Dionysus celebrate the power of the unconscious, the intuitive, what D. H. Lawrence called "blood-knowledge," and the deep sense of vitality and joyous existence we get when we're dancing, or making love, or intoxicated. Dionysus and his followers would laugh at

Socrates and his huddle of philosophers, and their ridiculous assertion that "the unexamined life is not worth living." On the contrary, they would suggest, the more you examine life, the more it withers and dies under your microscope.

They would say that the last people you should turn to for advice on life are philosophers. Look at them: weak, pale, stammering creatures, visibly unhealthy, palpably out of touch with their bodies and their societies. Nature has cursed them with weakness and timidity, so they wreak their revenge on nature by constructing their own artificial and self-conscious version of happiness. "Only virtue is happiness," the philosophers insist, and cough. But we Dionysiacs know they're lying, we who know the genuine joy that comes from the body, from hunting and dancing and love. The next time a philosopher tells you to practice rationality and self-control, laugh at them and pull their beard.

I used to love the Dionysiac tradition. When I was at university studying English Literature, my favorite books were D. H. Lawrence's *The Rainbow* and Friedrich Nietzsche's *The Birth of Tragedy*. Nietzsche's book is a tirade against Socrates's optimistic rationality, which Nietzsche blames for killing off the old deep connection he claimed we once enjoyed with Dionysus. In place of Pan's wild dance, we now have "philosophy," "psychology," "scientific rationality," "economics," and other soul-killing inventions. We should revolt against the Enlightenment rationality that Socrates spawned, and return to the intuitive, physical, unconscious world of Dionysus. This sounded good to me back then (now it strikes me as funny that two such sickly and bookish intellectuals as Lawrence and Nietzsche should have made such a big thing of the body, strength, and virility).

Unfortunately, however, my teenage Dionysiac revels left me somewhat damaged. Dionysus is great for a party, but he's never there to pick up the bill. When I started to suffer from post-traumatic stress disorder, I turned to my favorite writer, D. H. Lawrence, for advice. It seemed to me that I was suffering from what Lawrence saw as the great sickness of modern civilization: overthinking. I was stuck in my head, stuck in repetitive negative thoughts, and was cut off from the deep vital springs of my unconscious, my "blood-knowledge," or some such thing. If only I could stop thinking! So what was the cure? Lawrence didn't really have a cure for the illness he diagnosed. In his novels, he is incredibly unsympathetic to anyone who's suffering from neuroses or trauma. We often meet damaged men in his books (he was writing during the First World War, when many young men came home traumatized), and we're typically told they are "broken," "dead," "empty," "destroyed," and that there's no hope for them. They should probably be put out of their misery. This was not much consolation to me. It made me think there was no hope for me either, and I should just kill myself. But I didn't. Instead, after a few years, I managed to get better thanks to ancient Greek philosophy and CBT, which showed me that what was causing me suffering was not a psychic wound in my Dionysiac life force, but my own beliefs. Through a Socratic process of self-examination, I became aware of my beliefs, and learned how to challenge them and change them. I got better through Socrates, not Dionysus.

Lawrence would hate CBT. He would say, "It's all in the head, in rationality, it doesn't connect to the deep springs of our life-blood. It's not the cure for our modern malaise — it's the sickness itself. It's just another attempt to control the savage beast of our psyche using our technocratic reason. It's the machine." Likewise, Nietzsche would look on Positive Psychology and its cult of happiness with genuine horror. "They're the Last Men of history," he would exclaim. "Out of the twilight of the gods, they have invented happiness." I have some sympathy with this view. There are more things in heaven and earth than are dreamt of in Positive Psychology. Nonetheless, I think Lawrence, Nietzsche, Jung, and the other irrationalists of that era put the cart before the horse. Our unconscious, our dream-life, our automatic-emotive system, follows our thoughts and beliefs. If our beliefs are toxic, then our entire psychic life will be toxic. And if we want to get healthier, we cannot do it by trying to escape from our heads, by trying to return to a primitive unconsciousness, as Lawrence tried to do. The answer is not to escape conscious thinking. It is to stop thinking stupidly, badly, destructively. When we do that, it means we can free our psyche from overthinking. We can start thinking less, and simply enjoy the moment, the body, the flow.

Socrates still has something to learn from Dionysus too. At the end of his life, Socrates told his followers he had a recurring dream telling him to "make and cultivate music."[3] He wasn't sure what the dream meant, but perhaps it was telling him that rational philosophy is not enough, and that sometimes we should pay homage to the wilder gods of our nature.

Notes

EPIGRAPH

Letter to Francesco Vettori, December 10, 1513.

1. MORNING ROLL CALL:
SOCRATES AND THE ART OF STREET PHILOSOPHY

1. I do not mean to single out my college tutors for criticism. They were exceptional academics who steered half of my year to Firsts. My criticisms are of the British university system as presently constituted. The number of undergraduates reporting mental health difficulties rose 450 percent over the past decade, according to the Higher Education Statistics Agency, while the dropout rate for undergraduates in 2011 was over 20 percent. Pastoral care in British universities is far behind what is provided in American universities. I also think the education provided at British universities is narrower and less conducive to human development: I would like to see less specialization forced on students, greater opportunity to study subjects other than one's degree (along the lines of the American system), more obvious support for students' mental health and well-being, and also the opportunity to consider and debate wider questions of life and how to live it well. Students have a great desire to discuss such questions: that's why two of the most popular courses at Harvard are Tal Ben-Shahar's Positive Psychology course and Michael Sandel's course on Justice. My ideal course would combine the best of these two courses: useful techniques from the science of well-being,

combined with the opportunity for ethical reasoning about the meaning of life.

2. The course was called "Overcoming Social Anxiety: Step by Step," by Dr. Thomas Richards.

3. You can find the interviews with Ellis, Beck, and other cognitive psychologists on my website, www.philosophyforlife.org.

4. Plato, *Apology*.

5. For more on the therapy of philosophy, see particularly Martha C. Nussbaum's *Therapy of Desire*.

6. Marcus Tullius Cicero, *Tusculan Disputations*.

7. Plato, *Apology*.

8. Michel de Montaigne, "On Physiognomy," *Essays*.

9. See, for example, John Bargh's *The Automaticity of Everyday Life*, Daniel Kahneman's *Thinking: Fast and Slow*, Philip Zimbardo's *The Lucifer Effect: Understanding How Good People Turn Evil*, and Dan Ariely's *Predictably Irrational: The Hidden Forces That Shape Our Decisions*. On the illusion of free will, see further discussion in chapter 6.

10. James Gross and Kateri McRae, "The Reason in Passion," chapter 10 in *Handbook of Self-Regulation: Research, Theory and Applications*.

11. Ost, "Cognitive Behavioural Therapy for Anxiety Disorders: 40 Years of Progress," *Nordic Journal of Psychiatry*, 2008; 62.

12. Hollon et al., "Treatment and Prevention of Depression," *Psychological Science in the Public Interest*, 2002; 3: 39–77. Some studies suggest that other forms of psychodynamic or talking therapy are just as effective as CBT in the treatment of emotional disorders. This suggests to me that the quality of the therapeutic relationship, and the Socratic process of guided self-examination in all talking therapies, is a key factor in recovery. Perhaps the various "talking therapies" may be more similar than their bitter internecine feuds suggest. They do, after all, emerge from the same Socratic and Hellenistic foundation. Freud's idea that the goal of therapy is bringing the "pleasure principle" into harmony with the "reality principle" is quite in line with Epicurean or Stoic therapy. See Douglas Kirsner, "Freud's Stoic Vision." Other psychotherapists, such as Alfred Adler and Carl Rogers, also used versions of the Socratic method.

13. From a talk at the LSE by Kahneman. See a transcript at www.philosophy forlife.org.

14. Epictetus, *Discourses*.
15. Aristotle, *Nichomachean Ethics*.
16. Zeno of Citium, founder of Stoicism, quoted in Diogenes Laertius's *Lives of the Philosophers*.
17. For a discussion of whether the Socratic tradition is universal, essential, and ahistorical, see the appendices.
18. David Hume, "The Skeptic," *Essays*.
19. Christopher Phillips, *Socrates Café: A Fresh Taste of Philosophy*.
20. Alain de Botton, "A Point of View: Justifying Culture," *BBC News* magazine, January 7, 2011, www.bbc.co.uk/news/magazine-12136511.
21. For interviews with Long and Nussbaum, go to www.philosophyfor life.org.
22. John Stuart Mill, *On Liberty*.
23. Sir Isaiah Berlin, "Two Concepts of Liberty," *Liberty*. For Sir Karl Popper's defense of pluralism, see *The Open Society and its Enemies*.
24. See chapter 12 for a discussion of this "Neo-Aristotelian consensus."
25. Quoted in Jules Evans, "Teaching Happiness: The Classes in Happiness That Are Helping Our Children," *The Times*, February 18, 2008.
26. Martin Seligman, *Flourish: A Visionary New Understanding of Happiness and Well-Being*.
27. On Comte and the rise of Positivism in the UK, see Thomas Dixon, *The Invention of Altruism*.
28. John Stuart Mill, *On Liberty*.
29. Cameron also established a "nudge unit" or "Behavioral Insights Team" to turn the behavioral science of Richard Thaler into public policy. Watch his TED talk, "The Next Age of Government," www.youtube .com/watch?v=3ELnyoso6vI. Ten minutes in, he pays homage to a bevy of psychologists who inform his political vision, including Martin Seligman, Daniel Kahneman, and Robert Cialdini.
30. See the Office for National Statistics report, "Measuring What Matters," June 7, 2011: "There were considerably more contributions concerning belief or religion, in particular Christianity, than we had expected."
31. While I support many aspects of the "politics of well-being," the idea that we can measure "national *eudaimonia*" seems to me dangerously reductive. *Eudaimonia* means "virtuous happiness." I don't think clipboard-wielding bureaucrats can measure virtue, and I find it

strange that David Cameron, prophet of "post-bureaucratic government," should have asked them to try.

32. Aristotle, *Nichomachean Ethics*.

33. See Amartya Sen, *The Idea of Justice*.

34. Lucius Annaeus Seneca, *Moral Letters to Lucius*.

2. EPICTETUS AND THE ART OF MAINTAINING CONTROL

1. See "A Woman's Burden," *Time* magazine, March 28, 2003.

2. *American Psychologist* devoted a whole issue (Vol 66:1, January 2011) to
the program.

3. Martin Seligman, *Flourish: A Visionary New Understanding of Happiness
and Well-Being*.

4. See the Institute of Psychiatry's 2010 report on the mental health of UK
military personnel in Iraq, and the 2004 survey of the mental health of
US military personnel by the Walter Reed Army Institute of Research.

5. Quoted from a speech Cornum gave to US troops in Kuwait, September
10, 2010, reported here: www.dvidshub.net/news/56064/former
-pow-visits-resiliency-campus-kuwait-talks-comprehensive-fitness#
.TtJB7XHNX24.

6. Quoted in Marcus Aurelius, *Meditations*.

7. Schizophrenia provides an interesting challenge to the Stoics' conten-
tion that we always have some choice and control over our thoughts.
Surely schizophrenia is proof that we don't always have control over
our thoughts. In fact, the Stoics thought some people might be so sick
that they are beyond the reach of philosophy and can't be held responsible for their thoughts and actions — another example is people with
dementia. Today, however, many people with schizophrenia have shown
that they can learn to take a more detached and rational attitude to their
psychotic beliefs and to the voices they hear, learning to see them not
as all-powerful deities but as thoughts which they can choose to obey
or not to obey. This seems to agree with Epictetus's suggestion that we
always (or almost always) have a choice how to react to our thoughts
and beliefs. See, for example, www.hearing-voices.org. See also Aaron
Beck et al., *Schizophrenia: Cognitive Theory, Research and Therapy*, for a
cognitive approach to psychosis.

8. US Army Leadership Manual FM 6-22.

3. Musonius Rufus and the Art of Fieldwork

1. Epictetus, *Discourses*.
2. This and subsequent quotes from Musonius Rufus, "On Training," *Lectures and Sayings*.
3. Iamblichus, *Life of Pythagoras*.
4. Quoted in HDF Kitto's *The Greeks*.
5. Plutarch, "Life of Lycurgus," *Parallel Lives*.
6. Lucius Annaeus Seneca, "On Anger," *Essays*.
7. Epictetus, *Discourses*.
8. Edward Gibbon, *The History of the Decline and Fall of the Roman Empire*.
9. James Pennebaker, *The Secret Life of Pronouns*.
10. See, for example, St. Paul's Epistle to the Ephesians: "we wrestle not against flesh and blood, but against principalities, against powers, against the rulers of the darkness of this world, against spiritual wickedness in high places."
11. See, for example, Denis Diderot's *The Nun* or Jeremy Bentham's *An Introduction to the Principles of Morals and Legislation*.
12. Walter Mischel and Ozlem Ayduk, "Will-Power in a Cognitive Affective Processing System: The Dynamics of Delay of Gratification," chapter 5 in *Handbook of Self-Regulation*, edited by Kathleen Vohs and Roy F. Baumeister.
13. For the correlation between self-control and success in life, see Moffitt et al., "A Gradient of Childhood Self-Control Predicts Health, Wealth and Public Safety," *PNAS*, January 24, 2011; and also Vohs, Finkenauer, and Baumeister, "The Sum of Friends' and Lovers' Self-Control Scores Predicts Relationship Quality," *Social Psychological and Personality Science*, September 24, 2010.
14. Albert Bandura and Daniel Cervone, "Self-Evaluative and Self-Efficacy Mechanisms Governing the Motivational Effects of Goal Systems," *Journal of Personality and Social Psychology*, Vol 45(5), 11/1983.
15. David Eagleman, *Incognito: The Secret Lives of the Brain*.
16. Roy F. Baumeister, Dianne M. Tice, and Mark Muraven, "Longitudinal Improvement of Self-Regulation through Practice: Building Self-Control Strength through Repeated Exercise," *Journal of Social Psychology* 139, 1999.
17. See www.quantifiedself.com.

18. Tim Ferriss, *The Four-Hour Body.*
19. Xenophon, *Memorabilia of Socrates.*
20. Ibid.
21. Quoted in Jules Evans, "Teaching Happiness: The Classes in Happiness That Are Helping Our Children," *The Times*, February 18, 2008.
22. The phrase is from Rudyard Kipling's poem "If."
23. Lord Robert Baden Powell, *Scouting for Boys.*
24. Lord Robert Baden Powell, *Life's Snags and How to Meet Them.*
25. Lord Robert Baden Powell, *Rovering to Success.*
26. See www.defense.gov/speeches/speech.aspx?speechid=1494.
27. Epictetus, *Discourses.*

4. Seneca and the Art of Managing Expectations

1. Lucius Annaeus Seneca, *Moral Letters to Lucius.*
2. T. S. Eliot, "Shakespeare and the Stoicism of Seneca," *Selected Essays.*
3. See, for example, Nicholas A. Christakis and James H. Fowler, *Connected: The Surprising Power of Our Social Networks and How They Shape Our Lives.*
4. Lucius Annaeus Seneca, "On Anger," *Essays.*
5. Ibid.
6. Ibid.
7. Lucius Annaeus Seneca, "Consolation to Marcia," *Essays.*
8. Lucius Annaeus Seneca, "On Anger," *Essays.*
9. Lucius Annaeus Seneca, "On Providence," *Essays.*
10. For more on Major Jarrett's Warrior Resilience course, go to www .resilience.army.mil/MRTfacilitators.html. You can also see a video of him talking about the course on my website www.philosophyforlife.org.
11. You can watch a video about the event at www.philosophyforlife.org.
12. See Matthew Arnold's essay "Marcus Aurelius."
13. Wen mentions his fondness for Aurelius's *Meditations* in an interview with Fareed Zakaria on CNN, September 29, 2008.
14. Martha C. Nussbaum, *Upheavals of Thought: The Intelligence of Emotions.*

5. Lunchtime Lesson:
Epicurus and the Art of Savoring the Moment

1. Tom Hodgkinson, *How to Be Free.*
2. Ibid.

3. These and all subsequent quotes by Epicurus are from his *Letters and Collected Sayings*.

4. Lucius Annaeus Seneca, *Moral Letters to Lucius*.

5. Alan Watts, *Alan Watts Teaches Meditation*.

6. In fact, A. C. Grayling's *Humanist Bible* draws liberally on Lucretius for its opening chapters.

7. The quotations from Lucretius are from the beautiful translation by A. E. Stallings, from the Penguin Classics edition.

8. Read my interview with Greenblatt at www.philosophyforlife.org.

9. De Botton's essay on the School of Life is in the *Idler* 42: Smash the System.

10. Jefferson's letters contain several declarations of Epicureanism; for example, in a letter to William Short of October 31, 1819, he wrote: "I too am an Epicurean. I consider the genuine (not the imputed) doctrines of Epicurus as containing everything rational in moral philosophy which Greece and Rome have left us."

11. On Christopher Hitchens's fondness for Epicureanism, see, for example: www.slate.com/articles/news_and_politics/fighting_words/2007/12/bah_hanukkah.html.

12. Jeremy Bentham, *An Introduction to the Principles of Morals and Legislation*.

13. Bentham's student, John Stuart Mill, was rather more nuanced in his definition of utility, and thought the Epicurean emphasis on pleasant feelings could be combined with a more Aristotelian belief that some forms of pleasure are higher and qualitatively better than others — though this of course begs the question "higher according to who?" See Mill's *Utilitarianism* for a discussion of this. Lord Layard thinks Mill should have stuck closer to Benthamite orthodoxy.

14. Layard called for a "new secular spirituality" in a talk he gave at the RSA, which you can listen to here: www.thersa.org/events/audio-and-past-events/2011/happiness-new-lessons.

15. Mauss et al., "Can Seeking Happiness Make People Unhappy? Paradoxical Effects of Valuing Happiness," *Emotion*, 2010.

16. At the Franco-British Council conference, "Beyond GDP," February 2, 2011.

17. At the RSA event mentioned above.

18. See C. Daniel Batson, *Altruism in Humans*, for an excellent exploration of this issue.

19. The exchange was at the RSA event, which you can hear at the link above.
20. John Stuart Mill, *Bentham*.
21. Some of the most "meaningful" experiences life has to offer involve pain: the heartache we feel for our children (not to mention the worry and exhaustion of taking care of them); or the pain of falling in love. Lucretius warned us that sexual love involves a lot of anxiety and frustration. But I prefer that to a dull life of untroubled self-sufficiency.
22. Angus Deaton, "The Financial Crisis and the Well-Being of Americans," Hicks Lecture, Oxford, May 16, 2011.
23. A quote from Layard's speech at the Franco-British Council conference, "Beyond GDP," February 2, 2011.
24. Nozick's happiness machine, or "experience machine" as he called it, is mentioned in his 1974 book, *Anarchy, State and Utopia*, although it was mentioned before that in science fiction, such as Aldous Huxley's *Brave New World*, Philip K. Dick's *Do Androids Dream of Electric Sheep?*, and Woody Allen's *Sleeper*.

6. Heraclitus and the Art of Cosmic Contemplation

1. You can listen to my interview with Mitchell at www.philosophyforlife .org.
2. In Sagan's wonderful TV series *Cosmos: A Personal Voyage*, which you can watch on YouTube.
3. I should say that the interpretation of Heraclitus's philosophy I have put forward is just my interpretation, and that some academics think Heraclitus was much more pessimistic about humans' ability to "know" the *Logos*.
4. Epictetus, *Discourses*.
5. Pierre Hadot, *Philosophy as a Way of Life*.
6. Marcus Aurelius, *Meditations*.
7. Stephen Hawking and Leonard Mlodinow, *The Grand Design*. Some quotes also from a Q&A with Hawking in the *Guardian*, May 15, 2011.
8. See Thomas Huxley, *On the Hypothesis That Animals Are Automata, and Its History*; Anthony R. Cashmore, *The Lucretian Swerve: The Biological Basis of Human Behaviour and the Criminal Justice System*; Francis Crick, *The Astonishing Hypothesis*.
9. For a functionalist account of human consciousness, see Hilary Putnam,

Minds and Machines; and Roy F. Baumeister, E. J. Masicampo, and Kathleen Vohs, *Do Conscious Thoughts Cause Behaviour*. See also Roger Penrose's critique of functionalism in *The Emperor's New Mind: Concerning Computers, Minds, and the Laws of Physics*.

10. Roger Penrose, *The Emperor's New Mind: Concerning Computers, Minds, and the Laws of Physics*.

11. See Stephen J. Gould's 1979 paper "The Spandrels of San Marco and the Panglossian Paradigm" and his extended argument about consciousness with the functionalist Steven Pinker.

12. See the famous conclusion of Dawkins's book, *The Selfish Gene*: "We are built as gene machines and cultured as meme machines, but we have the power to turn against our creators. We, alone on earth, can rebel against the tyranny of the selfish replicators." See also Dawkins's 2006 program for Discovery Science, *The Big Question*.

13. On the hard problem of consciousness, see David Chalmers, *The Conscious Mind*. On the various theories of consciousness adopted by William James, see W. E. Cooper, "William James' Theory of Mind," *Journal of the History of Philosophy*, 28 (4): 571–93. See also Thomas Nagel, "Panpsychism," *Mortal Questions*; Galen Strawson, "The Self," *Journal of Consciousness Studies*, 4 (5/6): 405–28; Alfred North Whitehead, *Process and Reality: An Essay in Cosmology*. On the anthropic principle, see Bernard Carr and Martin Rees's essay "The Anthropic Principle and the Structure of the Physical World."

14. See Stephen Newmyer, *Animals, Rights and Reason in Plutarch and Modern Ethics*.

15. On the question of why animals play, see the fascinating work of Linda Sharp of the University of Stellenbosch. She summarises it here: blogs .scientificamerican.com/guest-blog/2011/05/17/so-you-think-you -know-why-animals-play.

16. Carl Sagan, *Cosmos: A Personal Voyage*.

7. PYTHAGORAS AND THE ART OF MEMORIZATION AND INCANTATION

1. Epictetus, *Discourses*.

2. Lucius Annaeus Seneca, "On Benefits," *Essays*.

3. Plutarch, "On Contentedness of Mind," *Moralia*.

4. Justus Lipsius, *Second Book of Constancy*.

5. You can see some of these philosophy tattoos at www.philosophyfor life.org.

6. Bertrand Russell, *A History of Western Philosophy*.

7. Emile Coué, *My Method*.

8. Epictetus, *Discourses*.

9. Iamblichus, *Life of Pythagoras*.

10. The story about the CEO of the mental health trust is told by Richard Layard, and quoted in a Guardian article by Darian Leader: www .guardian.co.uk/science/2008/sep/09/psychology.humanbehaviour.

11. Ibid.

12. Marcus Aurelius, *Meditations*.

13. Albert Ellis, *The Road to Tolerance: The Philosophy of Rational Emotive Behaviour Therapy*.

14. Quoted in James C. Collins, *Good to Great: Why Some Companies Make the Leap...and Others Don't*.

8. Skeptics and the Art of Cultivating Doubt

1. Adam Curtis, *The Century of the Self*, episode 3: "There is a Policeman Inside All Our Heads, He Must Be Destroyed."

2. For an idea of quite how big est was in the '70s, check out www.erhard seminarstraining.com.

3. Tom Wolfe wrote of the est movement, in his essay "The Me Decade and the Third Great Awakening": "The appeal was simple enough. It is summed up in the notion: 'Let's talk about Me.' No matter whether you managed to renovate your personality through the encounter sessions or not, you had finally focused your attention and your energies on the most fascinating subject on earth: Me. Not only that, you also put Me up on stage before a live audience. The popular 'est' movement has managed to do that with great refinement...just imagine...my life becoming a drama with universal significance...analyzed, like Hamlet's, for what it signifies for the rest of mankind..."

4. Landmark tells me: "Any time a program leader becomes aware of any participant experiencing what might be a medical or mental health issue, the program leader immediately recommends that the individual see a medical or mental health professional."

5. See David A. Clark and Aaron Beck, *The Anxiety and Worry Workbook: The Cognitive Behavioural Solution*: "Developing a 'Questioning' or

Skeptical Attitude to Your Initial Anxious Thought...Is a Key Element in Cognitive Therapy."

6. The documentary is called *Voyage au pays des nouveaux gourous* (Voyage to the Land of the New Gurus) and was shown on *Pièces à Conviction* on May 24, 2004.

7. Jon Ronson's journalism on the uses and abuses of psychiatry is another good example of this more rigorous Skepticism. See, for example, his book *The Psychopath Test: A Journey through the Madness Industry.*

8. Elizabeth Loftus and Katherine Ketcham, *The Myth of Repressed Memory: False Memories and Allegations of Sexual Abuse.*

9. DIOGENES AND THE ART OF ANARCHY

1. This and all subsequent quotes about Diogenes and other Cynics in the ancient world are from Diogenes Laertius, *Lives of the Philosophers.*

2. Jules Evans, "Albert Ellis: A Modern Diogenes," *Prospect Magazine,* August 2007.

3. www.people.com/people/archive/article/0,,20059903,00.html.

4. See Jackson's TED talk: www.youtube.com/watch?v=NZsp_EdO2Xk.

5. Bernard Mandeville, *The Fable of the Bees: or, Private Vices, Public Benefits.*

6. Epictetus, *Discourses.*

7. See Lovejoy et al., *Primitivism and Related Ideas in Antiquity.*

8. Charles Dickens, *Barnaby Rudge: A Tale of the Riots of Eighty.*

9. James Chanos spoke of his admiration for Diogenes in a speech to the Hellenic American Bankers Association in 2010.

10. New Testament, 1 Corinthians 4:13.

11. The epithet comes from Voltaire, quoted in Maurice William Cranston, *The Noble Savage: Jean-Jacques Rousseau, 1754–1762.*

12. Jean-Jacques Rousseau, *Discourse on Inequality.*

13. Henry David Thoreau, *Walden, or, Life in the Woods.*

14. See, for example, Guy Debord's *The Society of Spectacle.*

15. Susanne Elizabeth Shawyer, *Radical Street Theatre and the Yippie legacy: A Performance History of the Youth International Party, 1967–1968.*

16. Derek Wall, *Earth First! and the Anti-Roads Movement: Radical Environmentalism and Comparative Social Movements.*

17. Adam Curtis, *The Century of the Self,* episode 3: "There is a Policeman Inside All Our Heads, He Must Be Destroyed."

18. The song comes, of course, from *Les Misérables*, a musical about the 1832 student uprising in Paris.
19. William Wordsworth, *The Prelude* (1805 version).

10. Plato and the Art of Justice

1. www.meetup.com/platonism/members/6910692.
2. See the further reading recommendations for this chapter for several sources on shamanism.
3. See W. K. C. Guthrie's *History of Greek Philosophy, Volume III: The Fifth Century Enlightenment.*
4. On the rise of the sophists, see Eric Havelock, *The Liberal Temper in Greek Politics.*
5. Plato's triune theory of the psyche is explained in *The Republic.* For Paul MacLean's theory of the triune brain, see his book, *The Triune Brain in Evolution: Role in Paleocerebral Functions.*
6. See Alasdair C. MacIntyre, *The Unconscious: A Conceptual Analysis.* Plato's view of the unconscious was that it wasn't purely bestial and primitive, as Sigmund Freud believed. Plato thought that occasionally our divine self sends us messages through the unconscious via dreams, as Carl Jung later suggested. Jungian psychology owes much to Hellenic philosophy, particularly to Plato, and it would be interesting to work out a synthesis between it and cognitive therapy, which lacks a theory of the meaning or role of dreams.
7. The ideas and quotes from this paragraph come from *The Republic.*
8. Plato, *The Republic:* "in the soul of a person there is a better and a worse part. When the naturally better part is in control of the worse, this is what is meant by 'master of himself'... But when, as a result of bad upbringing or bad company, the better element, which is smaller, is overwhelmed by the mass of the worse element ... [a person is called] a slave to himself, undisciplined."
9. Plato discusses love and the ascent of the soul most beautifully in *Phaedrus, Symposium,* and *Phaedo.*
10. The allegory of the cave is from *The Republic.*
11. See, for example, Callicles's contempt for philosophers in Plato's *Gorgias.*
12. The quote is from the *Seventh Letter,* which scholars are still unsure whether to ascribe to Plato.

13. These and all subsequent quotes by Plato are from *The Republic*.

14. See, for example, Plato's *Phaedo*: "I do not mean to affirm that the description [of the afterlife] which I have given is exactly true — a man of sense ought hardly to say that. But I do say that, in as much as the soul is shown to be immortal, he may venture to think not improperly or unworthily, that something of the kind is true."

15. See in particular Sir Karl Popper, *The Open Society and Its Enemies*.

16. The Townend independent report into abuse at the two schools is available online here: www.iirep.com/Report/report.htm.

17. The headmaster at the boys' school when the abuse happened, Nicholas Debenham, who once caned two entire classes for insubordination on the way to the swimming pool, recently returned to SES to give a lecture on "The World, the Flesh and the Devil."

11. PLUTARCH AND THE ART OF HEROISM

1. The original Bobo doll experiments are described in Bandura and Ross's 1961 article, "Transmission of Aggression through Imitation of Aggressive Models" in the *Journal of Abnormal and Social Psychology*, 63, 575–82.

2. Plutarch, "On Moral Virtue," *Moralia*.

3. Plutarch, "The Education of Children," *Moralia*. (Plutarch's authorship of this essay is disputed by many scholars: I am not an expert, but suggest that, firstly, it is a very interesting essay in its own right and, secondly, is in line with Plutarch's educational theory and emphasis on the power of emulation and habituation, as expressed in the *Lives* and essays such as "On Moral Virtue.")

4. Ibid.

5. A good source for the economic, social, and emotional impact of absent fathers is the US National Fatherhood Initiative's website, at www .fatherhood.org, from where the following statistics have been sourced: according to the US Census Bureau of 2002, children in father-absent homes are five times more likely to live below the poverty line. A 2002 Department of Justice survey found that 39 percent of jail inmates grew up in mother-only households. Children growing up in single-parent homes are around 120 percent more likely to suffer some form of child abuse, according to a 1996 US Department of Health and Human Services report. Fatherless children are also twice as likely to drop out

of school, according to a 1993 US Department of Health and Human Services report. This is not to blame single mothers, who are often abandoned by irresponsible fathers; nor do I deny there are many instances of young people being brought up exceptionally well by single mothers.

6. This and all subsequent quotes by Plutarch from his *Lives of the Noble Greeks and Romans, or Parallel Lives.*

7. Niccolò Machiavelli, *The Prince.*

8. Interview in *New Statesman*, April 6, 2011.

9. Martin Gilbert, *Continue to Pester, Nag and Bite: Churchill's War Leadership.*

10. Plutarch, "On the Fortune or the Virtue of Alexander the Great," *Moralia.*

11. Perhaps the classic example of the swashbuckling hero of the British Empire is Charles George Gordon, variously known as "Chinese Gordon," "Gordon of Khartoum," and "Gordon Pasha." Gordon exemplified the English imperial hero's courage and penchant for fancy dress.

12. Zimbardo describes the Stanford Prison Experiment in *The Lucifer Effect: Understanding How Good People Turn Evil.* You can listen to an interview with Zimbardo about this experiment and his new Heroic Imagination Project on my website.

13. See www.heroicimagination.org.

14. For an example of the revival of Plutarchian history, see John McCain's book *Character is Destiny: Inspiring Stories Every Young Person Should Know and Every Adult Should Remember*, which describes character strengths through historical portraits.

12. ARISTOTLE AND THE ART OF FLOURISHING

1. This point is beautifully made in Patrick Leigh Fermor's account of his youthful voyage across Europe, *A Time of Gifts.* The difference between a tourist and a pilgrim, someone once said to me, is that a tourist moves through a market economy, while a pilgrim moves through a gift economy. In that sense, Leigh Fermor's journey was a secular pilgrimage.

2. Plutarch, "On the Fortune or the Virtue of Alexander the Great," *Moralia.*

3. See edge.org, March 15, 2011, edge.org/3rd_culture/leroi11/leroi11 _index.html.

4. See Ryan, Huta, and Deci, "Living Well: A Self-Determination Theory Perspective on Eudaimonia," *Journal of Happiness Studies* (2008)

9:139–170. Deci and Ryan's Self-Determination Theory is also a key influence on two recent books, Daniel Pink's *Drive: The Surprising Truth about What Motivates Us*; and Clark Skirky's *Here Comes Everybody: The Power of Organising Without Organisations*.

5. Robert Nozick, *Anarchy, State and Utopia*.

6. Sir Isaiah Berlin, *Two Concepts of Liberty*.

7. I'm thinking here in particular of the works of Michel Foucault, although it's notable that Foucault himself eventually moved away from a Nietzschean analysis of governmental power and toward an investigation of the government of the self in Hellenistic ethics — see late works like *The Care of the Self* (volume 3 of his *History of Sexuality*). What he never got time to investigate, sadly, was whether or how such an ethics could be a communal or even a political practice, rather than an individual pursuit.

8. See Alasdair MacIntyre's *After Virtue*, and Allan Bloom's rather less credible but nonetheless historically interesting *The Closing of the American Mind*.

9. See, for example, Martha C. Nussbaum, "Aristotelian Social Democracy" in *Liberalism and the Good*; and Michael Sandel, *Justice: What's the Right Thing to Do?*

10. Richard Reeves and Jen Lexmond, *Building Character* (Demos pamphlet).

11. Mary Riddell, "Can Ed Miliband Find an Antidote to the Politics of Fear and Loathing?," *Telegraph*, January 10, 2011.

12. See Charles Seaford's talk "The Benthamites versus the Aristotelians" on my channel on YouTube, www.youtube.com/watch?v=zmU9vo PPAYk.

13. Martin Seligman and Christopher Peterson claimed that Positive Psychology is the "social science equivalent of virtue ethics." See their book *Character Strengths and Virtues: A Handbook and Classification*.

14. Jules Evans, "Teaching Happiness: The Classes in Happiness That Are Helping Our Children," *The Times*, February 18, 2008.

15. See Martin Seligman's *Authentic Happiness and Flourish: A Visionary New Understanding of Happiness and Well-Being*.

16. See his 1998 American Psychological Association presidential address: www.ppc.sas.upenn.edu/aparep98.htm.

17. Tony Hsieh, *Delivering Happiness*.

18. Martin Seligman, *Flourish: A Visionary New Understanding of Happiness and Well-Being*.

19. www.actionforhappiness.org/news/happiness-a-message-to
    -world-leaders.
20. www.ppc.sas.upenn.edu/faqs.htm.
21. Martin Seligman, *Flourish: A Visionary New Understanding of Happiness
    and Well-Being.*
22. Martin Seligman, *Learned Optimism.*
23. See *Countdown with Keith Olbermann*, MSNBC, January 6, 2011,
    www.youtube.com/watch?v=GNfBPXi5rUA.
24. www.wellingtoncollege.org.uk/news-archive/archive/happiness
    -school-launches-10-point-well-being-programme-for-all.
25. He made this point at a talk at the RSA, July 6, 2011, www.thersa.org
    /events/audio-and-past-events/2011/flourish.
26. Jean Vanier, *Becoming Human.*

GRADUATION: SOCRATES AND THE ART OF DEPARTURE

1. Plato, *Phaedo.*
2. Lucius Annaeus Seneca, "On the Shortness of Life."
3. Marcus Aurelius, *Meditations.*
4. Adam Smith, letter to William Strahan.
5. Speech to Help for Hospices conference 2010. See also his Demos pamphlet, coauthored with Jake Garber, *Dying for Change.*
6. Lucius Annaeus Seneca, *Moral Letters to Lucius.*
7. Publius Cornelius Tacitus, *Annals.*
8. Marcus Aurelius, *Meditations.*
9. Alexander Murray, *Suicide in the Middle Ages: The Curse on Self-Murder.*
10. An exception is the atheistic philosopher A. J. Ayer, who was remarkably candid about his near-death experience.

APPENDIX 1. IS SOCRATES OVEROPTIMISTIC ABOUT HUMAN REASON?

1. From a talk at the LSE by Kahneman. See a transcript on my website www.philosophyforlife.org.

APPENDIX 2. THE SOCRATIC TRADITION AND NON-WESTERN PHILOSOPHICAL TRADITIONS

1. Bruno Cayoun, *Mindfulness-integrated CBT: Principles and Practices.*
2. Jesus's parable of the wise and foolish builders is in Matthew 7:24–7 and Luke 6:46–9.

APPENDIX 3. SOCRATES AND DIONYSUS

1. The idea of the Dionysiac tradition is informed by Sir Isaiah Berlin's theory of the irrationalist or anti-Enlightenment tradition in Western thought, as described in his essay *The Magus of the North.*
2. Mentioned in Friedrich Nietzsche, *The Birth of Tragedy out of the Spirit of Music.*
3. Plato, *Phaedo.*

Further Reading

1. MORNING ROLL CALL:
SOCRATES AND THE ART OF STREET PHILOSOPHY

You can find local Socrates Cafés at socratescafe.meetup.com. Philosophy in Pubs is at www.philosophyinpubs.org.uk. The London Philosophy Club is at www.londonphilosophyclub.com. And the School of Life is at www.theschooloflife.com.

On Socrates, the primary sources are Plato's *Dialogues*, and Xenophon's *Memorabilia*. Both are available free online, in translations by Benjamin Jowett and Edward Bysshe, respectively. A good secondary source on Socrates is W. K. C. Guthrie's chapter on Socrates in his *History of Greek Philosophy*. Two enjoyable recent books are Bettany Hughes's *The Hemlock Cup: Socrates, Athens and the Search for the Good Life* and Paul Johnson's *Socrates: A Man for Our Time*.

For criticism of Socratic rationalism, see Friedrich Nietzsche's *The Birth of Tragedy Out of the Spirit of Music*; Bernard Williams's *Ethics and the Limits of Philosophy*; and, from a psychological perspective, Daniel Kahneman's *Thinking: Fast and Slow*; and John Bargh and Robert Wyer's *The Automaticity of Everyday Life*. For a psychological criticism of the cognitive theory of emotions, see Antonio Damasio's *Descartes' Error: Emotion, Reason and the Human Brain*; and for a philosophical response, see Martha C. Nussbaum's *Upheavals of Thought: The Intelligence of Emotions*.

For introductions to CBT, four excellent books are Albert Ellis's *A Guide to Rational Living*; Aaron Beck's *Depression: Causes and Treatments*, and *Anxiety Disorders and Phobias: A Cognitive Perspective*; and David Burns's *Feeling Good: The New Mood Therapy*. There are many CBT books and courses written for self-help on particular emotional disorders, including the audio course that helped me, Dr. Thomas Richards's "Overcoming Social Anxiety: Step-by-Step."

On the philosophical roots of CBT, the best book is Donald Robertson's *The Philosophy of CBT*. More generally, three excellent books on ancient philosophy as therapy are Pierre Hadot's *Philosophy as a Way of Life*; Martha C. Nussbaum's *The Therapy of Desire: Theory and Practice in Hellenistic Ethics*; and Alain de Botton's *Consolations of Philosophy. Philosophy as Therapeia*, a collection of academic essays edited by Clare Carlisle and Jonathan Ganeri, is also very good. On the philosophical counseling movement, I recommend Lou Marinoff's *Plato Not Prozac*, Tim LeBon's *Wise Therapy*, and Peter Raabe's *Philosophical Counseling: Theory and Practice*. For more on the Socrates Café movement, read Christopher Phillips's *Socrates Café: A Fresh Taste of Philosophy*.

The best-known Positive Psychology books are Martin Seligman's *Flourish: A Visionary New Understanding of Happiness and Well-Being*; and Jonathan Haidt's *The Happiness Hypothesis: Finding Modern Truth in Ancient Wisdom*. For a good philosophical critique of Positive Psychology, see Mark Vernon's *Well-Being*, and Martha C. Nussbaum's essay, "Who Is the Happy Warrior? Philosophy Poses Questions to Psychology," which is available online. See also Kristjan Kristjansson's 2010 article in the *Review of General Psychology*, "Positive Psychology, Happiness, and Virtue: The Troublesome Conceptual Issues." On measuring well-being, I've been helped by the work of the new economics foundation, particularly their 2011 report "Human Well-Being and Priorities for Economic Policy-Makers," and Nic Marks's *The Happiness Manifesto*. On the different ways to define well-being, and the importance of moral reasoning and choice in the process, see Amartya Sen's *The Idea of Justice*. My interest in the politics of well-being was first inspired by a 1998 Demos pamphlet called *The Good Life*, which you can download here: www.demos.co.uk /publications/goodlife.

See also two fervent critiques of the politics of well-being: James L.

Nolan Jr.'s *The Therapeutic State: Justifying Government at Century's End*; and Kathryn Ecclestone's *The Dangerous Rise of Therapeutic Education*. For the latest developments in the politics of well-being, see my blog.

MORNING SESSION: THE WARRIORS OF VIRTUE

You can find other Stoics, sign up for a monthly newsletter, and even receive free Stoic tuition at www.newstoa.com.

A lively Stoic email list is groups.yahoo.com/group/stoics/.

There's a sizeable Stoic group on Facebook. Also worth a visit are www.wku.edu/~jan.garrett/stoa/,

www.thestoiclife.org, and

www.ibiblio.org/stoicism/.

You can see a video-talk by Thomas Jarrett, as well as some of my talks on Stoicism, and full-text interviews with many of the people interviewed in this section, at www.philosophyforlife.org.

The existing primary texts of Stoicism are all available free online: Epictetus's *Discourses*, and Marcus Aurelius's *Meditations*, both translated by George Long; Seneca's *Essays* and *Moral Letters to Lucius*, translated by John W. Basore; and the *Lectures* of Musonius Rufus, translated by Cora E. Lutz. Another important source on the early Stoics is Diogenes Laertius's *Lives of the Eminent Philosophers*, available online in a translation by C. D. Yonge.

Good academic explorations of Stoicism include A. A. Long and David Sedley's *The Hellenistic Philosophers*; A. A. Long's *Problems in Stoicism and Stoic Studies*; Margaret Graver's *Stoicism and Emotion*; Richard Sorabji's *Emotion and Peace of Mind: From Stoic Agitation to Christian Temptation*; Pierre Hadot's *The Inner Citadel: The Meditations of Marcus Aurelius*; and *The Cambridge Companion to the Stoics*, edited by Brad Inwood. For an attempt to build a modern Stoicism, read Lawrence C. Becker's *A New Stoicism*. For more accessible introductions to Stoicism, try John Sellars's *Stoicism*; William B. Irvine's *A Guide to the Good Life: The Ancient Art of Stoic Joy*; A. A. Long's *Epictetus: A Stoic and Socratic Guide to Life*; and Ronald Pies's *Everything Has Two Handles: The Stoic's Guide to the Art of Living*.

On Spartan culture, I enjoyed Paul Cartledge's *The Spartans: The World of the Warrior-Heroes of Ancient Greece*; as well as Plutarch's writing on Sparta.

You can find out more about Chris Brennan's use of Stoicism in the US Fire Service in his book *The Combat Position: Achieving Firefighter Readiness*.

LUNCH: PHILOSOPHY BUFFET

5. LUNCHTIME LESSON:
EPICURUS AND THE ART OF SAVORING THE MOMENT

You can join the global happiness movement at www.actionforhappiness.org; and at www.deliveringhappiness.com.

Epicurean meetup groups are at epicureans.meetup.com/.

Useful resources for budding Epicureans are found at www.epicurus.net and www.epicurus.info.

The Idler Academy's website is www.idler.co.uk/academy.

And the School of Life's website is www.theschooloflife.com.

Epicurus's *Principal Doctrines*, translated by Robert Drew Hicks, is available online. So are several verse and prose translations of Lucretius's *On the Nature of Things*, and Horace's *Odes*. For academic explorations of Epicureanism, I've been helped by David Sedley and A. A. Long's *The Hellenistic Philosophers*; Martha C. Nussbaum's *The Therapy of Desire: Theory and Practice in Hellenistic Ethics*; *The Cambridge Companion to Epicurus*, edited by James Warren; and, on Lucretius, Stephen Greenblatt's *Swerve: How the World Became Modern*. For a more contemporary take on Epicureanism, try Tom Hodgkinson's *How to Be Free*, Alain de Botton's *Consolations of Philosophy*, and Havi Carel's interesting and moving story, told in *Illness: The Cry of the Flesh*. You can read my interviews with Stephen Greenblatt, Tom Hodgkinson, and Havi Carel on my website.

On the "science of happiness," the reader is spoiled for choice. Daniel Gilbert's *Stumbling On Happiness* is very interesting; as is Jonathan Haidt's *The Happiness Hypothesis*. Richard Layard's *Happiness: Lessons from a New Science* is very influential, and for the book that most inspired him, read Jeremy Bentham's *An Introduction to the Principals of Morals and Legislation*. For a brilliant account of the history of our obsession with happiness, read Derrin M. McMahon's *Happiness: A History*.

EARLY-AFTERNOON SESSION: MYSTICS AND SKEPTICS

6. HERACLITUS AND THE ART OF COSMIC CONTEMPLATION

You can watch a video of my interview with Edgar Mitchell at www.philoso phyforlife.org, and find out more about the Institute of Noetic Sciences at www.noetic.org. For other accounts of astronauts' experience of space, read Frank White's *The Overview Effect: Space Exploration and Human Evolution*; or watch the beautiful documentary *In the Shadow of the Moon*.

You can find all the remaining fragments of Heraclitus's *On Nature* at the appropriately named www.heraclitusfragments.com. For academic studies of the Pre-Socratic philosophers, I recommend W. K. C. Guthrie's *History of Greek Philosophy, Volume 2: The Pre-Socratic Tradition*; Kirk, Raven, and Schofield's *The Pre-Socratic Philosophers*; and G. E. R. Lloyd's *Early Greek Science: Thales to Aristotle*. For a more accessible account, I recommend Carl Sagan's seminal TV series, *Cosmos: A Personal Voyage*, the seventh episode of which covers the Pre-Socratics. For the parallels between Heraclitus's philosophy and quantum physics, read Fritjof Capra's *The Tao of Physics*.

On the View from Above, I am indebted to Pierre Hadot's *Philosophy as a Way of Life*, and also to Donald Robertson's *The Philosophy of CBT*. You can watch a video interview of me talking to Donald about the View from Above on my website. For a famous exploration of the idea of "cosmic consciousness," read Richard Maurice Bucke's *Cosmic Consciousness: A Study in the Evolution of the Human Mind*.

Consciousness studies is now a huge field, in which I am no expert, but my philosophy group very much enjoyed Susan Blackmore's *Conversations on Consciousness*, which includes interviews with many of the leading thinkers in the field. John Searle's *The Mystery of Consciousness* is also a penetrating survey of the field. For two leading figures in that field, see Daniel Dennett's *Consciousness Explained*; and, from a different perspective, David Chalmers's *The Conscious Mind: In Search of a Fundamental Theory*. For a friendly debate between Stephen Hawking and Roger Penrose, see their exchange in Penrose's *The Large, the Small and the Human Mind*.

7. Pythagoras and the Art of Memorization and Incantation

There are a few Pythagorean meetup groups, which you can find here: pythagoreans.meetup.com

For a somewhat culty modern take on Pythagoreanism, check out the various groups around the world devoted to the teachings of G. I. Gurdjieff.

For a collection of philosophy maxims tattoos, see my website.

You can find all the lives and fragments of Pythagoras at www.complete pythagoras.net.

I used *The Pythagorean Sourcebook and Library*, edited by Kenneth Sylvan Guthrie. A good academic exploration of the man, the myth, and the philosophical movement is Christoph Riedweg and Steven Rendall's *Pythagoras: His Life, Teaching and Influence*. On maxims and memorization techniques, I am indebted to Pierre Hadot's *Philosophy as a Way of Life*. On Emile Coué's theories of autosuggestion, I was helped by Donald Robertson's *The Philosophy of CBT*. There are hundreds of books available on the Law of Attraction: if you close your eyes and really wish for it, one of them will magically appear on your bookshelf. For a good critique of the Secret, read Barbara Ehrenreich's *Smile or Die* (in the United States it's called *Bright-Sided: How Positive Thinking is Undermining America*). Vice-Admiral James Bond Stockdale told his remarkable story in *Thoughts of a Philosophical Fighter Pilot*.

8. Skeptics and the Art of Cultivating Doubt

You can watch a video I made of my visit to The Amazing Meeting on my website.

There are many websites for the budding Skeptic to visit, including: The James Randi Educational Foundation, www.randi.org/

And Michael Shermer's www.skeptic.com

Skeptic podcasts include:

The Skeptics' Guide to the Universe: www.theskepticsguide.org/

Skeptoid: www.skeptoid.org

Skepticality: www.skepticality.com

The Pod Delusion: www.poddelusion.co.uk

There are 435 Skeptic meetup groups around the world: skeptics.meetup .com/.

You can find the Skeptics in the Pub movement in the UK here: www

.skeptic.org.uk/pub; and there are other Skeptics in the Pub movements in Australia, New Zealand, the United States and, no doubt, elsewhere.

Sextus Empiricus's *Outlines of Pyrrhonism* is available online, as is Diogenes Laertius's *Lives of* Pyrrho and Carneades. A good academic introduction to ancient Skepticism is *The Cambridge Companion to Ancient Skepticism*, edited by Richard Bett. I was also helped, as usual, by David Sedley and A. A. Long's *The Hellenistic Philosophers*, and by Martha C. Nussbaum's *The Therapy of Desire: Theory and Practice in Hellenistic Ethics*. A brief, lively encapsulation of the Skeptic philosophical worldview is David Hume's essay "The Skeptic." An interesting book connecting ancient Skepticism and modern Skepticism is Jennifer Michael Hecht's *Doubt: A History*. Excellent modern books on Skepticism include Carl Sagan's *The Demon-Haunted World: Science as a Candle in the Dark*; Nassim Nicholas Taleb's *The Black Swan: The Impact of the Highly Improbable*; Daniel Kahneman's *Thinking: Fast and Slow*; and Michael Shermer's *How We Believe: Science, Skepticism and the Search for God*. I also enjoyed Jesse Bering's *The God Instinct: The Psychology of Souls, Destiny, and the Meaning of Life*. For a Skeptic take on self-help, read Richard Wiseman's *59 Seconds: Think a Little, Change a Lot*.

On Werner Erhard, Erhard seminars training and the Landmark Forum, see William Warren Bartley's *Werner Erhard: The Transformation of a Man, the Founding of est*; Tom Wolfe's essay, "The 'Me' Generation and the Third Great Awakening"; Charles Taylor's *A Secular Age*; and Adam Curtis's wonderful documentary *The Century of the Self*.

LATE-AFTERNOON SESSION: POLITICS
9. DIOGENES AND THE ART OF ANARCHY

I can't tell if the Occupy movement will still be going when you read this (have they occupied the White House yet?) but you can follow it or participate at these links:

www.occupywallst.org
www.occupylsx.com
www.meetup.com/occupytogether/
And for the movement that started it all: www.adbusters.org
There are also several anarchist meetup groups around the world:
anarchy.meetup.com

To prepare for the collapse, check out: collapsonomics.org/
Radio 4's *In Our Time* had a good discussion about Cynicism, here: www.bbc
.co.uk/programmes/poo3k9js.
You can see some of my photos from Occupy London on my website.

The Cynics lived more than they wrote. The best account of their antics is in
Diogenes Laertius's *Lives of the Philosophers*, which is available online translated by C. D. Yonge. Among academic works on Cynicism, I particularly
enjoyed *The Cynics: The Cynic Movement in Antiquity and its Legacy* by R.
Bracht Branham and Marie-Odile Goulet-Caze; and *Primitivism and Related
Ideas in Antiquity* by Lovejoy et al. For an account of Cynicism's evolution in
the Enlightenment, read Louisa Shea's *The Cynic Enlightenment: Diogenes in
the Salon*. On anarcho-primitivism in the modern age, I recommend *Against
Civilisation: Readings and Reflections*, edited by John Zerzan; *Dark Mountain,
Volume One and Two*, edited by Paul Kingsnorth and Dougald Hine; and if
you're feeling really militant, Derrick Jensen's *Endgame*.

On anarchist culture jamming, read Kalle Lasn's *Culture Jam: How to Reverse
America's Suicidal Consumer Binge — and Why We Must*; and for Situationist
philosophy, read Guy Debord's *The Society of Spectacle*, Raoul Vaneigem's
Revolution of Everyday Life; and, for an exploration of Situationism's influence
on punk culture, Greil Marcus's *Lipstick Traces: A Secret History of the Twentieth Century*. For a brilliant fictional take on anarcho-primitivist-situationism,
read (or watch the film of) Chuck Palahniuk's *Fight Club*. On shame attacking, see Albert Ellis's *How to Control Your Anxiety Before It Controls You*. Neil
Ansell tells the story of his hermitage in the Welsh hills in *Deep Country: Five
Years in the Welsh Hills*.

10. PLATO AND THE ART OF JUSTICE

There are several editions of Plato's *Dialogues* published. I've mainly quoted
from the nineteenth-century translations by Benjamin Jowett, which are available free online. There have been no shortage of academic books on Plato. For
this chapter, I found useful W. K. C. Guthrie's *A History of Greek Philosophy*;
Malcolm Schofield's *Plato: Political Philosophy*; Gregory Vlastos's *Platonic
Universe*; and Angela Hobbs's *Plato and the Hero: Courage, Manliness and the
Impersonal Good*. For a fairly damning critique of Plato's authoritarianism,
read Sir Karl Popper's *The Open Society and Its Enemies*; and for a response

and defense, read Leo Strauss's "Plato" in his *History of Political Philosophy*. For modern and popular reengagements with Plato, read Mark Vernon's *Plato's Podcasts: The Ancients' Guide to Modern Living*; and Lou Marinoff's *Plato not Proʒac: Applying Eternal Wisdom to Everyday Problems*.

The internet has a lot of great material on Plato, including several academics discussing his work on www.philosophybites.com/plato; YouTube has videos of Miles Burnyeat, Leo Strauss, Allan Bloom, and others lecturing on Plato; and you can find Alexander's Texan Platonists meetup group here: www.meetup.com/platonism/.

There's a lot of great material on neoplatonism at the International Society for Neoplatonic Studies' website, including translations of Plotinus, Damascius, and others, here: www.isns.us; and there's a neoplatonic yahoo mail-list here: groups.yahoo.com/group/neoplatonism/.

Neoplatonists tell me they particularly enjoy E. R. Dodds' commentary on Proclus's ideas in *The Elements of Theology*, as well as Pierre Hadot's *Plotinus, or the Simplicity of Vision*. On shamanism, I loved Mircea Eliade's dated but still fascinating *Archaic Techniques of Ecstasy*, and Piers Vitebsky's *Shamanism*. On shamanism in Greek culture, see E. R. Dodds's *The Greeks and the Irrational*, particularly chapter 5, "The Greek Shamans and the Origins of Puritanism."

On the School of Economic Science, see Dorine Tolley, *The Power Within: Leon MacLaren: A Memoir of his Life and Work*, and Brian Hodgkinson's *In Search of Truth: The Story of the School of Economic Science*. For a less sympathetic account, see *The School of Economic Science: The Secret Cult*, by Peter Hounam and Andrew Hogg. An interesting read is a novel by former St. James pupil Clara Salaman, *Shame On You*.

11. PLUTARCH AND THE ART OF HEROISM

Plutarch's *Parallel Lives* is available free online in several translations. I mainly used Bernadotte Perrin's from the Loeb Classical Library edition. His expansive *Moralia* is also available online, I particularly recommend "On Moral Virtue," "On the Fortune or Virtue of Alexander the Great," "Can Virtue Be Taught?," and "The Education of Children" — the authorship of the last essay is disputed, but it's a fascinating and trenchant essay. For academic explorations of Plutarch's philosophy and psychology, read Lieve Van Hoof's *Plutarch's Practical Ethics: The Social Dynamics of Philosophy*; and Tim Duff's *Plutarch's Lives: Exploring Virtue and Vice.*

For two Renaissance works that were deeply influenced by Plutarch's ideas on education, read Machiavelli's *The Prince* and Giorgio Vasari's *Lives of the Most Eminent Painters.* For the cult of the hero in the nineteenth century, read Thomas Carlyle's *Heroes and Hero Worship.* For an extended critique of the "great man" theory of history, see Leo Tolstoy's *War and Peace.*

On the revival of the Plutarchian idea of character in American education and public policy, see "Character Education Manifesto" of Boston University's Center for Character & Social Responsibility: www.bu.edu/ccsr/about-us /character-education-manifesto/.

For Plutarch's role in the modern character education movement, see Roger Kimball's article, "Plutarch and the issue of character" in *The New Criterion*: www.newcriterion.com/articles.cfm/plutarch-kimball-2286.

For an interesting history and critique of the "character education" movement in the United States, see Peter Smagorinsky and Joel Taxel's *The Discourse of Character Education: Culture Wars in the Classroom.*

For a UK perspective, see the Demos pamphlets, *Building Character* and *The Character Inquiry.*

On role models, see *Psychological Modeling: Conflicting Theories*, edited by Albert Bandura.

See also Philip Zimbardo's Heroic Imagination Project: www.heroic imagination.org. You can listen to my interview with Zimbardo on my website. For an interesting philosophical exploration of role-modeling and emulation, read Kristjan Kristjansson's article "Emulation and the Use of Role Models in Moral Education" in *The Journal of Moral Education.*

For an explicitly Plutarchian approach to character-building, see www .bostonleadershipbuilders.com.

And for two Plutarchian approaches to history, from both sides of the political spectrum, see John McCain's *Character Is Destiny: Inspiring Stories Every Young Person Should Know and Every Adult Should Remember*, and Gordon Brown's *Courage: Portraits of Bravery in the Service of Great Causes.*

You can read more about Louis Ferrante's journey from mafioso to campaigner for literacy in his memoir, *Tough Guy.* Rory Stewart is the author of two books: *The Places in Between* and *The Prince of the Marshes: And Other Occupational Hazards of a Year in Iraq.* You can watch a video of my interview with Rory on my website.

12. ARISTOTLE AND THE ART OF FLOURISHING

Most of Aristotle's surviving books are available in English translation online. There's a daunting body of academic work on his philosophy, and I'm not an academic expert, but the books I found accessible and useful for this chapter were *Essays on Aristotle's Ethics*, edited by Amelie Oksenberg Rorty; *The Fragility of Goodness* by Martha C. Nussbaum; and *Aristotle, Emotions and Education* by Kristjan Kirtsjansson. A good brief introduction to his philosophy is *Aristotle: A Very Brief Introduction* by Jonathan Barnes. For an Aristotelian approach to modern ethics and politics, a definitive work is *After Virtue* by Alasdair MacIntyre, and much of the argument of this chapter, and indeed this book, is informed by it. Another important and enjoyable work in the modern revival of virtue ethics is *Justice: What's the Right Thing to Do?* by Michael Sandel. See also *Virtue Ethics, Old and New*, edited by Stephen Mark Gardiner. I wrote a journal article called "All Our Leaders Are Aristotelian Now" on the rise of Neo-Aristotelian policy, in *Public Policy Quarterly*, February 2011.

On YouTube, you can watch Martha C. Nussbaum talk about Aristotle in her interview with Bryan Magee: www.youtube.com/watch?v=uNIPAwZVqb4.

And also Armand Leroi's excellent show on Aristotle's biology, Aristotle's Lagoon: www.youtube.com/watch?v=mIV4ka6lX8s.

Radio 4's *In Our Time* has shows on Aristotle's *Politics* and *Poetics*, both available online.

Philosophy Bites has interviews with philosophers on Aristotle, Aquinas and virtue ethics: philosophybites.com/aristotle/.

Mark Vernon produced a series of talks on Aristotle's philosophy of friendship, which you can download on iTunes here: itunes.apple.com/us /podcast/aristotles-philosophy-friendship/id170142977.

On Positive Psychology, see Martin Seligman's *Flourish*. For an interesting critique of it, see Nussbaum's article, "Who Is the Happy Warrior? Philosophy Poses Questions to Psychology," to which this chapter is indebted. You can download it here: mfs.uchicago.edu/institutes/happiness/prereadings /nussbaum_happy_warrior.pdf.

Jean Vanier has written several beautiful books, including *Made for Happiness: Discovering the Meaning of Life with Aristotle,* and *Becoming Human.* You can watch a video of my interview with Jean on my website, where you can also find some photos from my Camino trip.

GRADUATION: SOCRATES AND THE ART OF DEPARTURE

For an amusing exploration of death and philosophy, see Simon Critchley's *The Book of Dead Philosophers.* See also Steven Luper's *The Philosophy of Death* and Thomas Nagel's *Mortal Questions.*

On the Medieval and Renaissance debates over suicide, see Alexander Murray's *Suicide in the Middle Ages, Volume 2: The Curse on Self-Murder.* On the modern debate over assisted suicide, see Mary Warnock's *Easeful Death: Is There a Case for Easeful Dying?* and, as a sort of ultimate self-help book, Derek Humphry's *Final Exit: The Practicalities of Self-Deliverance and Assisted Suicide for the Dying.* See also the Demos inquiry into dying, and Charles Leadbetter and Jake Garber's pamphlet *Dying for Change.* See also the documentary by Sir Terry Pratchett, *Choosing to Die*: www.youtube.com /watch?v=_NUaoSyyyMg.

For philosophical explorations of the afterlife, see David Eagleman's *Sum.*

Acknowledgments

A BIG THANK YOU to all the people I've collared, cornered, pestered, and interviewed for this book, my blog, or for various articles over the last five years. I've been amazed and moved by people's helpfulness and patience. Thanks to Neil Ansell, Dan Ariely, Julian Baggini, John Bargh, Roy Baumeister, Aaron Beck, Alain de Botton, Christopher Brennan, Jesse Caban, Havi Carel, David M. Clark, Rhonda Cornum, Tom Daley, Michel and Pamela Daw, Paul Doran, Rob Lewis, Arthur Adler, and everyone involved with Philosophy In Pubs, Albert Ellis and Debbie Joffe Ellis, Louis Ferrante, Vinay Gupta, Maurice Glasman, Stephen Greenblatt, everyone at How the Light Gets In, Richard Heimberg, Dougald Hine, Tom Hodgkinson and the Idler Academy, Ryan Holiday, Leo Iermano, Ben Irvine, William Knaus, Kristján Kristjánsson, Kalle Lasn, Richard Layard, Charles Leadbetter and the Demos team, Darian Leader, Tim LeBon, Alaisdair Lees, Steven Leysen, Anthony Long, Martha C. Nussbaum, Antonia Macaro, Ian Mason and the School of Economic Science, Deb Beroset Miller and the Landmark Forum, Edgar Mitchell, Michael Perry, Ronald Pies, James Randi, Roberta Galluccio Robertson, Donald Robertson, Oliver Robinson and the Scientific and Medical Network, Charles Seaford and the New Economics Foundation, Jeremy Scott, Keith Seddon, Martin Seligman, Sophia Elizabeth Shapira, Nancy Sherman, David Steven, and everyone at Global Dashboard, Rory Stewart, Stefan Streitferdt, Sam Sullivan, Andrew Taggart, Charles Taylor, Jean Vanier,

Harriet Warden and the School of Life, Richard Weber, Brett Wheat Simms, Uri Wernik, Erik Wiergardt and Amielle Moyer, and Philip Zimbardo. Many of these interviews are available in their entirety on my website, www.philosophyforlife.org, and some of them are available in video form.

I've been inspired by many books while writing this, but particularly by Pierre Hadot's *Philosophy as a Way of Life*, Martha Nussbaum's *Therapy of Desire: Theory and Practice in Hellenistic Ethics*, Alasdair MacIntyre's *After Virtue*, and Donald Robertson's *The Philosophy of CBT*. I was also helped by Mark Vernon's books and excellent blog. I first discovered a love of the history of ideas through Sir Isaiah Berlin's essays, particularly *The Magus of the North*; Charles Taylor's *A Secular Age*; Norbert Elias's *The Civilizing Process*, and from Tom Wolfe's journalism and Adam Curtis's documentaries. Even further back, this book would of course be very slim without the original works of Epictetus, Marcus Aurelius, Lucretius, Plato, Aristotle, and all the other masters on whose shoulders I am hitching a lift.

Thanks to my teachers and tutors, particularly Hilary Stallibrass, Gilly Howarth, David Evans, and Lesel Dawson, and to my godmother Liz Archibald for all her love and encouragement over the years. A big thank you to Thomas Dixon and the Center for the History of the Emotions at Queen Mary, University of London, for being so welcoming to a random blogger without academic qualifications. Thanks to Filip Matous for bringing me on board with the London Philosophy Club. Thanks to my blog readers, who have given me great feedback over the years. Thanks to all the various editors who've commissioned me, particularly to Mary Wakefield and Tatiana Doudar. Thanks to my loyal friends for supporting me in the bad times and accepting me in the crazy times. Particular thanks for their encouragement with the book and/or life in general to Louisa Tomlinson, Harry Glass, Neil Robertson, Ed Dowding, Richard Orange, Kate Hannay, William Flemming, Katharine Fortin, Toby Guise, Maria Petrova, Claudia Hernandez, Oliver Robinson, Jack Wakefield, Clare McNeil, Anna-Louisa Psarras, Jonty Claypole, all the Manders, Sebastian Ling, and Joe Drury. Thanks to the amazing team at Rider Books, particularly to Judith Kendra, Alice Latham, and Amelia Evans. Thanks to my agent, Jonathan Conway, for his wit, wisdom, and lifestyle tips. Thanks to The Literary Consultancy for introducing me to my editor, the wonderful Sue Lascelles, who got me a book deal and helped me build this book: I'm in your debt! Thanks to my wonderful family for all their support — I dedicate this book to them, with love.

A note on translation: I've tried to avoid using Greek or Roman terms whenever possible. However, I've kept the ancient Greek word "psyche," which can be translated as mind, personality, soul, or something that incorporates all three — I think it's more useful and comprehensive than any of its translations. I've generally used nineteenth-century translations of the ancient texts, by classicists like George Long and Benjamin Jowett, as they're freely available on the internet. The notes at the back include recommendations for further reading and links to good material on the internet, including a lot of extra material on my website, www.philosophy forlife.org.

Index

About the Author

JULES EVANS RUNS THE WELL-BEING PROJECT at the Center for the History of the Emotions at Queen Mary, University of London. He is a BBC New Generation Thinker and a co-organizer of the London Philosophy Club, the largest philosophy club in the UK, and gives talks and workshops on practical philosophy around the country. He writes for publications such as the *Wall Street Journal*, the *Times*, the *Spectator*, *Prospect* and *Psychologies* and has worked with organizations including the New Economics Foundation, the Rockefeller Foundation, and the School of Life, the philosophy school in London. His blog, www.politicsofwellbeing.com, enjoys a loyal following around the world.

NEW WORLD LIBRARY is dedicated to publishing books and other media that inspire and challenge us to improve the quality of our lives and the world.

We are a socially and environmentally aware company. We recognize that we have an ethical responsibility to our readers, our authors, our staff members, and our planet.

We serve our readers by creating the finest publications possible on personal growth, creativity, spirituality, wellness, and other areas of emerging importance. We serve our authors by working with them to produce and promote quality books that reach a wide audience. We serve New World Library employees with generous benefits, significant profit sharing, and constant encouragement to pursue their most expansive dreams.

Whenever possible, we print our books with soy-based ink on 100 percent postconsumer-waste recycled paper. We power our Northern California office with solar energy, and we respectfully acknowledge that it is located on the ancestral lands of the Coast Miwok Indians. We also contribute to nonprofit organizations working to make the world a better place for us all.

Our products are available wherever books are sold.

customerservice@NewWorldLibrary.com
Phone: 415-884-2100 or 800-972-6657
Orders: Ext. 110
Fax: 415-884-2199
NewWorldLibrary.com

Scan below to access our newsletter
and learn more about our books and authors.